AN INTRODUCTION TO

Early

John Mansley Robinson

SENIOR FELLOW IN PHILOSOPHY, MARLBORO COLLEGE

Greek Philosophy

THE CHIEF FRAGMENTS AND ANCIENT
TESTIMONY, WITH CONNECTING COMMENTARY

HOUGHTON MIFFLIN COMPANY · BOSTON

New York · Atlanta · Geneva, Ill. · Dallas · Palo Alto

The author is indebted to the following publishers for
permission to reprint material now in copyright:

Harvard University Press and The Loeb Classical Library: Diodorus Siculus, *Diodorus of Sicily*, tr. C. H. Oldfather (New York and London, 1933), Bk. I, Ch. 7-8.

Humanities Press Inc. and Routledge & Kegan Paul Ltd.: E. A. Burtt, *The Metaphysical Foundations of Modern Science*, 2nd rev. ed. (New York and London, 1932), portions of pp. 75 and 85.

Random House, Inc.: Aristophanes, *Clouds*, lines 366-411, 816-830, 960-1023, 1062–1082, 1409–1432, from *The Complete Greek Drama*, ed. Whitney J. Oates and Eugene O'Neill, Jr. (New York, 1938), Vol. II, pp. 556-557, 572-573, 579-581, 582, 595-596.

To

ZENOBIA

around whom

the first draft

was written

PREFACE

WHITEHEAD observes somewhere that "the safest general characterization of the European philosophical tradition is that it consists of a series of footnotes to Plato." The judgment is sweeping but sound, and it is confirmed by the practice of making the study of Plato central to most college and university courses in the history of ancient philosophy.

But (to adapt a phrase of Newton's) if Plato saw further than most men it was because he stood on the shoulders of giants. Anaximander, Pythagoras, Parmenides, Democritus — these were the men who laid the foundations and filled out the framework of Greek philosophy. The problems Plato faced were problems they had created, and the fund of general ideas at his disposal for dealing with these problems he inherited from them. It is in his struggle with these recalcitrant materials that the depth and power of Plato's philosophical genius is most strikingly revealed.

This is partially understood; yet the great figures of early Greek philosophy are rarely studied as they ought to be, and for good reason. Of the works they produced not one has survived intact; what firsthand knowledge of their contents we possess we owe to later writers who quote from them. Where even these remains are wanting we are forced to rely upon secondhand, late, and often unreliable reports of them. These accounts form a mass of material difficult to assess and difficult to interpret; around it has grown up a formidable body of highly specialized and technical literature. This being so, it is no great wonder if the average instructor hurries over this material as quickly as decency permits in order to reach the firmer ground provided by the dialogues of Plato.

Yet the problem of dealing with it is not an impossible one. It is, in large part, a question of ordering the material — of presenting it as the record of a concerted attempt to answer certain fundamental questions. This is the point of view from which I have set myself to write this book. The student will find in it the materials upon which any understanding of early Greek philosophy must be based; but he will find them presented in the form of a continuously unfolding process of thought.

I will first say a word about the evidence and then about the principles of interpretation I have followed. The evidence on which our knowledge of early Greek philosophy is based is of two sorts: there are the fragments (the words of the early philosophers themselves), and there are the reports of the philosophers' teaching which we find in later writers. These two sorts of evidence are of very unequal value. The testimony of later writers is almost always unsatisfactory; none of it has the authority of the fragments themselves. I have tried, therefore, to work from the fragments as far as possible, and to include as many of these as I could.

In earlier thinkers the lack of firsthand evidence presents a serious problem. In Anaximander's case we have part of a single sentence (there is no agreement as to how much of it is Anaximander's) and two or three doubtful phrases to go by. In such a case we have no choice but to fall back on later testimony. It is not, in fact, until we come to Heraclitus that we have any considerable number of fragments to work with. But from this point on the reader will find that I have tried, so far as possible, to dispense with secondary materials (except for purposes of illustration) and to argue directly from the fragments themselves. They are, after all, our primary source of knowledge of early Greek philosophy.

To help the student distinguish the fragments from other materials the former have been printed in boldface type. All materials have been assigned numbers, and the source from which each is taken has been indicated in the list of references at the back of the book. The student who cares to make use of this list in the light of the Note which precedes it will find that he is able to exercise some slight control over my weighting of the evidence.

With one or two exceptions these materials have been translated afresh. This was not necessary; most of them already exist in good English translations, and the extent of my debt to these translations will be all too obvious to those familiar with them. The labor was undertaken for my own good, to force myself to come to grips with problems arising from the texts themselves. I quickly found the truth of the saying that translations are like women: the beautiful ones are not faithful, and the faithful ones are not beautiful. For the most part I have sacrificed beauty to faithfulness. If I have taken occasional liberties with the texts of Plato or Aristotle, I have held my hand in the case of the fragments. Here I have tried to preserve, rather than to remove, all significant ambiguity. Except as noted in the list of references, I have followed the readings of Diels-Kranz for the fragments and the doxographic tradition, and those of the various editors of the Loeb Classical Library texts for other authors.

It is impossible, of course, to translate without interpreting; so it is only right that I should say something about the principles of interpretation which I have followed in this book. I am not speaking of the interpretation of particular fragments, or even of particular authors. There is scarcely a passage of any importance in Parmenides, for example, which scholars would interpret the same way. If I have avoided all reference to such problems of interpretation it is not because I am unaware of them, or because I do not think them important, but because they seem to me to be out of place in a book for beginners. The student who is curious to see for himself what goes into the interpretation of a Greek text will discover what he is looking for in the Bibliographical Essay to be found at the end of the book.

I have consulted few specialist studies during the actual writing of this book. I wished to write directly from the texts themselves, and with the student, not the scholar, in mind. In doing so I have had two things forcibly impressed upon me. The first is the unity of Greek philosophy. The Greek philosophers addressed themselves to a single set of closely connected philosophical problems, they approached these problems from certain assumptions held in common, and they employed in their solution a limited range of philosophical ideas. I believe that this fact is of the greatest importance for philosophers. I do not think that anyone who has thought very long or hard about metaphysical problems can fail to realize in the end that the framework within which we think about these problems is Greek. Nor do I think any attempt to go behind that framework has much chance of succeeding if it does not begin by recognizing this fact.

Secondly, I have been impressed by the developmental aspect of Greek philosophy. The general framework within which the Greek philosophers worked may be said to have been established by Anaximander at the very beginning. But the exploration of that framework, the realization of the problems inherent in it, and the attempt to solve them was the work of successive generations of philosophers. This development took place at an astonishing rate during the period dealt with in this book; nor is it clear that it has even yet come to an end. These two convictions — of the unity and of the development of Greek philosophy — do not admit of summary proof; but it is only proper to say that they have left their mark everywhere upon the final form of this book.

Above all I have tried to make a book that would be useful to beginners. If any reader cares to suggest ways in which it can be made more useful still, I shall be grateful.

J.M.R.

Newfane Hill
Newfane, Vermont

CONTENTS

Part Four THE UNSEATING OF ZEUS

PART ONE

THE LAYING OF THE FOUNDATIONS

Hesiod

Anaximander

Anaximenes and Xenophanes

Pythagoreanism

THE LAYING OF
THE FOUNDATIONS

Hesiod

Anaximander

Anaximenes and Xenophanes

Pythagoreanism

ONE

Hesiod

The earliest known works to be composed in the language written and spoken by the Greeks of the classical period are the poems of Homer and Hesiod, which date from the eighth century B.C. The poems of Homer are concerned with the foreground of human life — with particular men and what they did and suffered. Only occasionally do we catch a glimpse, behind these struggling figures, of the larger order in which they live and move and have their being. The poems of Hesiod are another matter. Hesiod's *Theogony* is directly concerned with this larger order. It deals with the origin of the world, the birth of the gods and the kingship of Zeus. It is only in Hesiod's *Works and Days* that man occupies the center of the stage, and even here Hesiod's concern with man is entirely different from Homer's. He is concerned with man as such, in his relations to the social order, to the gods, and to the necessities of life. With such questions the Greek philosophers, too, were concerned, and the answers which they gave to them were deeply colored by their reading of Hesiod. If we are to start at the beginning, we must start with Hesiod.

THE SEPARATION OF EARTH AND SKY

Hesiod's *Theogony* is an account of the origin of things. In it Hesiod tells us how the existing world-order arose, and how the gods, and after them the generations of men, came into being. This preoccupation with origins, with beginnings, is typical of the whole of early Greek philosophy. It rests on an assumption so natural that

3

we are apt not to notice that we are making it at all. This assumption is that there must have been a time when the present world-order did not exist; for only on this assumption is its existence something that must be accounted for. The efforts of the earliest Greek philosophers were directed mainly to the solution of this problem.

Hesiod's description of the origin of the world-order is brief and obscure, but it is of the greatest importance for the subsequent development of Greek philosophy:

> **1.1** First of all was Chaos born;
> Then, after him, wide-bosomed Earth,
> a sure, eternal dwelling-place
> for all the deathless gods who rule
> Olympus' snowy peaks.
> Next, Tartarus of the dark mist was born
> in a nook of the wide-wayed earth;
> then Love, most beautiful by far
> of all the immortals, the looser of limbs,
> who overcomes, of all the gods
> and all mankind, the mind within them
> and their clever counsels.
> From Chaos there sprang Erebos
> and dark-robed Night.
> From Night the Upper Air was born
> and Day, borne in her womb,
> the offspring of her love for Erebos.
> The Earth's first offspring,
> equal to herself, was Heaven
> filled with stars, to cover her entire
> and be a sure, eternal dwelling-place
> for the blessed gods.
> Then she bore the lofty hills
> the happy haunts of goddess nymphs
> who dwell in mountain glens.
> Without sweet union of love
> she bore the sea, Pontus,
> unharvested, with raging swell of surge
> and, having lain with Heaven, bore
> the deeply whirling Ocean River stream.

We are so familiar with the idea of order being produced out of chaos that we tend to assume unconsciously that in this passage, too, "Chaos" stands for that pre-existent state of affairs out of which the world-order comes into being. But Hesiod distinctly says that Chaos came into being; moreover, he seems to be referring in his use of the word to some feature of the world-order itself. In fact, *chaos* is derived from a root meaning "gap," and it refers here to the region between earth and heaven. This is certainly the meaning which the word has, at any rate, later in the *Theogony*, where Hesiod describes the battle between the Titan and the Olympian gods. From out of the sky, he says, Zeus hurled his thunderbolts, and the land was engulfed in flame:

1.2   The whole earth seethed with it,
    and the streams of the Ocean river,
    and the unharvested sea.
    The blazing vapor engulfed
    the earthborn Titans.
    A flame unquenchable pierced through
    the shining upper air.
    A blazing beam of thunder flash
    and lightning blast
    blinded their eyes, despite their strength.
    The wondrous blaze confounded Chaos.
    To the eyes the sight was such
    and the sound was such to the ears
    as the collision of Earth
    might seem with the mighty Heaven above.

Chaos, here, is clearly the region between earth and heaven, which is filled with the burning heat of the thunderbolts and the noise of their passage.

THE PRIMORDIAL UNITY

Hesiod's account, then, begins with the opening up of a gap between heaven and earth. But the opening of this gap presupposes a pre-existing state of affairs in which earth and heaven are one. Hesiod himself does not refer to this earlier stage, but traces of it survive in later writers:

1.3   Not from me but from my mother
    comes the tale how earth and sky
    were once one form, but being separated,
    brought forth all things, sending into light
    trees, birds, wild beasts,
    those nourished by the salt sea
    and the race of mortals.

The suggestion implicit in the opening words, that the tale is an old one handed down from generation to generation, is confirmed by the existence of creation myths much older than Hesiod, in which the first step in the creation of the world-order is the splitting in two of a primordial unity. In the Babylonian *Enuma elish*, for example, earth and sky are at first not distinguished; nothing exists but the primeval waters. The hero Marduk, after a great battle, kills Tiamat, the goddess of the waters, and divides her body into two halves. One of these he sets overhead to be the sky with its sweet waters; the other he sets opposite to it to be the earth with its salt sea. In *Genesis*, too, the earth is at first "without form and void; and darkness was upon the face of the waters." But God "divided the waters which were below the firmament from the waters which were above the firmament" to create heaven and earth.

At first, then, there was no distinction between earth and sky, but they were "one form." It was the creation of Chaos which made possible their emergence as distinct entities. This accounts for Hesiod's assertion that earth came into being *after* Chaos; for before Chaos came into being the form of earth was not yet visible as such, but was blended with the form of heaven in a single whole. It is their separation that marks the beginning of the creation of the world-order.

What caused this separation to take place? In 1.1, at any rate, we are not told. But later in the *Theogony*, in a myth describing the mutilation of Heaven by his children, Hesiod returns to the events of this earlier time. Heaven, he says, hated his children from the beginning:

> **1.4**   The minute that each child was born
> he would hide them all away
> in a hidden place of Earth
> and conceal them from the light.
> Heaven exulted in his evil work,
> but mighty Earth, within her heart,
> groaned from pressure's pain,
> and conceived a crafty plan
> of wicked treachery.
> Straightway she created the spark
> of hard grey flint, and made
> a mighty sickle of it.
> Then she told her children
> of the plan and spoke
> encouraging words to them
> born of her heart's distress:
> "Children of mine, born of a wicked father,
> obey me if you will, that we might punish

the vile and wicked outrage of your father
who was the first to plan such deeds of shame."
So she spoke; but fear laid hold of all
and not one said a word.
But mighty Cronus, crooked in his counsel,
took courage, and addressed his mother thus:
"Mother, I undertake to do this deed;
for I do not respect our ill-named father,
who was the first to plan such deeds of shame."
So he spoke; and mighty Earth rejoiced
within her heart, and in an ambush
made him lie, concealed.
She placed within his hand a sickle,
jagged sharp, and then revealed her plan.
Great Heaven then approached, and in his train
came Night; he longed for love and lay
spreading himself entirely over Earth.
Then from his ambush, his own son
stretched out his left hand; with his right
he seized the monstrous sickle,
long, and jagged sharp, and swiftly chopped
and cut his father's genitals,
and hurled them far behind him.
Nor did they fall in vain.
For every bloody drop that poured forth
Earth received; and as the seasons changed
she bore the powerful Furies
and the mighty Giants ablaze with armor,
holding in their hands long javelins.

This version of the story, like the first, assumes that in the beginning there was no gap between heaven and earth. This was because heaven covered earth completely, so as to prevent the emergence of her children. The myth of the mutilation of heaven is clearly an attempt to explain the separation of the two and the appearance of Chaos. As an explanation it may seem worthless, but it serves to reveal an important fact about the primordial unity, namely, the existence within it of opposing principles, male and female. Their existence is important because otherwise nothing would happen; the process of creation could never begin from a completely undifferentiated unity.

The myth seems crude to us because, like so many primitive myths, it uses sexual imagery in a context in which such imagery no longer seems to us to have any place. But to Hesiod the use of such imagery was natural; for the coming into being of Chaos is a kind of birth, and all birth presupposes the union of male and female.

This imagery is sustained throughout. From the division of earth and sky Love is born, the desire of male and female — the sundered parts of the original whole — for one another:

> **1.5** Holy sky desires to penetrate the earth.
> Love seizes earth with longing for this marriage.
> And rain, falling from her bedfellow the sky,
> impregnates earth; and she brings forth for men
> pasture for their flocks, and grain for them.

In these lines from Aeschylus it is by means of rain, falling across the gap which separates them, that Earth is impregnated by Heaven. In Hesiod she receives the bloody drops that fall from his mutilated body, and from this union springs the first generation of gods.

THE STRUCTURE OF THE WORLD-ORDER

Of this generation the firstborn is Ocean, the great river which Hesiod describes elsewhere as "flowing backward upon itself" as it circles the outer rim of earth. It is possible that this conception of a ring of water surrounding the earth originated in Mesopotamia, where it figures in the Babylonian epic of creation and has some physical basis in the situation of the fertile lands that lay between the Tigris and Euphrates rivers. Certainly it did not fit the geographical situation of the Greeks, and the historian Herodotus, who found the conception still current in his own day, was clearly puzzled as to what basis it could possibly have in experience:

> **1.6** The Greeks claim that Ocean flows around the whole earth, beginning where the sun rises; but in fact they offer no evidence to support this.

Equally without basis in observed fact is the existence beneath the earth of Tartarus. In **1.1** Hesiod simply mentions it as coeval with heaven; but in his account of the battle between the Titan and Olympian gods he describes it at some length. It is the place into which the defeated Titans are at last driven:

> **1.7** As far beneath the earth
> as heaven is above,
> so far away from earth

is dank and misty Tartarus.
If a brazen anvil were to fall
from heaven, it would fall
nine days and nights continuous
until, upon the tenth,
it reached the earth.
And if an anvil made of bronze
should fall from earth
nine days and nights continuous,
upon the tenth at last
it would reach Tartarus.
Around it runs a wall of bronze,
around it night has poured
her triple necklace chain.
Above it grow the roots of earth
and the unharvested sea.
There the Titan gods are hid
beneath a dark and misty gloom
by Zeus the cloud commander's plans,
in a dank place where ends the mighty earth.
They may not leave this place;
Poseidon set upon it doors of bronze
and a wall runs round it on all sides.
There Gyes lives, and Cottus,
and great-souled Obriareus,
the trusty guardians of Zeus
who bears the aegis.
There, each one in order, loathsome and dank,
are the wellsprings and the boundary marks
of gloomy earth and murky Tartarus
and of the starry heaven
and the unharvested sea.
Even the gods abhor this place —
a mighty chasm, whose floor no man would reach
when once he entered its gates
until a year had run its course,
for whirlwind after whirlwind
would toss him to and fro with deadly blast.
This place of portent even the immortals dread.
The dreadful house of black-robed Night
stands shrouded with a pall of cloud.
Before her home stands Iapetus' son
immovable; upon his head, and with unwearied hands
he holds aloft the vault of heaven.

Here Night and Day draw close
and greet each other as they pass
beyond the mighty threshold made of bronze.
One leaves the house just as the other enters,
and home never contains the two together
but one is always roaming over the earth
while the other stays at home
awaiting the time for her journey.

This description will hardly bear detailed analysis; it is not entirely consistent, and seems to involve geographical impossibilities. But the picture that emerges from it is clear enough. Tartarus lies "as far beneath the earth as heaven is above." It is separated from earth by a "mighty chasm" corresponding exactly to the gap which separates earth from sky. But the latter is filled with light, the former with darkness; the sun never shines on it, but it is dank and gloomy and storms rage in it. The floor of Tartarus is solid and presumably curved to meet the descending dome of the sky. From the upper limit of this whole to the lower the distance is so great that it would take an anvil twenty days to fall from top to bottom of it. Such, in its main outlines, is Hesiod's world, finite and symmetrical:

Along its vertical axis heaven and Tartarus stand in opposition; along its horizontal axis the stream of Ocean flows back upon itself; and at the center, equidistant from all these, lies earth, "a sure, eternal foundation for the blessed gods" and men.

THE APPORTIONING OF THE WORLD-ORDER

Much of Hesiod's *Theogony* is devoted to the story of Zeus, father of the Olympian gods. Because of a prophecy that his own son would displace him, Cronus, the son of heaven, ate his children as fast as Earth brought them forth. But when Zeus was born, his mother hid him away and gave Cronus a stone to swallow in his stead. In time the prophecies were fulfilled: through treachery Cronus was forced to disgorge his children one by one, and led by Zeus they drove out the first generation of gods, the Titans, and hurled them into Tartarus.

> **1.8** Now when the blessed gods
> had ended their hard labor —
> judging by strength in battle
> their quarrel with the Titans
> for whom should have more honor —
> they stirred up Zeus, far-seeing,
> to rule and reign the gods,
> because Earth bade them do it.
> So he shared out among them
> the honors each should have.

The distribution of honors to which this passage refers is of great importance for later thought. Hesiod himself does not explain it, but there is a passage in Homer which helps to bring out its significance very clearly. It occurs in Book 15 of the *Iliad* where Zeus, enraged at the interference of Poseidon in the battle between Greeks and Trojans, sends a messenger to command him to withdraw from the plain of Troy. Poseidon angrily protests:

> **1.9** No, no; good though he be, he spoke insolently
> if he would restrain me by force against my will
> when I am his peer in honor. For we three are brothers,
> sons of Cronus whom Rhea bore:
> Zeus and I, and Hades, lord of the world below.
> All was divided in three; each received his share of honor.
> I had the gray sea as my dwelling when we cast lots;

Hades, the shadowy world; Zeus, the broad heavens
among the upper air and clouds. The earth
is shared by all of us, along with high Olympus.
Wherefore I will not live by Zeus' will;
strong though he be, let him rest content with his share.
Let him not threaten me with his strength, as though I were
  wicked.
Better for him to scold his sons and daughters,
the children whom he begat, for they of need
must listen to his rage.

The basis for this protest is evident. Each of the three brothers has received an equal share — Poseidon the sea, Zeus the sky, and Hades the realm of darkness — earth being reserved for their common use. With these shares go certain rights and privileges which define the place of each in the scheme of things. These are the "honors" which in Hesiod's version of the story Zeus distributes among the gods after the defeat of the Titans. They determine, as it were, the spheres of influence of the gods, and any attempt at encroachment upon the sphere of one god by another is fiercely resisted as an injustice, for it constitutes a threat to the balance of power established by the original apportionment.

THE GENERATIONS OF MEN

In his *Theogony* Hesiod is concerned with the birth of the gods; in *Works and Days* he is concerned with that of men:

1.10 First of all, the immortals who dwell on Olympus
created the golden race of mortal men.
These lived in Cronus' time
when he held sway in heaven.
Like gods they lived their lives
with hearts released from care,
released from pain and sorrow.
They never felt the misery
of age; with never-failing limbs
they banqueted with pleasure,
remote from every ill.
Their death was like a sweet subduing sleep.
All good things were theirs.
The fruitful earth poured forth
her fruits unbidden in boundless plenty.
In peaceful ease they kept their lands

with good abundance,
rich in flocks, and dear to the immortals.
Now the earth has covered over
these men who are called
"pure spirits who dwell on earth,"
"good men," "defenders from evil,"
"warders of mortal men" (who keep watch
over lawsuits and wicked deeds
and roam the earth enveloped in mist),
"givers of wealth."

This is Hesiod's account of the Golden Age so often referred to in Greek literature, when the first men, fresh from the hands of the gods, lived a life like that of the gods themselves, free from hardship, suffering, and toil. The spirits of these men, long departed, still roam the earth, says Hesiod, and watch over men; but they themselves were mortal and passed away to be replaced by another generation.

1.11 Next after these the gods who dwell in Olympus
made a race of silver men
far baser than the first,
unlike the race of gods, in stature
and in spirit.
A child was nurtured at his mother's side
a hundred years, an utter simpleton,
playing a child's part in his house.
But when he was full grown
and reached the prime of life
he lived a meager span of years
in sorrow for his folly.
For they could not restrain themselves
from sin and wrong,
nor would they serve the gods
nor sacrifice upon the holy altars
of the blessed ones,
which is man's lawful duty.
Then Zeus the son of Cronus
engulfed them in his rage
because they paid no honors to the gods,
the blessed ones who dwell upon Olympus.

With the second generation of men we enter the realm of historical fact. Though we do not know with certainty who these men of silver were, it is not hard to guess. For Hesiod says that they paid no honor to the gods of Olympus, and this description would fit well enough the peoples whom the Greeks found already occupying the land when they came down from the north bringing with them their own gods, the gods of Olympus. It was Olympian Zeus himself who destroyed this second generation of men and created the third:

1.12 Then the earth engulfed these men
who are called by mortals
"blessed gods of the underworld,"
men of inferior rank, but still
honor attends them too.
Then Father Zeus devised another race,
a third, of mortal men,
a race of bronze, in no way like the silver,
dreadful and mighty, sprung from shafts of ash.
The all-lamented sinful works of Ares
were their chief care.
They ate no grain, but hearts of flint
were theirs, unyielding and unconquered.
Great was their strength,
invincible the arms
which grew from mighty shoulders
on strong limbs.
Bronze were their weapons,
their houses too were bronze,
with bronze they worked.
Black iron did not exist.
Subdued by their own hands
nameless they went to icy Hades'
dank and drear abode.
Black death laid hold upon them;
in spite of their great strength
they left the sun's bright light.

We know who these men were. They came out of the north about 2000 B.C., bearing weapons of bronze. They settled the mainland, built the great Mycenaean fortresses, and left behind them the documents in Linear B which we now know to be an early form of Greek. We can trace the extension of their power southward to Crete and eastwards to the coast of Asia Minor, where they sacked the city of Troy toward the beginning of the twelfth century B.C.

The expedition against Troy and the men who took part in it form the subject of the Homeric poems. Already in these poems the heroes whose exploits Homer celebrates loom larger than life-size. Hesiod looks upon them as a race apart, and treats them as forming a fourth generation of men:

1.13 Then the earth engulfed this race,
      and Zeus the son of Cronus made
      another race, the fourth
      he set upon the fruitful earth.
      This was more just, and nobler
      than the last — a godlike race
      of heroes, who are called
      "half-gods,"— the race before our own
      upon the boundless earth.
      Some of these men, grim war
      and battle strife destroyed,
      some fighting round the seven-gated city,
      Thebes, the land of Cadmus,
      for the flocks of Oedipus;
      others, brought to Troy by ships
      across the great surge of the mighty sea,
      for fair-haired Helen's sake.
      There death came as the end
      to some of them, and with his pall
      he shrouded them.
      Father Zeus, the son of Cronus,
      gave the rest to live their lives
      apart from men, and made them dwell
      at the far corners of the earth.
      And there they live, beside the surge
      of the deep Ocean in the blessed isles
      with hearts released from care,
      these heroes blest.
      Three times each year the earth
      in fruitfulness bestows on them
      her fruits, as sweet as honey.
      Far from the gods they live;
      their king is Cronus, whom
      the father of the gods and men
      released from bondage.
      Still, upon these last attend
      honor and glory.

But the generation of heroes was short-lived. The Dorians, with their iron weapons, swept them out of existence, destroyed the

Mycenaean strongholds, and took the land for themselves. These were the fifth generation, the generation of Hesiod himself:

1.14 Then Zeus, farseeing, made another race
of men, the fifth, who live
upon the fruitful earth.
Would that I had no share
in this fifth race of men.
Would that I had died before
or afterwards been born.
This is the race of iron.
Not for a day do they cease
from toil and labor, not for a night
does their corruption cease.
The gods will give them
bitter sorrow to endure.
Yet still some good things
shall be mingled with the bad.
Zeus will destroy this race too
of mortal men, as soon as infants
at their birth have gray hair
on their temples;
when father and children can be
no longer like-minded,
nor guest agree with host,
nor friend with friend;
when love no longer exists
from brother to brother
as once it did.
Then they will swiftly dishonor
their aging parents, and chide them
with harsh rebukes, in bitterness,
with no respect for gods.
They will not repay their aged parents
for their childhood care,
but take the law in their own hands.
One man will sack another's city;
favor will not be shown to him
who keeps an oath, is just,
or good. The evil-doer's
arrogance will win men's praise.
Right shall depend on might
and piety will cease to be.
The wicked will slander the noble

and do him harm, and forswear himself.
Among all wretched men
envy will go her way
with shrill and evil tongue
delighting in disaster,
her face a face of hate.
And then the time will come
when, to Olympus from the wide-wayed earth,
enveloped in white robes
to hide their lovely flesh
Shame and Respect shall go,
leaving mankind, to join the blessed gods.
Bitter heartache they bequeath
to mortal men, nor leave
defense from evil.

Hesiod's account of the generations of men in *Works and Days* bears a certain resemblance to his account of the generations of gods in his *Theogony*. But there is an important difference between them. The Olympian gods are directly descended from the gods of the first generation. Moreover, the first generation of Titan gods is directly descended from heaven and earth, so that they issue as it were from the womb of nature itself. Their birth is but an extension of the process by which the world-order itself comes into being. This is not true of man. The generations of men not only form a discontinuous series but are brought into being by special acts of creation. Man is not a product of nature but a creation of the gods, and his destiny is bound up with theirs.

THE JUSTICE OF ZEUS

The Dorian invasion ushered in a Dark Age beyond which Hesiod, though he lived at the close of it, could see nothing but dissolution and death. In the violence of the great and the strong it seemed to him that he saw already the beginning of the end:

1.15 Now I will tell a story
for the ears of kings
who know it well.
Thus spoke the hawk
to the nightingale,
the bird of lovely throat,
bearing her high in the clouds

clenched in his crooked claws.
Pitifully she wept,
pierced by his curving claws.
But he, disdainful overlord,
addressed her thus:
"Wretch, why do you weep?
One mightier than you
now holds you fast.
You go wherever I take you,
singer though you are.
Food I shall make of you,
if I will, or let you go.
Foolish is he who wishes
to strive with those who are stronger.
He loses victory and gains
the pain of shameful suffering."
So spoke the hawk,
the swift of flight,
the long-winged bird.

Strength extorts what it will; weakness concedes what it must. Such is the philosophy of the overlords. But it is a false philosophy, Hesiod asserts; for Zeus has given justice to men, and it is by justice, not violence, that men must live:

1.16 Listen now to justice, and forget,
    completely, violence.
    For Cronus' son set up
    this law for men.
    Fish, flesh, and fowl
    each other may devour,
    for right is not in them.
    But right he gave
    to men, and this
    is best by far.

Zeus has not only given justice to men; he casts down the unjust and rewards those who follow justice:

1.17 Those who give to every man,
    those from abroad and those from home,
    straight judgments, and do not transgress
    the just — their city flourishes,

their people prosper too.
Peace, the children's guardian,
patrols the land, and Zeus, far-seeing,
does not plan cruel wars against them.
Upon the men who judge with honesty
famine and disaster never wait;
they work at their appointed tasks
with merriment.
For them the earth brings forth
a plenteous livelihood.
The mountain oak trees bear
on their high branches acorns,
and in the middle, bees.
Their woolly sheep are laden down
with heavy fleeces.
The children that their women bear
are like their parents.
They abound with good things in plenty.
They never take to the sea,
for the earth, the giver of grain,
supplies their every need.

Those who delight in violence
and wicked, sinful deeds,
far-seeing Zeus, the son of Cronus,
plans to punish.
Often a whole city suffers
for the actions of a man
who sins and plans outrageous crimes.
Upon such men the son of Cronus
brings great suffering,
with plague and famine too.
The people perish.
The women bear no children,
the houses dwindle through the plans
of all-contriving Zeus.
At other times, the son of Cronus
did destroy a mighty army
of these men, or else their walls,
or wrecked their ships upon the sea.

THE MORALITY OF PRUDENCE

If a man would avoid disaster, then, let him avoid injustice:

1.18 That other road is better
which leads toward just dealing;
for justice conquers violence,
and triumphs in the end.

This is the voice of prudence. When we say, "Honesty is the best policy," we mean that honesty pays; and when Hesiod says that justice is better than injustice, he too means that it pays, for it "triumphs in the end." If violence paid, that would be the better way; for a man would be foolish to be just if there were nothing to be gained by it. Hesiod puts it with disarming candor:

1.19 The eye of Zeus, all-seeing and all-knowing,
beholds us even now, if thus he wills.
The sort of justice that this city deals in
within herself will not escape his notice.
For otherwise I'd not myself be righteous,
nor have my son be so;
for it is bad to be a man of justice
if the less just's to have the greater right.

If the just man were to receive less benefit from being just than from following violence, it would clearly not be in his interest to be just. For no man is just simply for justice's sake, because justice is good in itself, but because it is the will of Zeus, who is able to detect injustice and punishes those who practice it.

We see the same mentality at work in the admonitions with which Hesiod intersperses his directions for plowing, planting, and harvesting. It is the mentality of the small peasant farmer, to whose way of life and station the virtues of hard work and thrift are appropriate:

1.20 If your heart within you yearns for riches,
do as I tell you; work unceasingly.

1.21 Don't put it off until tomorrow, or the next day.
No man fills his barn by shirking work
or putting off the job. It's keeping at it
gets the work done. The man who puts it off
contests with ruin.

1.22 If you add little to little
and do it often,
soon the little will grow
and become big.

1.23 Get good measure from your neighbor;
give good measure back.
Return as much, or better, if you can,
so that when you are yourself in need
you will find him able to supply it.

These admonitions reflect a way of thinking very different from that of the heroic age. The world of Homer is a world in which men are moved by considerations of honor; the world of Hesiod is one in which men are moved by self-interest. It is a simple view of life, but a limited one. With the passage of time it was to prove full of difficulties — as full of difficulties, indeed, as Hesiod's conception of the world-order as a whole.

TWO

Anaximander

Aristotle says that the founder of Greek philosophy was Thales, a citizen of Miletus, one of the Ionian Greek city-states on the coast of Asia Minor. But it is clear that Aristotle had no firsthand knowledge of his views, and it is quite impossible, from the evidence available to us, to give a connected account of them (Appendix A). To all intents and purposes the history of Greek philosophy begins with Thales' fellow citizen and younger contemporary Anaximander.

2.1 Apollodorus says in his *Chronicles* that Anaximander was sixty-four years of age in the second year of the fifty-eighth Olympiad [547/6 B.C.] and that he died shortly afterwards.

This would put the date of his birth about 612 B.C. and the period of his maturity about a hundred years after that of Hesiod.

Unlike Thales, Anaximander committed his views to writing. Of his book on the nature of things only a single sentence has come down to us; and apart from this single sentence we know of the contents of his book only from later and confused accounts of it. But even these confused reports show that in it Anaximander laid the foundations of Greek philosophical thought.

THE INFINITE

Aristotle, in his review of earlier thinkers in the first book of his *Metaphysics*, distinguishes sharply between those who, like Hesiod,

23

wrote concerning the gods, and those who, coming later, addressed themselves to the investigation of nature. The distinction is sound; despite the "somewhat poetical language" in which (according to Simplicius) Anaximander's book is written, there is no mistaking its difference from Hesiod's *Theogony*. At the same time it is easy to overestimate this difference; for the problem around which Anaximander's thought revolves is the same problem around which Hesiod's revolves — the problem of origins.

This is quite clear from all the accounts of Anaximander's thought which have come down to us:

> **2.2** Anaximander . . . asserted that the source and element of existing things is the "infinite." He was the first to introduce this name for the source. He says that it is neither water nor any of the other so-called "elements," but of another nature which is infinite, from which all the heavens and the world-orders in them arise.

> **2.3** It is eternal and "ageless" and encompasses all the world-orders.

The infinite is first and foremost the *source* of existing things; it is *that out of which* they come. In this respect it corresponds to the original union of earth and sky of which Hesiod speaks. But by calling it "infinite" Anaximander has taken a step beyond Hesiod. For Hesiod does not tell us whence this union of earth and sky arose; it is not even clear that the question occurred to him. It has occurred to Anaximander, however, and his answer is decisive for the history of Western thought: that out of which existing things arise can have neither beginning nor end. Therefore, the question whence it came into being does not arise; it did not come into being at all.

Aristotle, in a passage in which he clearly has Anaximander in mind, puts it this way:

> **2.4** Everything either *is* a beginning or *has* a beginning. But there is no beginning of the infinite; for if there were one, it would limit it. Moreover, since it *is* a beginning, it is unbegotten and indestructible. For there must be a point at which what has come into being reaches completion, and a point at which all perishing ceases. Hence, as we say, there is no source of *this* [the infinite], but *this* appears to be the source of all the rest, and "encompasses all things" and "steers all things," as those assert who do not recognize other causes besides the infinite . . . . And this, they say, is the divine; for it is "deathless" and "imperishable" as Anaximander puts it, and most of the physicists agree with him.

The life of the world-order is, as we shall see (**2.41**), limited at both ends. It comes into existence and passes away. But that out of which it arises and into which it passes away is "ageless" and "imperishable," without beginning or end. It will be evident from this that when Anaximander speaks of the source of existing things as "infinite," he is thinking in temporal rather than spatial terms. No doubt he thought of it as vast by Hesiodic standards; for it is *that in which* the world-order arises as well as *that out of which* it arises (**2.3**). But the problem which Anaximander was trying to solve did not require it to be infinite in extent.

THE FORMATION OF THE WORLD-ORDER

In Hesiod's *Theogony* the formation of the world-order begins with the separation of earth and sky. Anaximander, too, conceives the process as one of separation:

2.5   The opposites, which are present in the one, are separated out from it, Anaximander says.

2.6   The "opposites" are the hot, the cold, the dry, the moist, and the rest.

The hot, the cold, the wet, and the dry are not, as one might suppose, simply qualities; for as yet no distinction existed in Greek thought between a thing and the power which it has to affect another thing. The opposites are therefore indistinguishable from what later came to be called the "elements": earth, air, fire, and water. It is these that are contained in the primordial unity. Aristotle speaks of them as "separated out" from the "one," *i.e.*, from the infinite (**2.5**), and in an important sense this is true. For the emergence of the world-order as a distinct entity within the body of the infinite implies a separation of the elements which go to make up the world-order from that which "encompasses" them. But the statement is also misleading, for in order for the world-order to arise out of the mixture of earth, air, fire, and water, it is also necessary that these be separated *from one another*.

This aspect of the process is more clearly brought out in the one account of the formation of the world-order which has come down to us:

2.7   He says that something productive of hot and cold was separated off from the eternal at the coming into being of this world-order, and that a sphere of flame from this formed around the air about the earth, like bark around a tree. When this was broken up and enclosed in rings the sun, moon, and stars were formed.

The "eternal," here, is the infinite; so much is clear from **2.3**. What is separated off from the infinite, then, must be that portion of it which is to form the world-order. But to speak of this portion as "productive of" the opposites is misleading; for the hot, the cold, and the rest are present in the infinite from the beginning (**2.5**), and must therefore be present in that portion of it out of which the world-order arises. The "production" of the opposites, therefore, can only refer to the emergence of fire, air, and earth as distinct entities — much as in the *Theogony* earth and sky emerge as such only with the opening of the gap between them.

But the result of the separating-out is twofold. Earth, air, and fire emerge not only as distinct masses but as occupying different positions in the world-order. For **2.7** makes it clear that they come to be arranged in concentric circles, with earth at the center and fire at the outside. The reason for this particular arrangement, Aristotle says, is the same in all the earlier thinkers. They make the earth travel to the center of the world-order under the influence of a vortex motion:

> **2.8** All of them say that this is the cause, arguing from what happens in liquids and in air where the larger and heavier things always travel to the center of a vortex. Hence all who hold that the heaven came into being say that the earth travelled to the center for this reason.

Since Anaximander clearly held that the world-order comes into being, the process described in **2.7** must have been due to a vortex motion similar to that which we see "in liquids and in air."

The Vortex Motion

Aristotle's account of this phenomenon is very meager; but some light is thrown upon it by a Greek medical writer of the fifth century B.C. in a treatise dealing with the formation of the child in the womb:

> **2.9** If you attach a small tube to a bladder and introduce earth, sand, and fine particles of lead into the bladder through the tube, pour water in over them, and then blow through the tube, the contents will at first be mixed together by the water. But after a while, if you continue to blow through the tube, the lead will go to the lead, the sand to the sand, and the earth to the earth. And

if you allow the bladder to dry and tear it open and examine the contents, you will find that like has gone to like.

The air, as it enters the bladder, falls into a rotary motion, and this by degrees is communicated to the mixture of water, earth, sand, and lead. The result is a separating-out of the mixture in which, as the author puts it, "like goes to like," *i.e.*, sand goes to sand, earth to earth and lead to lead. But since "the larger and heavier things always travel to the center of a vortex," these masses will evidently form a series of concentric circles arranged according to weight.

Now this state of affairs exactly corresponds to the arrangement of earth, air, fire, and water in the existing world-order. Earth, which is heaviest, is situated in the middle; water, which is next heaviest, encircles it as Ocean; beyond lies air; outermost of all is the fiery circuit of the heavens. From this similarity of effects the early Greek philosophers argued backward to a similarity of causes. If what happens in liquids and in air is due to rotation, what happens in the process of world-formation must also be due to rotation.

If Aristotle is right (**2.8**), Anaximander must have been the first to offer such an explanation of the origin of the world-order. The fact is important because it marks the transition from the mythical and poetic mode of thought characteristic of Hesiod to the very different mode of thought which (despite backslidings) comes increasingly to dominate the thinking of the early Greek philosophers. It is not the use of analogy as such that is significant; Hesiod too relies on analogy in his account of the formation of the world-order. But the analogy with which he worked was drawn from human life. Earth and Heaven are not elemental masses in Hesiod; they are persons, and the forces which operate to bring about their separation and reunion are not physical but psychological. In short, Hesiod's account of the origin of the world-order is from first to last anthropomorphic. Anaximander's account represents, in principle, a complete break with this mode of thought. The analogy with which he works is purely mechanical, and the forces which operate to bring about the formation of the world-order are entirely impersonal. In taking this step, Anaximander crossed the line that divides Hesiod from the Greek philosophers. The implications of the step were only slowly realized, and in the process of making them explicit the foundations of Greek religion and morality were to be wholly undermined; but the history of the working-out of these implications is to a large extent the history of Greek philosophy.

THE HEAVENLY BODIES

In the process of world-formation the hot travels to the periphery, where it forms a sphere of flame (**2.7**). This in turn is broken up and the parts enclosed in "circles" to form the sun, moon, and stars. A number of passages refer to these circles:

2.10 The heavenly bodies come into being as a ring of fire, which has been separated off from the fire in the world-order and enclosed by air. There are vents — pipe-like passages — at which the heavenly bodies appear; hence eclipses occur when the vents become stopped up.

2.11 The heavenly bodies are wheel-shaped masses of compressed air filled with fire, which emit flames at various points from small openings.

2.12 Anaximander says that the sun is like a chariot wheel . . . the rim of which is hollow and filled with fire. At a certain point on it the fire shows through an opening, as through the nozzle of a bellows.

Anaximander's problem, clearly, was to account for the fact that the fire in the world-order does not appear to us as a single ring of flame but as a multitude of distinct points of light in the heavens. He solved this problem by making two assumptions: first, that the original band of fire had at some time in the distant past broken up into narrower bands (**2.7**); and second, that the air surrounding these narrower bands had become opaque because of the action of the fire on them, except for certain "vents" at which the flame within was still visible. The second of these assumptions was not quite as groundless as it appears; the principle on which it depends was to be taken up and developed in a very striking manner by Anaximander's successor Anaximenes (Chapter Three). But Anaximander's application of it to his theory of the heavenly bodies was too cumbersome to maintain itself.

Of more lasting importance for later thought were his views of their sizes and distances from the earth:

2.13 Anaximander was the first to take up the subject of sizes and distances.

2.14 He placed the sun highest of all, below that the moon, and below these the fixed stars and planets.

2.15 The sun, he says, is equal to the earth; but the ring on which its vent lies, and by which it is carried around, is twenty-seven times the size of the earth.

2.16 The moon is a ring eighteen times as large as the earth. It is like a chariot wheel the rim of which is hollow and full of fire, like the ring of the sun; and it is placed obliquely [to the plane of the earth] like the other.

The order in which Anaximander places the rings bearing the heavenly bodies seems odd; but it is in fact quite natural. The moon is cooler than the sun, as is evident from the fact that we get no heat from it. Consequently, it must be further from the outermost ring of flame than the sun, and therefore closer to us. But the stars and planets have an even smaller share of the hot in them, for they give even less light and heat than the moon. Consequently, they must be closest of all to the cold earth.

Still more curious are the figures which Anaximander assigns to the diameters of these rings. The two that we are given appear to be members of a series of multiples of nine in arithmetical progression. But there is evidently a gap in the series, and this gap exactly corresponds to the position occupied by the ring which bears the fixed stars in the series of rings bearing the heavenly bodies. If we assume that the diameter of this circle is nine times the diameter of the earth, we get the completed series nine, eighteen, twenty-seven. In **2.17**, moreover, we are told that the diameter of the earth is three times its depth. These figures certainly do not represent the results of observation and measurement. They seem, rather, to represent a fundamental assumption about the nature of the world-order, namely, that its structure can be expressed in the language of mathematics. The assumption is only implicit; the task of making it explicit, of justifying it and of grasping its implications, fell to the Pythagoreans (Chapter Four). But this development, like so many others, seems to have had its roots in the cosmology of Anaximander.

EARTH

At the center of the vortex lies the earth, a sedimentary deposit, as it were, of the process of separation:

2.17 He says that the earth is cylindrical in shape, and that its depth is one-third its breadth.

2.18 In form it is concave, round like the drum of a column. Of its [two] surfaces, we walk upon one and the other is opposite to it.

Anaximander's conception of the earth is very similar to Hesiod's. Its comparison to the drum of a column (presumably the comparison is

Anaximander's own) helps to explain the use of the term "concave." Greek columns were constructed out of drum-shaped pieces of stone, the upper and lower surfaces of which were made concave and convex respectively in order to ensure proper seating when the drums were placed on top of one another. The comparison therefore suggests that the upper surface of the earth, upon which we stand, is slightly hollowed out so as to form a basin — the Mediterranean basin, in fact, which was the center of the Greek world.

Hesiod, however, offers no explanation for the earth's remaining where it is, suspended midway between heaven and Tartarus. Anaximander evidently felt that some explanation was called for:

> **2.19** Anaximander says that the earth is suspended aloft, and that it rotates at the center of the world-order.

> **2.20** There are some who say, like Anaximander among the ancients, that it stays where it is because of its equilibrium. For what is stationed at the center, and is equably related to the extremes, has no reason to go one way rather than another — either up or down or sideways. And since it is impossible for it to move simultaneously in opposite directions, it necessarily stays where it is.

> **2.21** Anaximander seems to say that the earth remains where it is both because it is supported by air and because of its equilibrium and "indifference."

Since the earth shares in the rotation of the whole, it is not surprising to find it described as rotating at the center (**2.19**). This, however, would not account for its being "suspended aloft," and the explanation offered in **2.20** only increases the difficulties. According to this account (which comes to us from Aristotle) the fact that the earth occupies a point equidistant in every direction from the periphery of the world-order means that it has no reason to move in one direction rather than another; hence it remains where it is. This explanation does away at a single stroke with the notion of an absolute up and down, and it would be remarkable if Anaximander had put it forward at the very beginning of Greek philosophy.

There are strong reasons, however, for doubting whether it is Anaximander's at all, for it ignores a distinction of fundamental importance for all those who used the vortex hypothesis. It was not difficult for these thinkers to account for the position of the earth at the center of the plane of rotation. It was sufficient to suppose that the same forces that made the earth travel to the center in the first place continued to act on it. But the use of the vortex hypothesis depended on the assumption that the earth is heavy in an absolute sense, and on this assumption it is absurd to say, as Aristotle does, that it has no reason to go one way rather than another. For, being heavy, it has a tendency to fall out of the plane of rotation. Anaximander saw this quite clearly and solved the problem (as **2.21** shows) by supposing the earth to be supported from underneath by air. In this, as we shall see, he was followed by the majority of his successors; for the assumptions underlying Hesiod's description of the behavior of an anvil in free fall (**1.7**) held good down to the time of Plato.

THE FIRST MAP

When the earth was first formed, it was not as we see it now:

> **2.22** At first [according to certain of the natural philosophers] the whole region about the earth was watery. But as the sun dried it out, the water that evaporated gave rise to winds and the solstices of sun and moon, while the water that was left became the sea. Consequently they believe that the sea is even now drying up and becoming less, and that eventually a time will come when it will be all dried up.

> **2.23** Of this opinion were Anaximander and Diogenes [of Apollonia], according to Theophrastus.

As the water receded, the great land masses appeared. These Anaximander set out to distinguish in the first known map:

> **2.24** Anaximander the Milesian . . . was the first to undertake to draw the inhabited world on a tablet. After him the Milesian Hecataeus, a widely travelled man, made it more accurate, so that it was an object of wonder.

It was presumably this map, as revised by Hecataeus, which Herodotus ridiculed in his *Histories*:

> **2.25** I have to smile when I see how many up to now have drawn maps of the earth, and not one of them has explained the matter sensibly. They draw Ocean flowing around the earth (which is drawn as though with a compass), and make Asia and Europe the same size.

> **2.26** I am amazed at those who have mapped out and divided up the earth into Libya, Asia, and Europe; for the differences between them are considerable. Europe is as long as the other two put together, and in my opinion is not to be compared with them for breadth.

2.27 Nor can I imagine . . . why the boundaries set for them should be the river Nile in Egypt and the river Phasis at Colchis.

2.28 If we were to fall in with this way of thinking we should have to consider all Egypt, from the cataracts and the city of Elephantine to the sea, to be divided down the middle and to have two names, since part of it would be in Libya and part in Asia!

As for Ocean:

2.29 I know of no river of Ocean. I fancy that Homer, or one of the older poets, invented the name and introduced it into his poetry.

From these passages it is a fairly simple matter to reconstruct Anaximander's map in its broad outlines. It showed the earth's surface as a round disk divided into three equal parts: Europe, Asia, and Libya. These were separated by three great waterways: the Nile, the Phasis, and the Mediterranean itself, radiating out like the spokes of a wheel from the sacred stone on the island of Delos in the Aegaean sea to the river of Ocean, flowing around the rim.

What Herodotus objects to, plainly, is the symmetry of this scheme — a symmetry which he insists is entirely artificial, and which is obtained only by making Europe smaller than it really is, and by arbitrarily making half the Egyptians Libyans and the other half Asians. But it is precisely this feature of the scheme which most strikingly confirms its origin in Anaximander; for it is a product of that same tendency to impose order and proportion on all things which finds expression in the system of the heavenly bodies.

THE ORIGIN OF LIFE

The animals which inhabit these land masses, according to Anaximander, had their origin in the sea:

2.30 He held that the first animals arose in moisture, being enclosed in spiny "barks," but that as they grew older they emerged onto the drier land and there (the "bark" having ruptured) lived a different sort of life for a short time.

The notion that life arose spontaneously in the ancient seas, only afterwards emerging from them onto the dry land, strikes the modern reader as a startling anticipation of the findings of modern science; and this impression is heightened by a number of passages which deal specifically with the origin of human life:

2.31 He says further that in the beginning man was born from animals of a different sort, arguing from the fact that whereas animals are soon able to fend for themselves, the young of humans are dependent for a long period of time. Hence, if man had been in the beginning as he is now, he would never have been able to survive.

2.32 Anaximander of Miletus held that there arose from warm water and earth creatures which were either fish or fish-like. Inside these human beings were formed, remaining there like fetuses until the time of puberty. At this time the creatures broke open, and men and women already capable of getting food for themselves emerged.

2.33 He says that the first human beings arose inside fishes, and that having been nurtured there like sharks, and having become able to fend for themselves, they emerged and took to the land.

The impression that Anaximander anticipated Darwin is quite mistaken, however. Anaximander is very far from supposing that human beings "evolved" in our sense of that term. On the contrary, he thinks of them as coming into being in the form which they have today. This is precisely his problem. Human beings as we know them must be protected and fed during infancy for a much longer period of time than the young of other animals; hence Anaximander must provide for the survival of the *first* generation of men by some extraordinary means. The significance of these passages does not lie, therefore, in the mention of fish-like creatures; they are only there because the facts seem to require them — like the tubes of compressed air that surround the heavenly bodies. It lies rather in the contrast between Anaximander's theory of the origin of man and Hesiod's. In Hesiod the generations of men are created one after another by the gods; in Anaximander their coming into being is a natural process, continuous with that which brings the world-order itself into being. As the mixture of the opposites separates out simply because forces capable of effecting separation are present, so life begins simply because the physical conditions sufficient to produce it are present in the heat and the moisture.

THE INJUSTICE OF THE OPPOSITES

The single sentence of Anaximander's book that has come down to us is preserved by Simplicius. Immediately after **2.2** he continues:

> **2.34** Into those things from which existing things have their coming into being, their passing away, too, takes place, **according to what must be; for they make reparation to one another for their injustice according to the ordinance of time,** as he puts it in somewhat poetical language.

It is not immediately evident what "those things" are from which existing things arise. The infinite as such cannot be meant; so much seems clear from the use of the plural. On the other hand, in some sense existing things *must* arise from the infinite — if not from the infinite as such, then from those powers which are contained in the infinite and are separated out from it in the formation of the world-order. These are the opposites: "the hot, the cold, the moist, the dry, and the rest" (**2.6**). For the opposites are not conceived of in early Greek thought simply as the qualities of existing things; they are thought of as constituting them. It is from the opposites, then, that existing things arise.

The point is important, for the words which follow — "they make reparation to one another for their injustice according to the ordinance of time" — refer not (as one might expect) to existing things but to "those things" from which existing things arise. It is the opposites which "make reparation to one another for their injustice"; and the conception is one which we find elsewhere in early Greek thought. We find it, for example, in Alcmaeon of Croton, who laid the foundations of Greek medical theory early in the fifth century B.C.:

> **2.35** Alcmaeon says that the essence of health lies in the "equality" of the powers — moist, dry, cold, hot, bitter, sweet, and the rest — whereas the cause of sickness is the "supremacy of one" among these. For the rule of any one of them is a cause of destruction . . . while health is the proportionate mixture of the qualities.

The principle involved is stated still more clearly by a medical writer of the late fifth century. The opposites, he says, are to be found *in* the body as well as outside it:

> **2.36** All of them are present in the body, but as the seasons revolve they become now greater now less, in turn, according to the nature of each. The year has a share of all things — the hot, the cold, the dry, and the wet — for no one of the things which exist in the world-order would last for any length of time were it not for all the rest. On the contrary, if a single thing were to fail, all would disappear; for all things come into existence from the same necessity and are sustained by one another. So also with the body; if any of the things which have come into being together were to fail in it, a man could not live.

The opposites of which the body is made up are at war with one another. For the hot lives at the expense of the cold; it can only occupy a body by driving out its opposite. In this sense all change implies the wronging of one opposite by another. On the other hand, health lies in the maintenance of a balance of opposites; it can be preserved, there-fore, only if, for every wrong done, compensation is rendered and the balance restored. Unless this took place according to nature, one of the warring opposites would eventually destroy the rest and the body would perish.

As the writer of **2.36** points out, the same situation prevails in the world-order at large; for it too is comprised of the same opposites, and we can see for ourselves how first one and then the other dominates as the seasons succeed one another. Moreover, the succession of the seasons is an orderly one; each of the opposites makes reparation for the wrong it has done "according to the ordinance of time," *i.e.*, as the year revolves.

Here too the uncompensated encroachment of any one of the opposites would result in the destruction of the whole, the world-order itself.

THE LAW OF COMPENSATION

But what is the necessity that compels the opposites to make reparation to one another for their injustice? One thing is certain: the roots of our confidence in the law of compensation lie deep in human nature. We feel "instinctively" that an unusually mild autumn will have to be "paid for" by an unusually severe winter. In the same way we feel "instinctively" that no run of good luck can possibly last, and that the longer it does last the more certain it is that it will end badly. This is the root from which tragedy grows; for in the reversal of fortune which overtakes the tragic hero the same law of compensation is at work. But it is not yet tragedy; for tragedy was the invention of the Greeks, and the assumption basic to Greek thought is that nothing happens without a reason. If a man exalted above his fellows and to all appearances secure in his happiness is brought low, there must be a reason for it, and the Greeks were not long in finding one.

The classic case is that of Polycrates, tyrant of Samos. About 540 B.C. Polycrates seized power in Samos with the aid of his brothers. Having secured his position by the exile of one brother and the murder of the other, he made a pact of friendship with Amasis, the ruler of Egypt, and embarked on a policy of conquest. From the start his luck was phenomenal. Everything he set his hand to succeeded, and it was not long before he enjoyed a prosperity second only to that of the lords of Syracuse themselves.

> **2.37** Amasis was not unaware of the great good fortune of Polycrates, and it caused him some concern. When he saw that it continued to increase, he wrote the following letter, which he sent to Samos:
>
> "Amasis to Polycrates: It is gratifying to learn that a friend and ally is doing well, but these great successes of yours do not please me. For I know that the gods are jealous, and I wish for myself and those connected with me success in some things but failure in others — a life of ups and downs rather than one of unbroken good fortune. For no one, to my knowledge, ever experienced unbroken good fortune without coming to a bad end. If you will listen to me you will take steps to meet the danger in the following way. Decide what it is that is most precious to you and would cause you the greatest pain if you were to lose it, and throw it away, so that it will never again be seen among men. And if you do not find, after doing this, that your successes alternate with failures, continue to do as I have suggested."

Polycrates, when he read this, decided that the advice of Amasis was sound, and he began to consider which of his treasures it would grieve him most to lose. He hit on a signet ring that he used to wear — an emerald set in gold, the work of Theodorus, son of Telecles, of Samos — and determining to throw this away he caused a galley to be manned, went on board, and ordered it to sea. When he was far from the island he drew off the signet ring in the sight of all and flung it into the water. Then he sailed back and went to his house, where he lamented his loss.

On the fifth or sixth day after this, a fisherman who had caught a large, fine fish — one worthy, he thought, to be offered to Polycrates as a gift — brought it to the door and asked to be admitted to Polycrates' presence. And when this was granted he offered the fish, saying, "King: I am a man who has to work for a living, but it did not seem right to me to take this fish to market. It seemed to me worthy of you and your greatness, so I have brought it here to give to you." Polycrates was pleased by what the fisherman said and answered, "You have done well, and I thank you twice over — for your words and for your gift. In return, I invite you to supper with me."

The fisherman went home, pleased at the honor done him; but the servants, cutting open the fish, found the signet ring in its belly. Seeing what it was, they brought it joyfully to Polycrates and, presenting it to him, explained how they had found it. Polycrates, seeing the hand of providence in this, wrote a letter to Amasis telling him what he had done and what had come of it, and sent it off to Egypt. When Amasis read Polycrates' letter he saw that it was impossible for one man to save another from his destiny, and that Polycrates, whose luck held so consistently that even what he threw away he found again, would come to a bad end.

And so it proved: for not long afterwards Polycrates sailed to Magnesia at the invitation of the Persian governor and was brutally murdered there, thus fulfilling Amasis' expectations.

In this story an attempt is made to deduce the law of compensation, as applied to human affairs, from a higher principle: the jealousy of the gods. As Xerxes' advisor puts it to him, on the eve of his master's ill-fated invasion of Greece:

2.38 You see, my lord, how god strikes with his thunderbolts those living creatures who are exalted above their fellows, and does not suffer them to vaunt themselves. The small ones do not provoke his anger; it is always the highest buildings and the tallest trees on which his bolts fall. For god delights to put down all those who are exalted.

But from the point of view of tragedy this explanation of the law of compensation is not entirely satisfactory, for it lacks a moral dimension. Herodotus, in telling the story of Polycrates, does not suggest that Polycrates deserved his fate, or that it was in any way connected with the crimes by means of which he had achieved his position. Polycrates is no more guilty than the tree is that is struck by lightning merely because it is taller than its fellows. The tragic element enters only when the law of compensation is seen as a *moral* law:

> **2.39** Above all, happiness depends
> on wisdom. It is never right
> to sin against the gods. Great blows
> repay great words of boasting men,
> and teach us wisdom in old age.

There is not only a reason for the downfall of the tragic hero; the reason lies in the man himself. His fall is seen as a just punishment, visited upon him by the gods, for the overweening pride which success brings in its train. This is the pride — the lack of regard for the rights of others, even those of the gods themselves — which Agamemnon displays in the destruction of the altars of the gods at Troy, and for which he pays the penalty at the hands of Clytemnestra.

THE STEERING OF ALL THINGS

Tragedy, then, is based on the law of compensation seen as working for justice in human affairs. In this moralized form the law is already implicit in Hesiod (**1.17**), where its operation depends upon the will of Zeus. In Anaximander it is made to work not only in human affairs but throughout the world-order. The law of compensation becomes a law of nature; but in doing so it undergoes a curious transformation. For the orderliness which it guarantees is no longer contingent upon the will of Zeus; it is grounded in the nature of things as such.

A look at **1.9** will help to make the nature of this transformation clearer. Poseidon's protest at the highhandedness of Zeus is based on the claim that in so acting Zeus is threatening the whole order of things. But the order which is threatened is, in Homer, one which has been fixed by the agreement of the gods themselves; the rights and privileges of the gods as individuals are at stake. In Anaximander the gods as individuals have disappeared; the opposites, in the concrete form which they assume as earth, sea, and sky, have taken their place. And the order which is threatened by their "injustice" is the order of nature itself, free of dependence upon the will of individuals.

The disappearance of the gods is no accident; it is the result of the investigation of the natural order itself. We can see the process at work in Anaximander's explanation of thunder and lightning:

> **2.40** These are caused by wind; for when wind that has been shut up in a dense cloud bursts forth, owing to its fineness and lightness, the discharge produces the thunderclap while the rent that is made, seen against the darkness of the cloud, is the flash.

According to tradition these things are the work of Olympian Zeus. It is Zeus who gathers the storm clouds, Zeus who hurls down the fiery thunderbolts on those who provoke his anger. But for Anaximander they are not the work of Zeus but arise from the operation of purely natural causes.

The disappearance of Zeus does not mean the failure of justice in the world-order. The task of guaranteeing order now falls upon the infinite. As the ultimate source of existing things, it is the source of the justice which prevails among them; for it " 'encompasses all things' and 'steers all things' " (**2.4**). It would be a mistake to think of this activity as wholly impersonal. With the office of Zeus the infinite has inherited the titles and privileges of that office. It is not only "ageless" and "imperishable" and "divine" but in some sense a living intelligence. The notion of order never quite lost, either for Anaximander or his immediate successors, the implications which it has in human affairs, where order has always to be created and maintained by intelligence. But the first step toward an impersonal conception of nature had been taken.

THE DEATH OF THE WORLD-ORDER

The life of the world-order, like that of the body, is limited. Having come into existence, it must necessarily pass away, returning again into the infinite from which it sprang:

> **2.41** For from this all things came into being and into it all things pass away. In this way innumerable world-orders arise and perish again into that from which they came.

> **2.42** These world-orders, Anaximander supposed, are dissolved and born again according to the age which each is capable of attaining.

The death of one world-order is followed by the birth of another; for as the infinite out of which they come has no beginning or end, so the succession of world-orders must be without beginning or end. The grandeur of this conception goes beyond anything in Hesiod. It represents a vision of the existing world-order which reduces it to a mere incident in the unending process of change.

> **2.43** Was there a time before motion began? — a time before which it had no existence? Does it cease again, so that nothing moves? Or is it the case that motion neither comes into existence nor passes away, but always was and always will be, and is a deathless and unfailing source of existing things — the life, as it were, of all things constituted by nature?

> **2.44** Anaximander held that motion, through which it comes about that the heavens arise, is eternal.

The eternal motion to which **2.44** refers does not seem to be any particular motion, such as the rotation which results in the separating out of the opposites to form a world-order. It seems to be simply the process of change itself, conceived as without beginning or end. This is the "life" of the infinite. Against its immensity human life shrinks to a point. Anaximander passes over in silence the affairs of men which so concern Hesiod in *Works and Days*. In time the affairs of men would come to occupy the attention of philosophers, and the problems which they posed would displace those with which Anaximander was concerned. But the answers to these questions would be worked out within the limits established by his thought. For it was Anaximander who created the framework within which early Greek philosophy developed from start to finish. This framework was subjected to severe strains — how severe we shall have occasion to see hereafter. But the framework held, and the history of Greek philosophy is largely the history of the exploration of the possibilities inherent in it.

THREE

Anaximenes and Xenophanes

The work begun by Anaximander was carried on by his associate and fellow citizen, Anaximenes. For the most part Anaximenes was content to work within the lines laid down by his predecessor, but in one important respect he broke with him. This was in his theory of the nature of the infinite.

THE INFINITE

3.1   Anaximenes of Miletus, son of Eurystratus and associate of Anaximander, also says that the underlying nature of things is one and infinite. But he does not regard it as indeterminate, as Anaximander does, but as determinate, calling it air; and he says that it differs in respect of thinness and thickness in different things. When dilated it becomes fire; when compressed, wind and then cloud. When it is compressed further it becomes water, then earth, then stone. The rest are produced from these. He too makes motion eternal, through which for him also change comes about.

Like Anaximander, Anaximenes held that the source of existing things is infinite; but whereas Anaximander held that the infinite is neither earth, air, fire, nor water, but a mixture of these, Anaximenes identified it with air. It is difficult to see why he took this step unless it was from a desire for simplicity. Anaximander had been forced to account for the existence of the opposites in the world-order by assuming that they were contained in the infinite from the start. Anaximenes seems to have believed that he could account for the same facts without making this assumption. It should be possible, he thought, to deduce them from the existence of air alone.

Compression and Dilation

The mechanism by means of which he proposed to do this is sketched in **3.1**, but it receives further elaboration in other passages:

> **3.2** The form of air is as follows. When it is most evenly distributed it is invisible to the eye; but it is made visible by cold or heat or moisture or motion. It is in constant motion; for things that change would not do so unless there were motion. When it is compressed or dilated it appears different. When it is dilated and becomes rarer, it becomes fire. Winds, on the other hand, are air that has been compressed. Cloud is produced from air by "felting"; when compressed further it becomes water; when compressed still further, earth; and when compressed as far as possible, stone.

> **3.3** He says that what is contracted and compressed is cold, while what is dilated or "loosely-packed" (this is the word he himself uses) is hot. Thus it is quite proper to say of a man that he blows both hot and cold; for when the breath is compressed by the lips it is chilled, whereas when it issues from a relaxed mouth it is hot because of its dilation.

Anaximenes seems to have fixed on air as having no strongly marked characteristics of its own. In its normal state, when it is "most evenly distributed," we are unaware of its existence, despite the fact that it surrounds us on every side. When it is compressed, however, it makes itself known. For example, it becomes cold — as is obvious from the fact that in blowing on hot food to cool it we compress the air by compressing our lips. Since the food is cooled, it is clear that the air which chills it must be cool. On the other hand, when air becomes dilated, as it does when we breathe with open mouth on our hands to warm them, we can feel that it is hot.

But compression and dilation bring about other changes as well — changes which Anaximenes accounts for by the analogy of felting. When hair is compressed to make felt, a qualitative change takes place; instead of being soft and fluffy, as it was when loosely-packed, the hair becomes dense and resistant to penetration. Air, according to Anaximenes, behaves in just the same way. When it is closely packed it becomes dense and resistant to penetration, as is plain from the fact that when we walk into the wind we have to push our way through it. Moreover, the denser it is the heavier it is (**3.2**), so that as it becomes further and further compressed it sinks toward the center of the world-order. Lastly, the denser it is the darker it becomes. We see this in Anaximander, where the rings of fire which constitute the heavenly bodies proper are rendered invisible because the air which encloses them has been made dark through compression.

Air, therefore, when it is compressed, becomes colder, denser, heavier, and darker, and the more so the more it is compressed. When it undergoes dilation, on the other hand, it becomes hotter, rarer, lighter, and brighter; in fact it takes on the properties of fire, just as when compressed it takes on those of water and earth. The opposites of Anaximander have been brought into being by the process of thickening and thinning.

No doubt Anaximenes intended his theory to be a simplification of Anaximander's and nothing more. But in fact it opened up new possibilities; for it is clear that on this theory the difference between hot and cold reduces to the difference between one density and another. But the density of air depends on how much there is of it in a given amount of space; consequently it ought in principle to be possible to account for all changes of quality in terms of changes of quantity. That Anaximenes did not see the implications of his own theory is clear; but he stood on the threshold of a development that was to have momentous consequences for later thought.

THE VORTEX

Of the formation of the world-order we are told almost nothing.

3.4   When the air is felted, he says, there first comes into being the earth, which is quite broad and for this reason "rides" upon air.

3.5   The heavenly bodies were produced from earth through the rising up of vapors which, when dilated, became fire. Of the fire thus borne aloft the heavenly bodies are composed.

Anaximenes' account of the heavenly bodies is considerably simpler than Anaximander's. The cumbersome wheels of compressed air have disappeared, and their place has been taken by local concentrations of fire, formed by the dilation of vapors arising from the earth. But of the critical phase in the formation of the world-order, the formation of the earth itself, we are left in ignorance; nor is there any mention of the vortex motion which, according to Aristotle, his predecessors used to explain why the earth travelled to the center in the beginning (**2.8**). Yet if Aristotle is right there should be indications of it in Anaximenes too, and if we look more closely at the evidence we see that its presence is implied by his account of the motions of the heavenly bodies:

> **3.6**   Anaximenes says that the sun is flat "like a leaf."

> **3.7**   The earth is flat and rides upon the air. The sun, moon, and other heavenly bodies, all of which are fiery, likewise ride upon it owing to their flatness.

The likening of the heavenly bodies to fiery leaves immediately calls to mind Aristotle's reference to "what happens in liquids and in air" (**2.8**). For what happens in air is that leaves caught up in an eddy of wind are borne aloft and whirled about exactly as the heavenly bodies are carried about by the air on which they ride.

This means, of course, that they are carried horizontally around the earth:

> **3.8**   Anaximenes says that the heavenly bodies do not move *under* the earth, as others have supposed, but *around* it — as a felt cap is turned on one's head. And the sun is hidden [at night] not because it is beneath the earth but because it is concealed by the higher parts of the earth . . . .

> **3.9**   An indication that the northerly parts of the earth are high is the opinion of many of the ancient meteorologists that the sun does not pass under the earth but around its northerly part, and that it disappears and causes night because the earth is high toward the north.

The analogy of the felt cap is almost certainly Anaximenes' own, and the point of it must be that the sun and moon revolve about the central earth in the plane of the vortex motion. This, however, creates an obvious problem; how are we to account, on the vortex hypothesis, for the alternation of night and day? Anaximander had solved this problem by placing the rings bearing the sun and moon obliquely to the plane of the earth (**2.16**), but he did not explain (as far as we know) how this state of affairs came about, unless he thought of it simply as a chance result of the breaking up of the original sphere of flame (2.7). Anaximenes seems to have been dissatisfied with this solution, and his own explanation is both simpler and more drastic.

At first sight the boldness of his explanation is not apparent; for the natural interpretation of 3.8 and 3.9 is that the sun, as it passes laterally around the earth, is screened by mountains to the north which intercept its light. But in fact this interpretation leaves the problem exactly where it was; if the sun were low enough on the horizon to be hidden by mountains at night, it would travel from east to west close to the southern horizon, not overhead as it obviously does. There is, however, another way of taking these passages, and that is to suppose that the earth itself is tilted relative to the plane of rotation in which the sun is carried around, so that the sun is hidden at night not by mountains to the north (which are not in fact mentioned in either passage) but by the uptilted rim of earth itself. The notion that it is the earth that is tilted relative to the plane of rotation carries with it so many difficulties that it seems rash to suppose that Anaximenes could have put it forward seriously. Yet in his successors it is the standard answer to the problem which it was designed to solve.

Sky and Earth

The "other heavenly bodies" mentioned in 3.7 are presumably the planets, for the fixed stars present a somewhat different problem:

> 3.10 Anaximenes says that they are fixed in the crystalline [vault of the heavens] like ornamental nail heads.

The fact that Anaximenes likens the movement of the heavens not simply to that of a cap but to that of a *felt* cap may be purely accidental (3.8); but in view of the prominence of the felting process in his thought this is not very likely. The comparison, if it is to be taken seriously, must mean that the outermost heaven is of a dense nature, hardened perhaps by the action of fire, like the air which encloses Anaximander's rings of fire, to form a crystalline shell. Fixed in this shell the stars would shine at night from the reflection of the sun's rays on the other side of the uptilted earth like bronze nail heads glinting in the dark vault of a fire-lit hall.

At the center of this sphere lies the equally solid earth, a flat, circular disk.

> 3.11 Anaximenes says that it is like a table.

Being dense, it is heavy; but it does not fall, for its weight is supported by the air beneath:

> **3.12** The flatness of the earth is the cause of its staying where it is; for it does not cut the air beneath it but covers it like a lid. This seems to be the way of flat-shaped bodies; it is difficult even for the wind to move them because of their power of resistance. The same immobility, they say, is produced by the flatness of the surface which the earth presents to the air which lies beneath it.

To anyone who has scaled a paper plate the phenomenon will be familiar. The idea of treating the earth in this way was not new; it had been advanced by Anaximander (**2.21**). But Anaximenes saw in it the basis for a theory of earthquakes as well; for if the earth is flat, and not very deep, it should not take very much to make it rock:

> **3.13** Anaximenes says that the earth, through being soaked and dried out, cracks and is shaken by the impact of falling peaks that have broken loose. This is why earthquakes occur during droughts and heavy rains; for during a drought the earth is dry and (as just explained) cracks. Then, when rains make it excessively wet, it falls apart.

AIR AND INTELLIGENCE

According to tradition, earthquakes were the work of Poseidon, whom Homer describes as "earth-holder" and "shaker of earth." In ascribing them to heavy rains Anaximenes was continuing the work begun by Anaximander of substituting physical explanations of natural phenomena for religious ones. The same is true of his explanation of the rainbow:

> **3.14** Anaximenes says that the rainbow is produced when the rays of the sun fall on dense, thick air. Hence the leading edge of it appears red, being burnt by the sun's rays, while the rest is dark where the rays have been overpowered by the moisture.

In Homer the rainbow is Iris, the goddess whom Zeus sends to Poseidon with his threatening message (**1.9**). In Anaximenes it is a natural phenomenon the production of which is as impersonal a process as that which results in earthquakes.

Yet the divine plays as important a role in Anaximenes' thought as it does in Anaximander's. The attributes of divinity have merely been transferred to the infinite:

3.15 Anaximenes says that air is a god.

3.16 Just as our soul (being air) controls us, so breath and air encompass the whole world-order.

That air is a god is obvious enough; for by air Anaximenes means the infinite, and the infinite is divine because it is, in Anaximander's words, "deathless" and "imperishable" (**2.4**). But according to Anaximander the infinite also encompasses all things and steers them, and in **3.16** we get a further insight into the way in which it does so.

The belief that air is the principle of life in living creatures is based on the fact that when breathing ceases, life, too, ceases. Thus Homer writes of the wounded Sarpedon, fallen in battle before Troy:

3.17 His soul left him, and mist covered his eyes.
But he recovered his breath, and the blast of the north wind, blowing, gave him life, though he was sorely spent in spirit.

It is the air in us, then, which is soul. But the soul is not only the principle of life; it is the principle of sensation as well. As Aristotle puts it:

3.18 That which has soul in it seems to differ from that which does not chiefly in two respects: in moving and in having sensation. These two characteristics of soul we have more or less inherited from our predecessors.

But it puzzled Aristotle that his predecessors seemed to make no distinction between having a soul and possessing intelligence. Thus he complains of Anaxagoras (Chapter Nine), whose thought belongs to a period later even than that of Anaximenes:

3.19 In many places he says that mind is the cause of beauty and order, but at other times he says that the soul is. For he says that mind exists in all living things, great and small, noble and ignoble, whereas in fact mind (at any rate in the sense of intelligence) does not appear to exist in all living things alike — even in all men.

It is evident from such passages that the Greeks did not at first distinguish between sensation and thought; so that if air is soul it is the principle not only of motion and sensation but of intelligence as well. If the movements of living things take place not in a random manner but in an orderly one, it is because their soul, being air, "controls" them.

Now the point of 3.16 is that the infinite air which encompasses the world-order is related to it exactly as air — the air which surrounds us and which we breathe — is related to us. As air directs and controls the movements of living creatures, so also it controls and directs the life of the world-order, maintaining in it that cosmic justice without which it would fail.

MICROCOSM AND MACROCOSM

The whole argument is based on the analogy between microcosm and macrocosm. What is true of living creatures is true of the world-order at large; for

> **3.20** The living creature is a world-order in miniature.

Galen, who quotes this saying, adds that it was the opinion of "those among the ancients who were versed in natural philosophy," and this statement is borne out by all that we know of the beginnings of Greek philosophy. The notion is first hinted at in Anaximander. Anaximander's use of the vortex motion to bring about the formation of the world-order represents a departure, and a very striking one, from traditional modes of thought. Yet there are curious parallels between his account of the formation of the world-order and his account of the formation of the first men. He seems to have used the same word, "bark," to describe both the membranes which enclosed the first men (**2.30**) and the sphere of flame that surrounded the world-order in the beginning (**2.7**). Moreover, he speaks of the emergence of the first men in terms of a rupturing of these membranes, just as in his cosmogony he attributes the formation of the heavenly bodies to the breaking up of the fiery husk that surrounds the air about the earth. It appears, therefore, that Anaximander thought of the two processes as in some respects similar, and that to this extent he was not altogether free from the influence of biological analogies. It is the same with the medical writers; the theory of health as a balance of opposites is explicitly based upon the analogy between microcosm and macrocosm (**2.36**), while the aim of the author of the bladder experiment described in **2.9**, curiously enough, is to provide visual proof of the fact that the same laws which govern the behavior of the opposites in the world-order at large govern their behavior in living creatures also, where the same principle of "like to like" brings about the articulation of the fetus in the womb.

In Anaximenes this way of thinking finds expression in the full-blown identification of the air in us with the air which encompasses the world-order as a whole, and with this identification a clearer conception of the meaning of **2.34** emerges: justice is maintained in the world-order by a living and intelligent presence which, by controlling all things, preserves the whole in being.

DIOGENES OF APOLLONIA

The impression left by these scanty materials is strikingly confirmed by the fragments of Diogenes of Apollonia, a Milesian colony on the shores of the Black Sea. Diogenes wrote a hundred years after Anaximenes, and in places the fragments betray the influence of intervening thinkers; but in the main they simply restate the thought of the Milesians:

3.21 He too says that the nature of the whole is air, infinite and eternal. As it is compressed and dilated and undergoes change the forms of other things come into being.

Those things which come into being also pass away, but the infinite within which these processes take place is untouched by them:

3.22 So much seems clear: that it is great and strong and eternal and deathless and much-knowing.

Intelligence is expressly listed here, together with the other attributes of divinity, as a property of air:

3.23 It seems to me that that which has intelligence is what men call air, and that all men are steered by this, and that it has power over all things. For this very thing seems to be a god and to reach everywhere and to dispose all things and to be in everything.

3.24 For it would not be possible, without intelligence, to be divided up so as to have measure in all things — winter and summer, night and day, rain and wind and fair weather . . . .

This is the crux of the argument: where there is order there must be intelligence. And the source of this assumption is not far to seek; it lies in the analogy between microcosm and macrocosm:

3.25 For men and other animals live by breathing air. And this is for them soul and intelligence, as will be clearly shown in this work; and if this is taken away they die and intelligence fails.

In living creatures the source of all order is intelligence; and if this is so in living creatures it must be so in the world-order as a whole, for living creatures are but world-orders in miniature (**3.20**). The divinity which reaches everywhere and steers all things shares with men that which marks them off as living and intelligent things.

The first to grasp the religious implications of this development was Xenophanes, a native of Colophon, some forty miles north of Miletus. In 546 B.C., when Xenophanes was only twenty-five, Colophon, together with many other Greek city-states along the Ionian seaboard, fell to the Persians and Xenophanes fled westward. Eventually he made his way to Sicily, where he lived to a great age; but his thought bears the unmistakable imprint of his Ionian origins.

Two examples will suffice to show Xenophanes' relation to his predecessors: his account of the rain cycle, and his speculations on the significance of the fossil record.

The Rain Cycle

3.26 Xenophanes says that atmospheric changes are due primarily to the warmth of the sun. For when moisture is evaporated from the sea the sweet part of it, which is distinguished by its lightness, forms a mist and becomes cloud; and this falls as rain when felting takes place and winds scatter it.

3.27 The sea is the source of water and the source of wind. For there would be no winds to burst forth from the clouds were it not for the great sea, nor rivers nor showers of rain from heaven, but the great Pontus is the father of clouds, winds and rivers.

Water vapors, rising from the surface of the sea as it is warmed by the sun, form clouds; but when condensation takes place and they are dispersed by driving winds, they fall again as rain which the rivers once more carry to the sea.

The rain cycle theory appears here for the first time, but the mechanism which makes it possible is already familiar. It is the process of dilation and compression worked out by Anaximenes on the basis of the analogy of felting. Xenophanes has gone beyond Anaximenes in representing dilation and compression as two aspects of a single process. If evaporation did not take place, there would be no rain; if rain did not fall, the sea, which is fed by the rivers, would dry up. Evaporation and precipitation are thus brought into relation with one another within the wider framework of Anaximander's conception of change. Dilation and condensation are made to provide the mechanism by means of which sea and sky "make reparation to one another for their injustice according to the ordinance of time" (**2.34**).

THE FOSSIL RECORD

The same notion of cyclical change recurs in the following passages:

3.28 He asserts that the earth, being carried down continuously, little by little, is, over a period of time, advancing into the sea.

3.29 Xenophanes believes that a mixing of the earth with the sea is taking place, and that in time it will be dissolved by the moisture. He says that he has proof of this, namely, that shells are found inland and in the mountains. And he says that in Syracuse the impressions of fishes and seaweed have been found in the quarries, while at Paros the impression of a laurel leaf has been found deep in the rock, and in Malta flattened forms of all sorts of marine animals. He says that these were formed long ago when everything was covered with mud, and that these impressions were dried in the mud. All men are destroyed when the earth, having been carried down into the sea, becomes mud, after which there is a new beginning. And this periodic change takes place in all the world-orders.

3.30 For we are all born of earth and water.

Anaximander had said that the earth, originally moist, was gradually drying out, and that the sea (the remnant of the original moisture) would in time disappear (**2.22**). But Xenophanes maintained that the drying out of the earth was but one phase of a larger process in which it was counterbalanced by the earth's once more returning to its original state. This return, he insisted, was even now going on under men's very eyes; for the silting up of the great river mouths showed clearly that the earth was "advancing into the sea." Moreover, there was evidence to show that this had happened before; for the fossil remains of plants and animals in places as far apart as Paros (an island in the Cyclades) and Malta demonstrated that once before, long ago, the earth had turned to mud only to emerge again as the sea retreated. The process is thus a cyclical one, taking place in conformity with the law of compensation laid down by Anaximander himself.

THE GODS OF THE POETS

But the importance of Xenophanes for the history of thought does not lie in his contribution to the detail of the Ionian tradition. It lies rather in the revolutionary implications for religion which he perceived to be inherent in it.

If the founders of the tradition were aware of these implications, they gave no sign of it. In their explanations of earthquakes, thunder, and lightning, the question of the existence of the gods was passed over in silence. But if we compare Xenophanes' account of the rainbow with Anaximenes' (**3.14**), we see that there is a marked difference between them:

> **3.31** She whom men call "Iris," too, is in reality a cloud, purple, red, and green to the sight.

The effect of that "in reality" is to drive home in the most uncompromising way the contrast between popular belief and the truth concerning the divine. It is a theme to which Xenophanes returns again and again:

> **3.32** Mortals believe that the gods are begotten, and that they wear clothing like our own, and have a voice and a body.

> **3.33** The Ethiopians make their gods snub-nosed and black; the Thracians make theirs gray-eyed and red-haired.

> **3.34** And if oxen and horses and lions had hands, and could draw with their hands and do what man can do, horses would draw the gods in the shape of horses, and oxen in the shape of oxen, each giving the gods bodies similar to their own.

Poseidon, emerging armed from the sea onto the plain of Troy; Iris, gliding on sandaled feet to bring the message of Zeus to him — these are but the creations of the poets. And they reveal clearly the inability of men to conceive the divine except through images derived from their own experience. But the true nature of the divine is very different:

3.35 One god, greatest among gods and men, in no way similar to mortals either in body or mind.

In the phrase "greatest among gods and men" the older tradition lives on; but the phrase is an empty one. It is a mere formula, inherited from the older poets and used here only because Xenophanes happens to be writing in verse. There are not many gods; there is only one.

THE ONE GOD

The concentration of divine power in the hands of Zeus is already far advanced in Homer; so far advanced, indeed, as to call forth the bitter protest of Poseidon in **1.9.** In Hesiod it has gone still further; Zeus is no longer the receiver but the dispenser of titles and privileges. He is the very source of justice, and the father of men. The strict monotheism of Xenophanes, therefore, represents an extreme development of a tendency already at work in Greek thought. But it is very much more than that, as we can see at once from Xenophanes' description of his one god:

3.36 He sees all over, thinks all over, hears all over.

3.37 He remains always in the same place, without moving; nor is it fitting that he should come and go, first to one place then to another.

3.38 But without toil he sets all things in motion by the thought of his mind.

The gods of Homer are scarcely distinguishable from men, except for their greater power and their freedom from death. Their life is a faithful reflection of the life of the heroic society which brought them into being. Even Zeus, who is more remote and indirect in his dealings with men, is hardly more than a powerful chieftain. The Zeus of Hesiod is less personal, less human, than the Zeus of Homer; but the difference is one of degree rather than of kind. In Xenophanes the difference is one of kind: the one god is "not like men either in body or mind." He does not see and hear as men do, for he has no organs of sense but "sees all over, thinks all over, hears all over." Neither does he act as men do, for he has no arms or legs or other organs of locomotion but "remains always in the same place, without moving," effecting his will by means of thought alone. This is not the god of Homer and Hesiod; it is "the god of the philosophers," the god of Anaximander and Anaximenes, born of reflection upon the nature of things. The language of Xenophanes is the language of poetry, but the one god of whom he speaks is not the product of the poetic imagination; he is the product of reason, of an intellectual vision of the world-order itself — the starting point of the Ionian tradition:

> **3.39** Fixing his gaze upon the heaven as a whole, Xenophanes declared that the one, *i.e.*, god, exists.

> **3.40** The being of god is spherical, not like that of man. He sees all over and hears all over, but does not breathe. He is the totality of mind and thought, and is eternal.

The visible world has come into being and is doomed to perish. On this point the evidence is firm:

> **3.41** He says that there are innumerable world-orders, but that they do not overlap.

The world-order must come to an end before a new one can arise. But god is eternal; he does not come into being nor does he pass away. There can be no question, therefore, of his being identical with this or any other of the innumerable world-orders, but only with that feature which is common to them all: the presence of order in each which makes it a world-order.

But where there is order there is intelligence; for order is but intelligence made manifest (**3.24**). And this intelligence, conceived in abstraction from its manifestations, is the one god of Xenophanes — "the totality of mind and thought." He is "spherical" only in the sense that he is coextensive with the world-order, able to act everywhere in it without moving because he is suffused throughout it, the active principle of order itself, formally the same in all the worlds.

But the order which the Milesians saw in the world-order around them was a *moral* order. As the life of the city can endure only as long as men observe justice, so the world-order as a whole can endure only as long as the opposites "make reparation to one another for their injustice according to the ordinance of time" (**2.34**). Justice, therefore, is of the very nature of the divine. But if this is true, the stories told by the poets must be lies; for

3.42   Homer and Hesiod have attributed to the gods all those things which in men are a matter for reproach and censure: stealing, adultery, and mutual deception.

The gods of popular belief are not merely anthropomorphic; they are unworthy of the respect due to the divine:

3.43   It is proper for reasonable men to celebrate god with stories that are meet and with pure words. And when they have poured a libation and prayed for the power to do what is right (for it is of this that we stand most in need), then it is not unseemly for a man to drink as much as he can hold and still get home without help, unless he be very old. But among men he is to be praised who after drinking performs skillfully — telling not of the battles of the Titans or of Giants or of Centaurs (those fictions of the men of old) nor of violent civil war, in which there is no good, but to hold the gods in reverence: *that* is good always.

To require justice of the gods is not new; Hesiod had insisted on it in *Works and Days*. But this insistence was hardly compatible with the tales of "stealing, adultery, and mutual deception" with which he had filled his *Theogony*, and to Xenophanes the inconsistency was glaring.

HUMAN KNOWLEDGE

Not merely is Xenophanes' thought revolutionary; it proceeds on the basis of an assumption more revolutionary still — that the way to a knowledge of the divine lies through the contemplation of the world-order (**3.39**). Hesiod makes no such assumption; the origin and nature of the gods is revealed to him by the Muses, daughters of Zeus:

3.44 Tell how at first the gods
and earth were born,
the rivers and the boundless sea,
with swelling surge,
the shining stars and heaven
broad above.
Tell how they shared their riches
and dealt their honors out,
and how they came to hold
the many-valed Olympus.

The poetry of Xenophanes breathes a very different spirit:

3.45 The gods have not revealed all things from the beginning to mortals; but, by seeking, men find out, in time, what is better.

Only through patient inquiry does the truth come to be known; and there are limits, even then, to what men may know.

These limitations are due to the relativity of human knowledge. As Xenophanes puts it:

3.46 If god had not created yellow honey, men would think figs sweeter than they do.

As it is, the sweetness of honey prevents them from realizing how sweet figs actually are. All human knowledge is of this sort. Darkness would seem less dark to us but for the contrast which full daylight presents; winter less cold but for the heat of summer. It is in this sense that human knowledge is relative; and because it is relative it always falls short of the truth:

3.47 No man knows the truth, nor will there be a man who has knowledge about the gods and what I say about everything. For even if he were to hit by chance upon the whole truth, he himself would not be aware of having done so, but each forms his own opinion.

This does not mean that all opinions are equally correct. Xenophanes certainly thought that his own views were closer to the truth than those of the poets. But they are only closer — not truth itself.

3.48 Let these things, then, be taken as *like* the truth. . . .

For the truth itself is known only to god, who "sees all over, thinks all over, hears all over," and whose knowledge is absolute.

FOUR

Pythagoreanism

Pythagoras was a native of Samos, an island off the Ionian coast just north of Miletus. According to tradition he left Samos because of dissatisfaction with the tyranny of Polycrates. Like Xenophanes before him Pythagoras fled westward, and about 530 B.C. established himself at Croton, a Greek settlement on the east coast of southern Italy, opposite the Greek mainland. He was at this time forty years of age. At Croton he gathered around him a large number of disciples, through whom he exerted great influence on the affairs of the city and its neighbors. But the rule of the Pythagoreans was not to everyone's liking, and about the turn of the century dissatisfaction with it culminated in a general uprising, in which a number of the leading Pythagoreans were killed. Pythagoras himself managed to reach Metapontium, where he died not long afterwards.

For a long time the teachings of Pythagoras were kept secret:

> **4.1**   Down to the time of Philolaus it was impossible to obtain any knowledge of any Pythagorean doctrine.

It is therefore difficult to distinguish between the Pythagoreanism of the fifth century B.C., when Philolaus wrote, and the teachings of Pythagoras himself:

> **4.2**   What he taught his disciples no one can say for certain, for they maintained a remarkable silence. All the same, the following became generally known. First, he said that the soul is immortal; second, that it migrates into other kinds of animals; third, that the same events are repeated in cycles, nothing being new in the

57

strict sense; and finally, that all things with souls should be regarded as akin. Pythagoras seems to have been the first to introduce these beliefs into Greece.

The closing words of this passage suggest that the teachings in question did not originate with Pythagoras himself, and there is a persistent (though late) tradition that he learned them, or some of them, in the East, where he is said to have travelled after leaving Samos and before settling down in Croton. The tradition may be true, but it cannot be confirmed, and we must seek as best we can for the roots of Pythagorean thought in the Ionian tradition with which, at Samos, Pythagoras would have been familiar.

Soul and Body

According to that tradition the soul, the principle of life and movement within us, is simply "breath" — a detached portion of the same air which steers all things and encompasses the world-order (**3.16**). This air, the source from which existing things arise and into which they perish, is without limit, without beginning or end, deathless and imperishable. But if air is immortal, then the soul, being air, must also be immortal. This was a deduction which Pythagoras was quite capable of making for himself.

But if the soul is immortal, how is it related to the body, which is subject to dissolution and decay? Pythagoreanism really begins with the putting of this question, and Pythagoras' answer to it was momentous for the history of Western thought:

> **4.3** Because of its sins the soul is yoked to the body and buried in it as in a tomb.

The words are those of Philolaus, but there can be no doubt that the thought which they express goes back to Pythagoras himself and is fundamental to his teaching. The soul is alien to the body, and the relation between them is fleeting; the two belong to entirely different orders of existence.

This conception seems at first sight to have no basis in Ionian thought. Yet the following passage suggests that it grew out of that thought in a perfectly natural way:

> **4.4** The air about the earth is sluggish and unhealthy, and all things in it are mortal; but the uppermost air is always in motion and pure and wholesome, and all things in it are immortal and

therefore divine. The sun, moon, and other heavenly bodies are gods; for in them the hot predominates, and this is the cause of life . . . . The rays of the sun penetrate the cold and the dense ether (they call air "cold ether" and sea and moisture "dense ether"), even to the depths, quickening all things. All things live which have a share of the hot; hence plants, too, are living things. But not all have soul. Soul is a detached portion of the ether — of the hot and the cold both, for it has a share of the cold ether, too. Soul is distinct from life and is immortal, since that from which it is detached is immortal.

The physical setting here is perfectly familiar. Air, when compressed, is heavy and sinks toward the center of the world-order, where it becomes sea. When it is dilated it goes to the periphery, where it becomes fire. Both sea and fire, then, are forms of air or "ether," exactly as they are for Anaximenes. But the writer of the present passage distinguishes sharply between the "purity" of the upper air and the "unhealthiness" of the air about the earth. The bodies which inhabit the upper air — the sun, moon, and stars — move eternally; they are "immortal and therefore divine." But here below all is subject to corruption and decay. The difference between the two realms amounts to a radical breach in the natural order. For the history of Western thought it was fateful; for in the form which it was to receive at the hands of Aristotle it prevented the development of a rational system of celestial mechanics down to the time of Galileo. Yet the breach was inevitable; for in the absence of any conception of a realm *outside* the natural order, the Pythagoreans were compelled to account for the radical difference between soul and body in terms of a breach *within* that order as the Ionians had conceived it.

The division between "upper" and "lower" corresponds to the division between soul and body. The soul is no longer conceived as something whose function it is simply to animate the body. That function has been taken over by "the hot"; it is the vital heat in living creatures which is the source of their life. When this is lost, the body dies. But "soul is distinct from life and is immortal." It is not affected by the corruption which overtakes the body, but stands apart from it even in life, a detached portion of the divine in exile from its native land. Because it is in exile it yearns to return to that upper region from whence it came, to be released from the prison house of the body, and to rejoin once more the company of the blessed gods.

THE IMMORTALITY OF THE SOUL

The effect of this new conception of the soul was to undermine the traditional view of man's place in the world-order. For according to tradition the life of the gods is forbidden to men. In Pindar's words:

4.5   There is one race of men and one of gods,
and we both draw our breath from one mother.
A wholly divided power keeps us apart,
as if the one were nothing, while for the other
the safe and brazen citadel of heaven
remains forever.

The blessed gods alone possess everlasting life. Men are but the creatures of a day:

4.6   No man can win to happiness complete.
To none that I can name has Fate held forth
this gift unshaken.

4.7   In brief space the joy of mortals waxes;
in brief space it falls to the ground,
stricken by an adverse fate.
We are but creatures of a day.
What is man? What is he not?
Man is a dream of shadows.
But whenever a glorious gift of god appears,
bright is the light that rests on men
and sweet is their life.

4.8   If a man having wealth surpass all others in beauty,
displaying his strength by victory in the games,
let him remember the limbs he arrays are mortal
and that he will come to the end that all men come to,
clothing himself with earth.

4.9   Mortal thoughts befit mortal men.

The teachings of Pythagoras ran directly counter to this traditional view. Man is not the creature of a day; he has in him that which is immortal and makes him akin to the gods. And therefore, as Aristotle was later to put it:

4.10   We ought not to obey those who tell us that a man should think a man's thoughts, and a mortal the thoughts of a mortal. On the contrary, we should endeavor as far as possible to become immortal, and to do all that we can to live in accordance with what is highest in us.

TRANSMIGRATION

Plato says that Pythagoras taught "a way of life," and we can now see what the purpose of that way of life was. It was to live in accordance with what is highest in us, remembering always its divine origin. But this could be done in a variety of ways. It could, for example, be achieved through the observance of certain taboos, the chief of which was abstention from meat. This was clearly connected with the belief in the transmigration of souls.

That Pythagoras taught this doctrine is quite certain; for Xenophanes who was his contemporary, mockingly refers to it:

> **4.11** They say that once when a puppy was being whipped, Pythagoras, who was passing by, took pity on it, saying, "Stop! Do not beat it! It is the soul of a friend; I recognize his voice!"

What is less certain is the source of the idea, for it does not appear to be Greek. Herodotus says that it was Egyptian:

> **4.12** The Egyptians were the first to hold that the soul of man is immortal; that when the body perishes it enters into another animal that is being born at the same time; and that when it has gone the rounds of the animals who dwell on land and in the sea and in the air, it enters once more into the body of a man at birth. This takes three thousand years. Certain Greeks (some earlier, some later) have made use of this doctrine as if it were their own idea. I could name them, but will forbear.

In this Herodotus would appear to have been mistaken; the Egyptians did not believe in transmigration. But the belief could have reached Europe from the East, and the story referred to earlier, that Pythagoras travelled eastward as far as Babylonia before returning to settle at Croton, may actually be true.

Whatever its origins, the implications of the belief are clear. If the souls of men enter into the bodies of animals, it follows that we must view all creatures as akin (**4.2**). The eating of animal flesh, being a kind of cannibalism, will be forbidden, and the killing of animals for food will be considered murder, incurring the same bloodguilt as the slaying of one man by another:

> **4.13** Pythagoras forbade even the killing, let alone the eating, of animals which share with us the privilege of having a soul.

4.14 Some say that he was satisfied with honey alone, or a bit of honeycomb or bread (he did not touch wine during the day); or, for a treat, vegetables boiled or raw. Seafood he ate but rarely. His robe, which was white and spotless, and his bedclothes, which were also white, were of wool; for linen had not yet reached those parts. He was never observed to relieve himself, or to have intercourse, or to be drunk. He used to avoid laughter and all pandering to scurrilous jokes and vulgar stories.

4.15 Being asked, once, when a man ought to approach a woman, he replied, "When you want to lose what strength you have."

THE FUNCTION OF INQUIRY

These passages make it clear that there was more to the Pythagorean way of life than the mere observance of dietary rules. It sprang from a deeper source — a desire for purity which expressed itself (as this desire so often has in human affairs) in the form of asceticism. But what is distinctive in Pythagoreanism is not simply the desire for purity; it is the conception of philosophy as a method of achieving it — of bringing the soul into harmony with the divine.

Not only the conception but even the very word "philosophy" was Pythagorean:

4.16 The first to use it, and to call himself a philosopher [*i.e.,* a "lover of wisdom"] was Pythagoras. For no one, he said, *is* wise except god.

The lover of wisdom can never possess the object of his desire; but the pursuit of it becomes for him a way of life, and a source of happiness which is pure and unalloyed.

To the intellectual activity which this implies, Heraclitus (Chapter Five) bears witness:

4.17 Pythagoras, the son of Mnesarchus, practiced inquiry beyond all other men . . . .

It is evident, then, that from the very beginning the practice of "inquiry" was a prominent feature of the Pythagorean way of life and that it was connected in some way with the welfare of the soul. It is therefore somewhat surprising to learn that

4.18 "Inquiry" was the name which Pythagoras gave to geometry.

This can hardly be a mistake; the evidence for Pythagoras' interest in geometry is too strong for that:

4.19 It was he who brought geometry to perfection, Moeris having been the first to find the beginnings of its elements, as Anticleides says in the second book of his *Alexander*. He goes on to say that Pythagoras worked very hard at the arithmetical side of geometry, and discovered the musical intervals on the monochord. Nor did he neglect even medicine. Apollodorus the calculator says that Pythagoras sacrificed a hecatomb when he discovered that the square on the hypotenuse of a right-angled triangle is equal to the sum of the squares on the sides enclosing the right angle.

The connection between these activities and the purification of the soul is not at first sight clear; but a closer look at Pythagorean mathematics will help to make it so.

PYTHAGOREAN MATHEMATICS

The earliest Greek mathematical work which has come down to us is Euclid's *Elements*. This work, composed in the fourth century B.C., was based upon the investigations of earlier geometers, some of whom were certainly Pythagoreans:

4.20 Eudemus the Peripatetic ascribes to the Pythagoreans the discovery of the theorem that any triangle has its interior angles equal to two right angles. He says that they proved the theorem in this way:

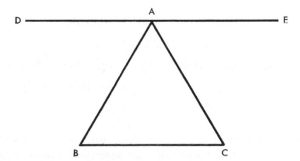

Let *ABC* be a triangle, and let the line *DE* be drawn through *A* parallel to *BC*. Now since *BC* and *DE* are parallel, and the alternate angles are equal, the angle *DAB* is equal to the angle *ABC* and the angle *EAC* is equal to the triangle *ABC*.

Let the angle *BAC* be added to them both. Then the angles *DAB*, *BAC*, and *CAE* (that is to say, the angles *DAB* and *BAE*, *i.e.*, two right angles) are equal to the three angles of the triangle *ABC*.

Hence the three angles of the triangle are equal to two right angles.

This proof, which differs from Euclid's (Book I, Proposition 32), shows that the Pythagoreans were already familiar with the properties of parallel lines, if indeed they did not discover them.

More famous is the discovery of the fact that in a right triangle the square on the hypotenuse is equal to the sum of the squares on the sides containing the right angle — the so-called "Pythagorean theorem." The original proof of this theorem must have been very different from that given by Euclid in his *Elements* (Book I, Proposition 47); for it was almost certainly based on the theory of proportionals which Proclus, in his summary of the development of Greek mathematics, ascribes to Pythagoras.

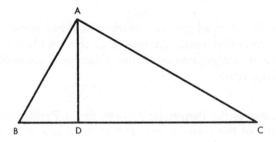

Let *AD* be drawn perpendicular from *A*. The triangles *ABD* and *ADC* are similar both to each other and to the triangle *ABC*. Consequently:

$$BA^2 = BD \cdot BC$$
$$\text{and} \quad AC^2 = CD \cdot BC$$
$$\text{therefore} \quad BA^2 + AC^2 = BC \cdot BD + BC \cdot CD$$
$$= BC \, (BD + CD)$$
$$= BC^2$$

According to **4.19** it was on the occasion of the discovery of this proof that Pythagoras offered a sacrifice of oxen; but Plutarch gives a different version of the story:

4.21 Among the most ingenious theorems, or rather problems, is this: given two figures, to apply [*i.e.*, to construct] a third equal to the one and similar to the other. It was in connection with this discovery, they say, that Pythagoras made his sacrifice. Certainly this theorem is more subtle and more elegant by far than that which proves that the square on the hypotenuse is equal to the sum of the squares on the sides enclosing the right angle.

The method of "application of areas" was indeed "more subtle and more elegant" than the Pythagorean theorem, and it proved a powerful instrument in the hands of the Greek geometers. For the Greeks possessed no algebra in our sense. They were compelled to solve algebraic problems by geometrical means; and the method of application of areas, which enabled them to solve second-degree equations, was an important contribution to this geometrical algebra. It formed the basis of Euclid's theory of irrationals and of Apollonius' treatment of conic sections.

THE REPRESENTATION OF NUMBERS

The statement that "Pythagoras worked very hard at the arithmetical side of geometry" (**4.19**) is further borne out by the tradition that he investigated the arithmetical problem of finding triangles having the square on one side equal to the sum of the squares on the other two:

> **4.22** There have been handed down certain methods of finding such triangles, one of which is ascribed to Plato, another to Pythagoras. The Pythagorean method proceeds from the odd numbers. It takes the given odd number as the lesser of the sides enclosing the right angle. From the square of this it subtracts a unit and takes half the remainder as the greater of the sides enclosing the right angle. Adding a unit to this, it takes the result as the hypotenuse. For example, starting with three: the square of this is nine, from which a unit is subtracted, leaving eight, half of which is four. If a unit is added to this, we get five, and we have found a right-angled triangle having as its sides three, four, and five.

That is, if n is "the given odd number," the sides of the triangle will be n, $\dfrac{n^2 - 1}{2}$, and $\dfrac{n^2 + 1}{2}$; what is asserted is that

$$n^2 + \left(\frac{n^2 - 1}{2}\right)^2 = \left(\frac{n^2 + 1}{2}\right)^2.$$

More interesting still for our purposes is the method by which Pythagoras probably arrived at this formula. The Pythagoreans appear to have represented numbers geometrically by means of pebbles arranged on a flat surface. "Square numbers," for example, were constructed by placing around the number one a series of *gnomons*, *i.e.*, sets of units arranged in the form of carpenters' squares:

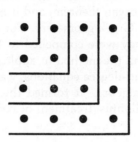

Suppose now that to a square of side *m* we add a further *gnomon*:

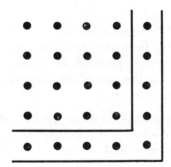

The *gnomon* will be equal to $2m + 1$. Assuming that this number is a square, let

$$2m + 1 = n^2$$

then

$$m = \frac{n^2 - 1}{2}$$

and

$$m + 1 = \frac{n^2 + 1}{2}.$$

It is thus possible to see from the figure that

$$n^2 + \left(\frac{n^2 - 1}{2}\right)^2 = \left(\frac{n^2 + 1}{2}\right)^2,$$

which is the formula required.

MATHEMATICS AND THE SOUL

The connection between these mathematical inquiries and the Pythagorean way of life is not, perhaps, obvious. But two passages will help to make it clearer:

> **4.23** According to most accounts, geometry was discovered first among the Egyptians, and originated in the measurement of areas; for it was forced upon them by the flooding of the Nile, which obliterated everyone's boundaries. Nor is it astonishing that the discovery of this and of the other sciences should have arisen from practical needs, since everything that is in process of development proceeds from the imperfect to the perfect . . . Pythagoras transformed this study into a form of liberal education, examining its principles from the beginning and tracking down the theorems immaterially and conceptually. It was he who discovered both the theory of proportionals and the construction of the cosmic figures [*i.e.*, the pyramid, cube, octahedron, dodecahedron and icosahedron].

> **4.24** We shall begin with what offers a more profitable field for theory and contributes to philosophy as a whole, imitating the Pythagoreans among whom this saying was current: "A figure and a basis; not a figure and a profit" — by which they meant that the geometry deserving of study is that which with each theorem establishes a basis for further advance, elevates the soul and does not allow it to descend to objects of sense in order to satisfy the common needs of mortals, and, in aiming at this, neglect the turning of the soul to things above.

Egyptian "geometry" was, as the name implies, the art of measuring land. It consisted mainly in the knowledge of certain practical rules which had been discovered empirically and for which it did not occur to the Egyptians to seek proof. It was in this form that geometry, according to tradition, passed to Greece. Pythagoras freed it from its connection with practice. In his hands it ceased to "satisfy the common needs of mortals" and became a liberal study — a pursuit worthy of free men. This meant not merely that it was a study for freemen as opposed to slaves, but a study capable of making a man free. For a free man is not simply one who is not a slave to another man, but one whose soul is not in slavery to the demands of his body. Mathematics, freed from its practical aims, becomes an instrument by means of which the soul is freed from these demands.

But it is also freed from the body in a deeper sense; for mathematical inquiry proceeds not by the use of the senses but "immaterially and conceptually." It is, as we should say, a formal, not an empirical, science. Thus the soul is freed not merely from the desires of the body but from all reliance upon the uncertain testimony of the senses. For the fact that the square on the hypotenuse of a right triangle is equal to the sum of the squares on the other two sides is guaranteed not by what happens when knotted ropes are stretched by surveyors but by the fact that it follows by rigorous deduction from first principles. In mathematics, therefore, the soul lives as it were a life of its own, and participates, as far as is possible for it while in the body, in the divine nature. It was a view which, through the influence of Plato, was to affect profoundly the whole development of Western thought.

THE WORLD-ORDER AS A HARMONY

Even more momentous in its consequences was the discovery of the musical intervals. These were discovered, according to **4.19**, by means of the monochord. The monochord, as the name indicates, is a one-stringed instrument. By stopping the string at one point, plucking it, then stopping it at another, and plucking it again, it is possible to establish a relation between the sounds produced and the length of the vibrating strings. Thus, in the accompanying figure, where C represents the point at which, in each instance, the string AB is stopped, the ratios of AB to AC, AC to CB and AC to CB are 2:1, 3:2, and 4:3 respectively:

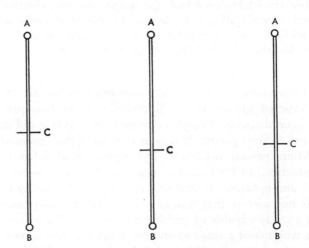

These correspond to the octave, the major fifth, and the major fourth — the chief "consonances" of Greek music. But they do not merely correspond to them; they make them what they are. And it was in recognizing this that the genius of Pythagoras lay, for it opened his eyes to the possibility that *all* order is at bottom capable of being understood and expressed in terms of number.

This conception was not entirely new. It underlies Anaximander's belief that the distance of the heavenly bodies from the earth forms a series of multiples of nine in arithmetical progression. But it was Pythagoras who actually established the existence of a mathematical order in nature. And he lost no time in applying his discovery to the whole of the natural order:

> **4.25** The so-called Pythagoreans, having applied themselves to mathematics, first advanced that study; and having been trained in it they thought that the principles of mathematics were the principles of all things. Since of these principles numbers are by nature first, they thought they saw many similarities to things which exist and come into being in numbers rather than in fire and earth and water — justice being such and such a modification of numbers, soul and reason being another, opportunity still another, and so with the rest, each being expressible numerically. Seeing, further, that the properties and ratios of the musical consonances were expressible in numbers, and that indeed all other things seemed to be wholly modelled in their nature upon numbers, they took numbers to be the whole of reality, the elements of numbers to be the elements of all existing things, and the whole heaven to be a musical scale and a number.

It is hardly necessary to insist upon the importance of this generalization for the history of science. Within two hundred years it was to give rise, in the hands of Archimedes, to a science of mechanics; and Galileo, at the opening of the modern period, took it as the starting point for his own work:

> **4.26** Philosophy is written in the great book which is ever before our eyes — I mean the universe — but we cannot understand it if we do not first learn the language and grasp the symbols in which it is written. This book is written in the mathematical language, and the symbols are triangles, circles, and other geometrical figures, without whose help it is impossible to comprehend a single word of it; without which one wanders in vain through a dark labyrinth.

Upon this assumption the foundations of classical physics were securely laid.

THE HARMONY OF THE SPHERES

The first attempts to give a mathematical description of the world-order were carried out by the Pythagoreans themselves. As we have seen, they considered the whole heaven to be "a musical scale and a number," and Aristotle, in his account of the motions of the heavenly bodies, gives a detailed account of this theory:

> **4.27** Some thinkers suppose that the motion of bodies so great must produce a noise, since even objects here on earth do so, though they are not equal in bulk to those, nor do they move at such high speeds. That the sun and moon and stars, so great in number and in size, and moving with so swift a motion, should fail to produce a sound correspondingly great, is (they say) incredible. On this assumption, then, together with the further assumption that their speeds, as determined by their distances [from the center] are in the ratios of the musical consonances, they say that the sound made by the heavenly bodies as they revolve is a harmony. And in order to account for the fact that we do not hear the sound, they say that it is with us from the moment of birth, so that we are unable to distinguish it from its opposite, silence; for sound and silence are only known by contrast. Consequently, what happens to us is similar to what happens to workers in bronze, who are so used to noise that they do not notice it.

The argument is exceedingly ingenious. Since a bit of wood tied to the end of a string and whirled about one's head will produce a noise, it stands to reason that the heavenly bodies, which are much larger and travel at incomparably greater speeds, must make an even greater noise. Now the pitch of the sound produced in this way is a function of the rate at which the body is moving. As the Pythagorean Archytas puts it:

> **4.28** The "rhomboi" which are whirled about in the mysteries produce a low note when whirled gently, but a high one when whirled vigorously.

But the rate of motion of the heavenly bodies is, in turn, a function of their distance from the earth, *i.e.*, from the center. This is a direct consequence of the nature of a vortex, in which the nearer an object is to the periphery the swifter its motion must be if it is to keep its position relative to objects closer to the center. If we assume that these distances are in the ratios of the musical consonances, the sounds produced must fuse in a vast "harmony," which we fail to hear only because it is constant.

The assumption that the distances of the heavenly bodies are in a certain ratio to one another derives, of course, from Anaximander. But there is something distinctively Pythagorean in the identification of these ratios with the musical intervals — something caught and expressed in its purest form, curiously enough, in Shakespeare's *Merchant of Venice*:

4.29   LORENZO

How sweet the moonlight sleeps upon this bank!
Here will we sit and let the sounds of music
Creep in our ears: soft stillness and the night
Become the touches of sweet harmony.
Sit, Jessica: look, how the floor of heaven
Is thick inlaid with patines of bright gold:
There's not the smallest orb which thou behold'st
But in his motion like an angel sings,
Still quiring to the young-eyed cherubins;
Such harmony is in immortal souls;
But, whilst this muddy vesture of decay
Doth grossly close it in, we cannot hear it . . . .

JESSICA

I am never merry when I hear sweet music.

LORENZO

The reason is, your spirits are attentive:
For do but note a wild and wanton herd,
Or race of youthful and unhandled colts,
Fetching mad bounds, bellowing and neighing loud,
Which is the hot condition of their blood;
If they but hear perchance a trumpet sound,
Or any air of music touch their ears,
You shall perceive them make a mutual stand,
Their savage eyes turn'd to a modest gaze
By the sweet power of music: therefore the poet
Did feign that Orpheus drew trees, stones, and floods;
Since nought so stockish, hard, and full of rage,
But music for the time doth change his nature.
The man that hath no music in himself,
Nor is not moved with concord of sweet sounds,
Is fit for treasons, stratagems, and spoils;
The motions of his spirit are dull as night,
And his affections dark as Erebus:
Let no such man be trusted.

In this version it is because our souls are imprisoned that they cannot hear the harmony of the spheres. The explanation is ancient, for it is preserved by Plutarch:

> **4.30** The ears of most souls are blocked and stopped up not with wax but with carnal obstructions and passions.

This explanation, rather than the more sophisticated and probably later one preserved by Aristotle, accords best with the spirit of Pythagoreanism. For it echoes the conviction upon which the Pythagorean way of life is based: that the soul is buried in the body as in a tomb (**4.3**) from which, through purification, it seeks release.

THE WORLD-ORDER AS NUMBER

From the first, the Ionians had concerned themselves with the origin of the world-order, and to judge from a curious passage in Aristotle the Pythagoreans too addressed themselves to this problem:

> **4.31** The so-called Pythagoreans make use of first principles and elements stranger than those of the natural philosophers. The reason for this is that they do not derive them from sensible objects; for the objects of mathematics (except for those of astronomy) do not move. Yet their discussions and inquiries are all concerned with nature. They bring the heaven into being, observe what happens with respect to its parts and their attributes and functions, and lavish their first principles and causes on it quite as if they agreed with the other natural philosophers that what is is just what is perceptible and contained in the so-called heaven — though, as I said, the causes and first principles of which they speak are adequate to deal with higher things as well and are better suited to these than to theories about nature.
>
> How motion can begin, if "limit" and "unlimited" and "odd" and "even" alone exist, they do not say; nor how it is possible, without motion and change, for coming into being and passing away to take place, or for the bodies which move in the heaven to do as they do. Further, even if one were to grant that magnitude results from these, or it were proved, how it is that some bodies are light and some heavy? For to judge by what they say, they are not speaking of mathematical bodies as opposed to sensible ones; hence, I suppose, they say nothing about fire and earth and bodies of this sort because they have nothing to say that applies *peculiarly* to sensible objects.

Two things stand out clearly in this rather confused passage: that the Pythagoreans "bring the heaven into being" out of numbers, and that Aristotle did not see how this was possible. His puzzlement is understandable; for by his time numbers had come to be thought of as intelligible rather than sensible objects. They belong, in Aristotle's words, to "the class of things without movement." It is not, therefore, clear to him how a world-order composed of things in motion can possibly be generated out of numbers. Yet it is clear that the Pythagoreans did think that this was possible, while it is not equally certain that they thought of numbers as things devoid of movement.

Some light is shed on this problem by the Pythagorean method of representing numbers by means of pebbles. As we have seen, this method was not without its uses; it must have suggested intuitively to Pythagoras the method of finding triangles which would satisfy the Pythagorean theorem. But it also led the Pythagoreans to think of numbers as having spatial magnitude and position. Aristotle himself recognized this in another passage:

> **4.32** They construct the whole heaven out of numbers. Not, however, out of numbers considered as abstract units; for they suppose the units to have magnitude. But how the first "one" was constructed so as to have magnitude, they seem to be unable to say.

From this view of numbers it was an easy step to the assumption that they possessed other physical properties. Aristotle might protest that even if numbers had magnitude it did not follow that they had weight, but the Pythagoreans clearly made no such distinction. The belief that all things were numbers was, for them, entirely compatible with the belief that "what is is just what is perceptible and is contained in the so-called heaven." And this, in Ionian fashion, the Pythagoreans thought of as coming into being through a process of generation.

The process of generation is described (again by Aristotle) as follows:

> **4.33** They say plainly that when the "one" had been constructed — whether from planes, or surface, or seed, or something else which they are unable to express — then straightway the nearest part of the unlimited began to be drawn in and limited by the limit.

THE GENERATION OF NUMBER

Since the world-order is, according to the Pythagoreans, a number, it may help to understand the generation of the world-order if we consider the generation of number. The number sixteen, we saw earlier, is generated by placing around a "one" a series of *gnomons* containing successive odd integers:

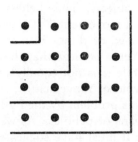

Now this process answers in a rough way to Aristotle's description of the world-order. For the addition of successive *gnomons* has the effect of bringing under control, *i.e.*, of bringing within bounds, a part of the space surrounding the original "one." This is clearly one way of setting a limit to what is unlimited.

We tend to think of the number sixteen as being made up of the dots only. But this is not the case; the number sixteen is represented by the *whole* of the figure. The space *between* the dots is as much a part of it as the dots themselves; for if the space were not there to hold them apart, the dots would run together into a single dot, and the number would no longer be sixteen but one. The dots, as it were, *organize* the space. They enclose it and limit it; and it is in this sense that the generation of the world-order also involves imposing a limit on what is unlimited.

Now Aristotle says of the Pythagoreans that

> **4.34** . . . they did not think of the limit and the unlimited as ele-
> mentary substances on a par with fire or earth or anything else
> of that sort, but rather of the unlimited itself and the "one" itself
> as constituting the very *being* of those things of which they are
> predicated. *This* is why, for them, number is the essence of all
> things.

Fire is real, but it is not *the* real; the "one" and the unlimited which it draws in and limits are the real. Only so can all things, including fire, be number. But the real is also identical with "what is perceptible and is contained in the so-called heaven" (**4.31**). Consequently limit and the unlimited must be perceptible, and to be perceptible they must possess physical properties.

The evidence indicates that this was the case:

> **4.35** The Pythagoreans, too, said that void exists, and that it enters the universe from the infinite breath as if it were being inhaled. It is the void which keeps things distinct, being a kind of separation and division of things that are next to each other. This is true first and foremost of numbers; for the void keeps them distinct.

By "void" Aristotle means empty space. But empty space cannot be inhaled; what enters the universe *is* the unlimited breath. The whole conception is derived from Anaximenes; the world-order inhales the air outside it just as we ourselves do.

The theory of respiration current among the Greek medical writers throws a good deal of light on this process:

> **4.36** The heart draws breath because it is the hottest part of the body. It is possible to see this in another way. If you light a fire indoors where there is no wind, the flame flickers — sometimes more, sometimes less — though no wind stirs that we can feel . . . . A candle flame behaves in the same way.

To us the explanation is simple: the fire warms the surrounding air, which rises, its place being taken by colder air from below. To the Greeks the explanation was simpler still: fire has the power to "draw" cold air and set it in motion. This power was thought to play an important role in the formation of the child in the womb:

> **4.37** Philolaus of Croton says that our bodies are brought into existence by heat. They have no share of cold, he says, and he adduces as evidence such facts as these. The seed is hot, and it is this which is fitted to produce the living creature. Moreover, the place into which the seed falls, *i.e.* the womb, is like it or even hotter; and what is like a thing has the same power as the thing it resembles. Since, therefore, the producing agent has no share of cold, and the place into which it falls has no share of cold, it is evident that the living creature which is produced is of this nature . . . . For immediately after birth it draws in the outside air, which is cold.

Now if the analogy between microcosm and macrocosm holds (**3.20**), we should expect to find that the world-order forms from the center outwards, as the child does in the womb; and this is exactly what we do find:

> **4.38** The world-order is one, and it began to come into being from the center; and from the center upwards to the same extent as downwards. For the regions above the center are merely the counterpart of those below . . . .

Moreover, we should expect that the center from which the world-order grows is fiery, and this too seems to be the case. Most people, says Aristotle, hold that earth is in the center:

> **4.39** But the Italian philosophers, the so-called Pythagoreans, affirm the contrary. For they say that fire occupies the center, and that earth, being one of the heavenly bodies, makes night and day as it moves around in a circle about the center. Further, they place another earth opposite this one, to which they give the name "counter-earth" — not seeking theories and causes to fit the facts but trying to force the facts into conformity with their theories and beliefs.
>
> There are many others who would agree that we ought not to assign to earth the central place, basing their belief, too, not on facts but on theories. For they suppose that to the most honorable thing belongs the most honorable place, that fire is more honorable than earth, that limit is more honorable than what falls between limits, and that periphery and center are limits. On these grounds they suppose that fire, not earth, lies at the center of the sphere.

In this passage Aristotle describes two quite different views. The first of these definitely asserts that the earth is a planet. The second merely asserts that there is fire at the center of the world-order — a view which is quite compatible with its being located at the center of the earth. That this was the traditional view is attested by Simplicius:

> **4.40** The more genuine members of the school say that the fire in the middle is the creative force which quickens the earth from within and warms its cold parts.

The belief in a fiery core at the earth's center would have gained considerable support from the existence of volcanoes and hot springs, both of which are common in southern Italy.

COSMOS AND HARMONY

In a general way, then, we can see how the world-order comes into being. The original "one," being fiery, sets the surrounding cold air in motion, drawing it in upon itself and limiting it. In this way number arises:

4.41 From numbers points, from points lines, from lines plane figures, from plane figures solid figures, from these sensible bodies, of which the elements are four: fire, water, earth, and air. These change and are wholly transformed; and from them arises a cosmos animate, intelligent, and spherical, embracing earth (itself spherical and inhabited all around) as its center.

It is animate because it is a living, breathing thing; intelligent, because it is capable of imposing order on what it takes in; spherical, because, as we saw, it grows outwards from the center equally in all directions. But above all it is a cosmos:

4.42 Pythagoras was the first to call what surrounds us a cosmos, because of the order in it.

The orderliness of nature is central to Greek thought from the start; but the word "cosmos" brings into sharper focus the implications which "order" had for the Greek mind. For the corresponding verb means not merely "to set in order," but "to set in an order which is fitting" and which is therefore beautiful. But in Greek there is no sharp distinction between "beautiful" and "good"; and "cosmos" suggests them both. It signifies not merely the regularity to be met with in the world-order, but in addition those aspects of it which the Greeks associated with the divine. This conception was, of course, part of the Ionian tradition from the first, but it is made explicit in Pythagoreanism.

The existence of a cosmos depends upon the observance of due proportion:

4.43 Light and darkness have an equal share in the cosmos; so too with hot and cold, dry and moist. When heat predominates, we get summer; when cold predominates, winter; when dry predominates, spring; when wet predominates, fall. When all have an equal share, we get the best seasons of the year . . . .

But the soul, too, is ordered by the observance of due proportion. For the soul, like the world-order, is a "harmony." As a young Pythagorean from Thebes puts it in Plato's *Phaedo*:

> **4.44** I imagine, Socrates, that you are well aware of our view of the soul, which is this: the body is in a state of tension, held together by heat, cold, dryness, moisture, and the like; and the soul is a blend or harmony of these same things when they are mixed together well and proportionately.

Any disruption of this harmony is an evil to the soul as well as to the body. And therefore, just as the art of medicine is called into being to treat the body in such cases, a corresponding art is needed which shall treat the soul:

> **4.45** For the most important thing in human life is the art of winning the soul to good . . . . Those who acquire a good soul are blessed, but if the soul is bad a man cannot rest or ever keep the same course.

Hence it was that

> **4.46** Pythagoras would chastise neither slave nor free man in anger. He called admonition a "re-tuning."

For it is by reasoning with a man that his soul is brought into that state in which alone it is stable and not subject to violent perturbations.

THE CITY AS A COSMOS

The city is itself a cosmos. It is a harmony of diverse elements, and the art of the ruler is directed towards the preservation of this harmony. It was at this point that the teaching of Pythagoras touched most nearly the lives of his fellow citizens; for the role played in the political life of Croton and its neighbors by the Pythagorean order was a very active one:

> **4.47** There Pythagoras gave laws to the Italians, and he and his disciples were held in great honor; for, being nearly three hundred strong, they administered affairs so well that the constitution was virtually an aristocracy [a "rule of the best"].

It is not difficult to gather from this and other passages the general tendency of Pythagorean politics. There is a story in Diodorus that in 511 B.C.

> **4.48** A leader of the mob named Telys arose among the Sybarites, who brought charges against the most prominent men and persuaded the Sybarites to exile the five hundred wealthiest citizens and confiscate their estates. When the fugitives went to Croton and sought refuge at the altars in the marketplace, Telys sent messengers to the people of Croton, commanding them either to deliver up the refugees or prepare for war. A general assembly was called and the question put to it whether to surrender the refugees or accept war with a foe more powerful than themselves. The council and the people were at a loss what to do. At first the opinion of the masses inclined towards giving up the refugees, because of fear of war. But when the philosopher Pythagoras advised them to shelter the refugees, they changed their minds and undertook to fight to protect them.

The story suggests that Pythagoras was not sympathetic with the aims of popular parties, and this squares with the conservatism for which the Pythagoreans were famous. On the other hand, the Pythagoreans do not seem to have identified themselves with the aristocratic faction. Cylon, who led the revolt against the Pythagoreans at the beginning of the fifth century B.C., was himself a member of this class, and **4.47** suggests that the rule of the Pythagoreans was intended to be a rule not of those who *called* themselves "best" — i.e., the old ruling class — but of those who really *were* "best."

The evidence suggests that the Pythagorean rule was neither democratic nor (in the traditional sense) aristocratic. It appears to have embodied principles of another order altogether, and in a very general way we can make out the outlines of that policy. Plato, in his *Gorgias*, makes Socrates say to Callicles:

> **4.49** Wise men, Callicles, say that heaven and earth and gods and men are held together by communion and friendship, and by orderliness and self-restraint and justice. And that is why they call the whole a "cosmos" and not an unbridled chaos. Now it seems to me that for all your wisdom you pay insufficient attention to these things, and have failed to see the enormous power of "geometrical equality" among gods and men. It is because you neglect geometry that you think men ought to take advantage of others.

These ideas are clearly Pythagorean. The world-order is a cosmos, an harmonious blend of divine elements bound together by order and justice. As Philolaus puts it:

> **4.50** Since the first principles are neither similar nor of the same kind, it would be impossible to make a cosmos of them unless some kind of harmony were somehow or other to come into being. Things which are similar and of the same kind have no need of harmony; but things which are neither similar nor of the same kind nor of equal rank must be linked together in such a harmony if they are to be part of a cosmos.

As the language of this passage indicates, the doctrine of harmony is meant to apply to the social order as well. This order too is made up of diverse elements: good and bad, well-born and base-born, rich and poor. If the social order is to reflect the nature of the world-order as a whole, these diverse elements must be bound together in harmony and friendship. Hence the great importance which Pythagoras attached to friendship:

> **4.51** He had a gift for friendship, especially when he found anyone who shared his views. He would straightway take to such a man and make a friend of him.

> **4.52** He was the first, Timaeus says, to say that "friends have all things in common," and that "friendship is equality." And his disciples actually put their possessions into one common stock.

Order and justice are possible only where this harmony, expressed in friendship and the sharing of goods in common, already exists.

Pythagoras represented this harmony by means of a figure:

> **4.53** To represent the constitution he arranged three lines with their ends touching so as to form a figure with one right angle — one side having the nature of the epitrite, another five such parts, and the third being a mean between the other two.

The figure described is clearly intended to be a right triangle having its sides in the ratio of 3:4:5. The short side and the hypotenuse represent the extremes which, in the city, are to be united; the intermediate side represents the mean which binds them together, for 5:4::4:3. Four is the square number which the Pythagoreans identified with justice; so that it is justice which, in a formal sense, binds the city together.

JUSTICE AS A PROPORTION

The principle of social order, then, is justice. But justice is founded upon "reciprocity":

4.54 The Pythagoreans used to define justice simply as reciprocity.

4.55 They thought it just that what a man had done he should suffer in return.

This definition of justice is quite in accord with the traditional Greek view of it as "giving every man his due," but the question now arises: how is this to be determined in distributing honors, wealth, and the other divisible assets of a community?

On this subject there were sharply opposing views. As Aristotle was to put it much later:

4.56 All agree that justice in distributions must be based on merit of some sort, but they do not all mean the same sort of merit. Democrats make the criterion free birth; oligarchs, wealth (by which they mean noble birth); aristocrats, virtue.

It seemed to the Pythagoreans that the soundest of these criteria was the third. But how could the distinction between the better and the worse elements in the city be maintained without sacrificing the principle of equality? The answer seemed to lie in the theory of proportions:

4.57 In the old days, in the time of Pythagoras and the mathematicians of his school, there were three means: the arithmetic, the geometric, and a third which was in those days called the "subcontrary" but was renamed "harmonic" by the circle of Archytas and Hippasus . . . .

4.58 The arithmetic mean is that in which three terms are proportional by virtue of a difference between them such that the first exceeds the second by the same amount by which the second exceeds the third. It turns out, in this proportion, that the ratio between the greater of the terms is less than the ratio between the lesser. The geometric mean is that in which the first term is to the second as the second is to the third. In this case the greater of the terms are in the same ratio as the lesser. The "subcontrary" mean, which we call the "harmonic," is such that by whatever part of itself the first term exceeds the second, the middle exceeds the third by the same part of the third. In this proportion the ratio between the greater of the terms is greater than the ratio between the lesser.

Thus b is the arithmetic mean between a and c if $a - b = c$, the geometric mean where $\dfrac{a}{b} = \dfrac{b}{c}$, and the "harmonic" mean where $\dfrac{a - b}{a} = \dfrac{b - c}{c}$.

Of these three means Pythagoras chose the second to represent justice in the world-order (**4.49**). Why did he do so? There is a passage in Aristotle which suggests the answer. We ought to distinguish, he says, between the mean with respect to the thing itself and the mean relative to us:

> **4.59** By the mean relative to us I mean that which is neither too much nor too little, and this is not one and the same for everybody. For example, if ten be many and two be few, then the mean relative to the thing is six, since six exceeds two by the same amount that ten exceeds six. This is the mean according to arithmetic proportion. But we cannot find the mean relative to us in this way. For if ten pounds of food are too many to eat and two are too few, it does not follow that the trainer will prescribe six pounds; for perhaps even this is too much or too little for the recipient. It is too little for a wrestler like Milo, but too much for a man just starting in training, and the same goes for running and wrestling. In the same way every man of understanding avoids excess and deficiency and seeks the mean — not the mean relative to the thing but to us.

It will be clear from this example that the arithmetic mean is too mechanical. It fails to take into account differences such as the difference between a professional wrestler like Milo and a mere beginner. It is the business of an expert in any art to take such differences into account, and politics is an art. The statesman, in distributing honors, must recognize that while men may be equal in their birth, they may also differ in their merits, and that in giving to each his due these differences must be taken into account. Thus, by elimination (for Pythagoras does not seem to have concerned himself with the "harmonic" mean) we are left with the geometric mean. In Aristotle's words:

4.60 The principle of justice in distributions, therefore, is the joining of the first term of a proportion with the third and the second with the fourth; and this sort of justice is a mean, whereas injustice is that which contravenes the proportion. For the proportionate is a mean, and the just is a proportion. The mathematicians call such a proportion "geometrical."

This formula preserves the differences recognized by the aristocratic conception of justice while at the same time admitting the democratic claim to equality. For proportion, as Aristotle puts it, is "equality of ratios." In other words, if A and B receive honors C and D, then $AC : BD : : A : B$; that is, their relative conditions after receiving them will be exactly the same as before. They will, in short, have received "equal" treatment.

PYTHAGOREAN THOUGHT

The problem of social justice, then, is at bottom a mathematical one. For it is in essence a problem of ordering things, and the key to all order is number — the assigning of limit to what otherwise remains indeterminate and confused. This is the office of reason, the fountainhead of order in the cosmos as in the city, in the individual as in the cosmos. And it is the essence of Pythagoreanism to hold that the real is a reflection of the order of reason. But this is also the essence of Greek philosophy as a whole.

The most striking feature of Pythagorean thought is the curious blend of the scientific and the unscientific which we find everywhere in it. This feature is often thought to be peculiar to Pythagorean thought, but in fact it is a characteristic which Pythagoreanism shares with the Ionian philosophy out of which it grew. What strikes us as scientific in the Ionian tradition is the use of mechanical analogies — the appeal to "what happens in liquids and in air," where heavy things go to the center, or to what happens in the manufacture of felt. From our point of view the use of such analogies represents an advance over "prescientific" modes of thought such as we find in Hesiod. We are apt to forget that these prescientific modes of thought persisted, side by side with the scientific, throughout the development of early Greek philosophy.

They found classical expression in the analogy between microcosm and macrocosm. There are clear traces of this analogy in the thought of Anaximander and Anaximenes, but it plays a recessive role there. Our attention is taken up with what happens in liquids because this way of thinking is closer to our own. In Pythagoreanism it is the other way around; the appeal to what happens "when you light a fire indoors, where there is no wind" is there, but we fail to notice it because of the dominant role played by the analogy of microcosm and macrocosm in Pythagorean cosmology.

What is peculiar to Pythagoreanism is not the use of this analogy, or the preoccupation with order — even of mathematical order; in these respects Pythagoreanism is largely a making explicit of what was implicit in the Ionian tradition. What is new in Pythagoreanism is its preoccupation with the soul. Here, too, it is rooted in Ionian thought; but the contemplation of the order of nature has now a new purpose, unknown to the Milesians: the freeing of the soul from its bondage to the body. This conception was to leave its impress upon the whole body of classical Greek philosophy, and, through Plato, upon the whole of Western thought.

PART TWO

THE POSING OF
THE PROBLEM

Heraclitus

Parmenides

Zeno and Melissus

PART TWO

THE POSING OF
THE PROBLEM

Heraclitus

Parmenides

Zeno and Melissus

FIVE

Heraclitus

The Ionians had taken as the starting point of their inquiry the visible world-order. Their aim was to understand this order: to determine its origin and the laws of its functioning. Even Pythagoras, who subordinated this inquiry to the freeing of the soul from its bondage to the body, did not radically alter the nature of the inquiry itself. It revolved still around the same center: the cosmos, the visible embodiment of reason.

This unanimity of approach was shattered, early in the fifth century B.C., by the appearance of Parmenides (Chapter Six). The methods Parmenides used, and the conclusions he reached, were so utterly opposed to those of the Ionians as to suggest a complete break with the whole tradition. Yet the *problem* with which Parmenides was concerned — the problem of "the one and the many" — grew out of the Ionian tradition in the most natural way, and the first to concern himself with it was himself an Ionian, Parmenides' predecessor Heraclitus.

Heraclitus was a native of Ephesus, midway between Colophon and Miletus. Around 500 B.C. he produced a book of which well over a hundred fragments have come down to us. The tone of these fragments is striking; they reveal a proud and passionate nature, harsh in judgment, impatient of the views of others, yet redeemed by a clear, intense, and profoundly religious vision of reality.

THE REJECTION OF POPULAR RELIGION

Heraclitus gives short shrift to his predecessors and contemporaries:

5.1   A knowledge of many things does not teach one to have intelli-

gence; otherwise it would have taught Hesiod and Pythagoras, or again Xenophanes and Hecataeus.

5.2   Wisdom is one thing: to understand the thought which steers all things through all things.

There is a fragment of the Greek poet Archilochus which runs:

5.3   The fox knows many things, the hedgehog only one. One big one.

Heraclitus is a hedgehog. To know many things — to know the causes of thunder and lightning and earthquakes — is good; but it is better to understand the one thing which underlies all of these — the thought that steers all things through all things. *This* is wisdom.

On the other hand, Heraclitus clearly owed more to Xenophanes than **5.1** would indicate, and nowhere is this more evident than in what he has to say of the religious conceptions and practices of his fellowmen:

5.4   The one and only wisdom is willing and unwilling to be called Zeus.

The wisdom of which Heraclitus speaks here is the "totality of mind and thought" which Xenophanes calls "god" (**3.40**); it is the intelligence which steers all things through all things. To the extent that it is divine it is willing to be called "Zeus," since this is the name that all men give to the divine. But it is also unwilling; and this unwillingness — the unwillingness of Heraclitus himself to invoke the name of Zeus — springs from a rejection of the anthropomorphic conceptions which it conjures up in men's minds:

5.5   The secret rites which are in use among men are celebrated in an unholy manner.

5.6   For if it were not in honor of Dionysus that they hold their processions and sing their hymn to the male organ they would be acting most shamelessly.

5.7   Though defiled with blood they purify themselves with blood — as though a man who had stepped in mud were to wash it off with mud. Such a man would be thought insane by anyone who saw him acting in this way. And they pray to these statues, as if a man were to talk to a house, not realizing what gods and heroes are.

The first two passages refer to rites associated with the mysteries of Dionysus, the third to those connected with the worship of the Olympian gods. Heraclitus condemns them without distinction, and the grounds on which he condemns them are familiar to us from Xenophanes; they are not only immoral, but they betray a complete misconception of the nature of the divine.

Hence Heraclitus' unwillingness to call the thought that steers all things "Zeus." Instead he chooses the fiery thunderbolt, which in Hesiod is the attribute of Zeus and the symbol of his might (1.2), to symbolize the divine:

> **5.8** Thunderbolt steers all things.

THE WORLD-ORDER AS A FLUX

If we approach Heraclitus from the side of the world-order, the influence of Xenophanes is still more marked:

> **5.9** Heraclitus describes change as a way up and down, and the world-order as coming into being in accordance with it. For fire, when it is contracted, becomes moist; when it is contracted still further it becomes water; and water, when it is contracted, turns to earth. This is the downward way. And earth liquifies again; and from it water arises; and from water the rest. For he refers nearly everything to the evaporation of the sea. And this is the upward way.

The process described in these lines is a familiar one; it is the process of dilation and compression by means of which Anaximenes brings about the transformations of air. But it is due to Xenophanes' influence that the process is so clearly conceived as a cyclical one, in which the evaporation of water from the sea is balanced by its return in the form of rain.

What is peculiar to Heraclitus is the sheer sweep of his vision of the world-order as a dynamic equilibrium of these opposite movements:

> **5.10** All things come into being through opposition, and all are in flux like a river.

> **5.11** Cool things become warm; what is warm cools; what is wet dries
> out; what is dry becomes moist.

In both Anaximander and Anaximenes (though perhaps more explicitly in the latter) the life of the world-order lies in continual movement; "for the things that change would not do so unless there were motion" (**3.2**). Heraclitus expresses the same idea in an arresting image:

> **5.12** This world-order, the same for all, no god made or any man, but
> it always was and is and will be an ever-living fire, kindling by
> measure and going out by measure.

The mechanism of dilation and compression is such that it does not matter, from a metaphysical point of view, which element is taken as fundamental: earth, air, water, or fire. One will do as well as another; for it is as easy, given earth as fundamental, to derive air from it as to derive earth from air. Anaximenes had fixed on air simply as having no character peculiar to itself "when it is most evenly distributed" (**3.2**). Heraclitus fastens on fire because it *does* have a peculiar characteristic; that of perpetual motion. It is this which fits it to serve as a symbol of the cosmic process as a whole. To express in a single image the involved movement of men massed in battle on the plain of Troy, Homer says that "they fought in the image of blazing fire." For the same reason Heraclitus likens the warring of the opposites, the process of becoming, to a vast conflagration in which the whole forever consumes and renews itself.

In another image he likens the world-order to a posset — a drink made of ground barley, grated cheese and wine:

> **5.13** Even the posset separates if it is not stirred.

For if it is not stirred, the ingredients quickly separate out, and the posset as such ceases to exist. So it is with the world-order; if the perpetual transformations of fire were to cease, becoming would fail and with it the world-order itself.

But the image with which Heraclitus' name has come to be associated in men's minds is that of **5.10**, where the world-order is likened to a river:

> **5.14** Heraclitus, you know, says that everything moves on and that
> nothing is at rest; and, comparing existing things to the flow

of a river, he says that you could not step into the same river twice.

You cannot step into the same river twice, because nothing is the same from one moment to the next. The waters into which you stepped but a moment ago have been carried away down the stream, and fresh waters have taken their place. So in the world-order the transformations of fire succeed one another continually, and nothing stands still.

The simile is an apt one, but in the form in which it is stated in **5.14** it is misleading. In this passage Plato makes Heraclitus say that you cannot step into the same *river* twice; but what Heraclitus actually says is:

> **5.15** Upon those who step into the same rivers flow other and yet other waters.

In this version the *waters* are different but the *rivers* are the same. In the midst of change they preserve their identity. They change, yet they remain the same; for there are always fresh waters flowing on to take the place of those which have gone before. So it is in the world-order as a whole; in the midst of change the everlasting fire remains one and the same, "kindling in measure and going out in measure."

Measure and Justice

The kindlings and goings-out of fire are simply the transformations of the upward and downward ways:

> **5.16** The changes of fire: first sea, and of sea half is earth, half fiery thunderbolt . . . . Earth is dispersed as sea, and is measured out in the same proportion as before it became earth.

> **5.17** All things are an exchange for fire, and fire for all things; as goods are for gold, and gold for goods.

The transformation of sea into earth is balanced by an equal and opposite transformation of earth into sea, the equilibrium of the whole being preserved by means of the equality of these exchanges, exactly as wares are exchanged for gold and gold for wares.

What is essential to maintaining this equilibrium is the observance of measure:

> **5.18** The sun will not overstep his measures; for if he does, the Furies, defenders of Justice, will find him out.

If the sun were to fail to turn back at the time of summer or winter solstice, the succession of the seasons would be disrupted and the whole natural order thrown out of balance. The avenging of all such violations of the natural order is the task of Furies. When the horses of Achilles prophesy his doom in Book 19 of the *Iliad,* it is the Furies who bid them be silent; it is not right that horses should talk. Neither is it right that the sun should overstep the limits set for it. The preservation of the whole requires the observance of measure in all things.

These ideas plainly go back to Anaximander. But Anaximander regards the destruction of one of the opposites by another as a kind of injustice. Heraclitus sees such destruction differently. The injustices of which Anaximander speaks are part and parcel of the cosmic process itself; without them there would be no alternation of winter and summer. The injustices which the opposites commit against each other are as essential to the well-being of the whole as the reparation which they make to one another. In the eyes of god, therefore, they are not injustices at all; for their occurrence is necessary to the functioning of the whole:

> **5.19** To god all things are beautiful and good and just; but men suppose some things to be just and others unjust.

The debt to Xenophanes is evident. Men can only know things through their opposites; this necessity is laid upon them by the nature of perception itself:

> **5.20** According to Anaxagoras [Chapter Nine] and Heraclitus, sensation proceeds by opposition . . . . In their view perception involves change, and a thing is not affected by what is like it, but only by what is unlike it. On this they base their belief; and they hold that what occurs in the case of touch bears them out. For when a thing is the same temperature as our body we do not feel it [as hot or cold].

Because of this fact all human knowledge is limited to the perception of contrast. But god is not bound by the laws of perception; "he sees all over, thinks all over, hears all over" (**3.36**). He is able, therefore, to perceive all things as they are in themselves, and seen from this point of view all things are just, for all are necessary — both the things that men think just and those that they think unjust.

The poets, in their ignorance, think that strife is unjust; but it is not:

> **5.21** Heraclitus rebukes Homer for saying, "Would that strife might perish from among gods and men!" He did not see that he was praying for the destruction of the whole; for if his prayers were heard, all things would pass away . . . .

> **5.22** It is necessary to understand that war is universal and justice is strife, and that all things take place in accordance with strife and necessity.

> **5.23** For fire lives the death of earth, and air lives the death of fire; water lives the death of air, and earth that of water.

> **5.24** War is the father and king of all . . . .

Not only Homer but Hesiod, too, rails against strife, saying that fishes devour one another because they do not have justice (**1.16**). But he fails to see that if fishes were not eaten by other fishes, and these by other fishes again, the balance of life in the sea would be completely disrupted. This is true not merely of living things but of the cosmic process as a whole; for the life of the cosmos is motion and change, and it is war that stirs the posset, war that brings about the perishing of sea that earth may live, and the other transformations of fire. Because it is the mainspring of the world-process, war is the father of all things and king of all. It has, in fact, assumed the titles of Zeus, fountainhead of all justice. War, too, is justice; in the eyes of god what men call "injustice" and what they call "justice" are one and the same.

THE "IDENTITY" OF THE OPPOSITES

The identity which underlies all opposition is insisted upon again and again in the fragments:

> **5.25** Sea water is very pure and very impure; drinkable and healthful for fishes, but undrinkable and destructive to men.

> **5.26** The path traced by the pen is straight and crooked.

> **5.27** In a circle, beginning and end are common.

The path which the pen traces across the page is crooked if you attend to the individual letters; but it is straight if you attend to the whole. In constructing a circle, the same point which serves as the beginning also serves as the end. The writing is both crooked and straight; the point, both beginning and end. In all of these examples the intention is the same: to illustrate the paradox of sameness in difference.

In the whole all opposition is transcended:

> **5.28** The god is day, night, winter, summer, war, peace, satiety, hunger, and undergoes change as fire, when it is mingled with spices, is named according to the aroma of each.

Even as the same fire, mingled with different spices, appears to us now as pleasant, now as unpleasant, so the god appears to us now as justice, now as injustice, now as life, now as death, but remains the same. To grasp this unity amid change is to grasp the fact that as it is the same river that flows towards us and recedes from us, so it is the same universal fire which in measure kindles and in measure goes out:

> **5.29** The way up and the way down are the same.

The *Logos*

There are few men capable of grasping this:

> **5.30** For the many do not understand such things when they meet with them; nor having learned do they comprehend, though they think they do.

> **5.31** Though the *logos* is as I have said, men always fail to comprehend it, both before they hear it and when they hear it for the first time. For though all things come into being in accordance with this *logos*, they seem like men without experience, though in fact they do have experience both of words and deeds such as I have set forth, distinguishing each thing in accordance with its nature and declaring what it is. But other men are as unaware of what they do when awake as they are when they are asleep.

> **5.32** Though they are in daily contact with the *logos* they are at variance with it, and what they meet with appears alien to them.

Logos can mean many things in Greek. It is derived from a verb meaning "to speak," and may refer simply to the words used by a speaker. But it may also refer to the thought expressed by what is said, conceived as existing in its own right apart from the words of the speaker. This is the sense in which Heraclitus uses it when he says:

> **5.33** Listening not to me but to the *logos*, it is wise to acknowledge that all things are one.

The *logos* to which he refers here is clearly thought of as having an independent existence, and **5.31** confirms this impression: the *logos* is that in accordance with which all things come into being. It is in fact "the thought that steers all things through all things" (**5.2**).

Though the *logos* confronts men at every turn, they do not grasp it but behave like men asleep, unaware of what goes on about them:

> **5.34** To those who are awake the world-order is one, common to all; but the sleeping turn aside each into a world of his own.

> **5.35** We ought not to act and speak like men asleep.

> **5.36** We ought to follow what is common to all; but though the *logos* is common to all, the many live as though their thoughts were private to themselves.

Just as men who are asleep turn aside in dreams from the world which is common to all into private worlds of their own, so men who are awake turn aside from the *logos* which is common to all into private worlds of their own. For "each forms his own opinion," as Xenophanes says (**3.46**), and each is pleased to think this opinion "his." But the truth does not lie in private judgment; it transcends opinion, and is the same for all. Its unity is grounded in the unity of the *logos* itself, in accordance with which all things take place.

But though the *logos* is common to all, knowledge of it is hard to acquire, for its features are ambiguous:

> **5.37** If you do not expect the unexpected, you will not find it; for it is hard to find and difficult.

> **5.38** Those who dig for gold dig up much dirt and find little.

This is only natural, for

5.39 Nature loves to hide.

5.40 The lord whose oracle is at Delphi neither speaks out nor conceals, but gives a sign.

5.41 The Sibyl with raving mouth, uttering things mirthless, unadorned, and unperfumed, reaches down a thousand years with her voice because of the god.

Herodotus, in his *Histories,* relates that when Croesus, king of the Lydians, meant to march against the Persians, he sent to the oracle of Apollo at Delphi to inquire whether he should do so. The answer, delivered through the mouth of the Sibyl, was that if he did a great empire would fall. Croesus, encouraged, marched against the Persians, and it turned out as the oracle had prophesied — except that the empire was his own. In such dark riddles as these does the god speak: neither speaking out or concealing, but giving a sign.

The oracle through which he speaks to all men is sense perception:

5.42 Those things of which there is sight, hearing, understanding, I esteem most.

But the deliverances of the senses are only "signs" which lead men astray unless they are correctly interpreted. When the intelligence sleeps, men fail to read them aright:

5.43 Eyes and ears are bad witnesses to men if they have souls that do not understand their language.

This is why the many are estranged from the *logos,* though it is common to all:

5.44 They do not comprehend how, though it is at variance with itself, it agrees with itself. It is a harmony of opposed tensions, as in the bow and the lyre.

5.45 In opposition there is agreement; between unlikes, the fairest harmony.

5.46 The hidden harmony is stronger than the apparent.

In the bow as in the lyre there is an equilibrium of forces, the pull of the frame against the taut string being balanced by the pull of the string against the bent frame. The result is a harmony of opposed tensions such as we find in the world-order. For in the world-order this harmony is maintained by the equality of the transformations of fire. From the point of view of the senses the aggregation of these transformations is a many, a plurality of changes proceeding in opposite directions along the upward and downward ways, and therefore as filled with discord. But from the point of view of reason it is one, its unity consisting in the equilibrium maintained by the equivalence of the transformations of fire. The world-order is thus both a one and a many:

5.47 Aggregations are wholes, yet not wholes; brought together, yet carried asunder; in accord, yet not in accord. From all, one; from one, all.

5.48 Changing, it rests.

The *Logos* in Man

To grasp the hidden connection that runs through all things and binds them together is to realize the impossibility of accepting some and rejecting others, of calling some "good" and others "bad." Men call those things "good" which they wish for themselves; but

5.49 It is not good for men to get all they wish.

5.50 It is sickness that makes health pleasant and good; hunger, satiety; weariness, rest.

5.51 Physicians who cut, burn, stab, and rack the sick demand a fee for it.

5.52 Beasts are driven to pasture with blows.

The cautery which the physician performs is painful; yet the physician demands a reward for it all the same, for by hurting the patient he makes him well. The patient, insofar as he fails to understand this, is no better than an ox that resists the blows of the drover, not realizing that it is being driven to pasture.

In truth, the many are as far from understanding what happens to them as oxen are:

> **5.53** It is not characteristic of men to be intelligent; but it is characteristic of god.

> **5.54** Man is called childish in comparison with the divine, just as a child is in comparison with a man.

> **5.55** Even the wisest of men appears to be but an ape in comparison with a god, both in wisdom and in beauty and in every other way.

Yet, as wide as the gap is between the human and the divine, the two are connected by a thread. For all men have a share in the intelligence by which all things are steered through all things:

> **5.56** According to Heraclitus we become intelligent by drawing in the divine *logos* when we breathe. We become forgetful during sleep, but on waking we regain our senses. For in sleep the channels of perception are shut, and the intelligence in us is severed from its kinship with the environment — our only connection with it being through breathing, by which we are, as it were, rooted in it. When it is separated in this way, the mind loses the power of remembering which it formerly had; but in the waking state it once more flows forth through the channels of perception as through so many openings, and making contact with the environment recovers the power of reasoning.
>
> Just as coals, when they are brought close to the fire, begin to glow, and die down when they are removed from it, so it is with that portion of the environment which sojourns in our own bodies. When it is separated from its source, it loses nearly all power of thought; but when it makes contact with it through the many channels of sense, it becomes of like nature to the whole.

It is for this reason that those who fail to perceive the one in the many are likened to sleepwalkers; for in sleep our contact with the *logos* is reduced to a minimum. But we can see, too, why we ought not to act and speak like men asleep (**5.35**); for all men breathe, and therefore all have a share of intelligence, however slight:

5.57 Thought is common to all.

5.58 It is common to all men to know themselves and to act with moderation.

SELF-KNOWLEDGE AND MODERATION

Over the doors of the temple of Apollo at Delphi two commandments were inscribed: "Know thyself!" and "Nothing in excess!" How closely related they were may be seen from a passage in which Aeschylus makes the ghost of Darius prophesy the destruction of the Persian host at Plataea in the summer of 479 B.C.:

5.59 Sand dunes of corpses will proclaim,
  even to the third generation,
  their silent message for the eyes of men:
  that never, being mortal, is it right
  for us to cast our thoughts too high.
  For insolence, in blossoming,
  has sown the sheaf of ruin
  from which a tearful harvest springs.
  Seeing such things deserved, remember, Athens!
  And Hellas, too! Let no man overlook
  the present good, lusting for more,
  and squander his great fortune.

To know ourselves is to remember who we are: that we are only men, and that being mortal we ought not to cast our thoughts too high. So much only is granted to men; to lust after more is to overstep the limit, and to bring upon oneself the wrath of Zeus which is certain destruction. It is better, therefore, to avoid excess and to observe moderation in all things.

The classical theory of conduct is founded upon these two precepts. It goes back at least to Hesiod, and it must have been familiar to the Milesians, for we find it echoed in their conception of the world-order as one in which any excess, any uncompensated predominance of one of the opposites over the rest, is fatal to the whole. The reparation which the opposites make to each other for their injustice is but a projection of the classical theory of conduct upon the world-order at large. But the Milesians were not concerned with human conduct as such; their interests lay in the origins of the world-order as a whole. The first of the Ionians to concern himself with conduct was Pythagoras.

Pythagoras was not opposed to the classical theory of conduct. On the contrary, he used the traditional formulas in his own teaching:

5.60 He rejects all excess, saying that one should not overstep due proportion either in drinking or in eating.

But he gave these traditional formulas a deeper meaning. The observance of moderation became, in his hands, the observance of limit as such, the curbing of impulse by reason, the ordering of the soul in accordance with the order which is manifest throughout the cosmos as a whole. In these ideas lay the germ of a complete theory of conduct grounded in Ionian physics, but Pythagoras did not pursue them. For him, the problem of human conduct was overshadowed by the more important problem of the soul's imprisonment in the body, and the means of releasing it from bondage. The task of developing these germinal ideas, therefore, fell to Heraclitus.

That the classical theory of conduct supplied the starting point for his thought is clear; "it is common to all men to know themselves and to act with moderation" (**5.51**). Heraclitus denounces insolence just as fiercely as his younger contemporary Aeschylus:

5.61 There is more need to stamp out insolence than a fire.

But in his hands the commandments of the god take on a deeper significance. They are no longer isolated precepts but are grounded in the very nature of things. If what is reason in us is a portion of the divine, it should be possible for us to arrive at an understanding of the *logos* by turning inward. Of his own search Heraclitus says:

5.62 I searched out myself.

The man who seeks out himself becomes conscious of a power that reaches out in every direction:

5.63 The soul has a *logos* which increases itself.

5.64 You would not find out the boundaries of the soul though you travelled every road, so deep is its *logos*.

For to know oneself is to know the thought that steers all things through all things; and this is nothing less than wisdom (**5.2**).

Yet the soul has its being in the world-order; for

5.65 Souls arise from the moist.

5.66 It is death to souls to become water; to water it is death to become earth. From earth comes water, and from water soul.

5.67 A dry soul is wisest and best.

5.68 When a man is drunk he is led stumbling by a beardless boy, not knowing where he is going, because his soul is moist.

A dry soul is wisest and best because it most fully shares the nature of fire, and is therefore able to grasp the *logos*. But drunkenness quenches the fire in us and clouds our wits, so that we are no better than children.

If the many prefer drunkenness it is because of the pleasure that it brings:

5.69 It is a delight to souls to become moist . . . .

Happiness, however, does not lie in such pleasures:

5.70 If happiness consisted in bodily pleasures we ought to call oxen happy who find vetch to eat.

But the desire for pleasure is hard to resist:

5.71 It is hard to fight against impulse; for what it wants it buys at the expense of the soul.

Because it buys what it wants at the expense of the soul, the wise man will not yield to it but will fight against it, acting with moderation. For all men have the power to act with moderation (**5.51**), and to do so is to conform to the *logos*:

5.72 Moderation is the greatest virtue, and wisdom is to speak the truth and to act according to nature, giving heed to it.

To act according to nature is to act in accordance with the law that governs the transformations of fire and determines their measures. The man who is governed by reason will, in short, reflect in his own life the larger life of the world-order, setting limits to his desires even as the *logos* sets limits to the passage of the sun from north to south and back again. The injunction "Nothing in excess!" understood in its deepest sense, is an injunction to follow the *logos*, to observe in oneself the order observed by nature, using to this end the same intelligence which, on a large scale, steers all things through all things.

Such a man will not seek his happiness in externals, for he will realize that such things are determined by chance:

> **5.73** [War] makes some slaves, some free.

> **5.74** Life is a child moving pieces in a game. The kingship is in the hands of a child.

Whether a man is born into slavery or into a hereditary kingship (as was Heraclitus himself) is not in his power. But happiness lies in conformity to the *logos*, and this is a matter which does lie in his power; for

> **5.75** A man's character is his guardian spirit.

The Fate of the Soul

Heraclitus does not speak of the soul as though it were alien to the body; yet he seems to believe that it outlives it, for he says:

> **5.76** There await men, after death, such things as they neither hope nor imagine.

The body reverts to earth; or, as Heraclitus puts it with brutal precision:

> **5.77** Corpses are fitter to be cast out than dung.

But the soul is fiery, and shares the nature of the divine:

> **5.78** He says that the soul, passing out into the soul of the all, returns to its own kind.

There is evidence, however, that not all men share the same fate:

> **5.79** For better deaths win better portions.

> **5.80** The souls of men slain in battle are purer than those who die of disease.

The sick waste away, and the soul grows weaker in them as they approach death; but men who die in battle are cut off in the prime of life, when they are most active and their souls most fiery, for the battle-fury is upon them.

But of these we hear no more. Perhaps they share the fate of those "pure spirits" who, according to Hesiod, watch over men and defend them from evil (1.10). But their fate is obscure, and no fragments have come down to us which would help to show the extent of Pythagoras' influence on Heraclitus' conception of the soul.

THE RULE OF THE BEST

He who desires to live in conformity with the *logos* will speak the truth (5.64); for even as the Furies, defenders of justice, will find out the sun if he oversteps his measures, so in the city

5.81   Justice will overtake the makers and witnesses of lies.

5.82   How could anyone escape the notice of that which never sets?

The law of the city is but a reflection of the *logos* which runs through all things:

5.83   It is necessary for men who speak with common sense to place reliance on what is common to all, as a city relies upon law, and even more firmly. For all human laws are nourished by the one divine law. For it governs as far as it will, and is sufficient for all things, and outlasts them.

Therefore,

5.84   The people ought to fight for the law as they would for their walls.

But if the law of the city is a reflection of the divine *logos*, the actual making of law can hardly be entrusted to the many; for the many are incapable of understanding:

5.85   For what understanding or intelligence have they? They believe what they are told by the bards of the people, and take the mob for their teacher, not realizing that "the many are bad, the good few."

> **5.86** Uncomprehending, even when they have heard, they are like the deaf. The old saying bears witness to them: "Though present they are absent."

This would not matter if the many were content to be ruled by those wiser than themselves. But they lack even the intelligence to realize that they ought to obey those whose understanding of the *logos* is greater than their own. And when a man appears who is not cut to their measure, they drive him out:

> **5.87** Dogs bark at those whom they do not recognize.

> **5.88** The Ephesians ought to hang themselves — every grown man of them — and leave their city to adolescents, now that they have expelled Hermodorus, the best man among them, saying, "Let there be no best man among us; or if there is, let him be so elsewhere and among others!"

For the many cannot grasp the fact that

> **5.89** To be obedient to the counsel of one man is also law.

They want the law to express the will of all, not realizing that it is not numbers that determine what is right or wrong, but intelligence. And one man of intelligence is worth all of the ignorant put together:

> **5.90** One man is worth ten thousand to me, if only he be best.

In the rule of the best we seem to hear an echo of Pythagoreanism, but the resemblance is in fact only superficial.

> **5.91** For the best men choose one thing above all the rest: everlasting fame among mortal men. But the many have glutted themselves like cattle.

The language of this passage is not Pythagorean; it is Homeric. It opens a door suddenly into the world of heroic values which we meet with in the *Iliad*, and the choice with which it confronts men is the choice of Achilles:

5.92 Two fates are bearing me to the issue of death.
If I stay here and attack the Trojans' city,
my homecoming is lost but immortal glory will be mine.
If I return to my beloved country, lost is my goodly glory
but my life will be all too long,
and death will not swiftly take me.

Faced with this choice, Achilles does not hesitate. It is nobler to die bravely in battle, and to win thereby "immortal glory," than to live long in comfortable security:

5.93 For gods and men honor those slain in battle.

Such are those who are "best" — distinguished from the worst in death even as in life. For the world of Homer is not a democratic world. The best are exalted above the many even as Agamemnon is exalted above his followers:

5.94 Like some great bull that towers above the herd,
conspicuous among the mass of cattle;
so Zeus made Atreus' son stand out that day,
pre-eminent among the mass of men.

In this world the aristocracy found the highest expression of its own ideals; and Heraclitus, who belonged to it by birth, shared these ideals. The virtues he celebrated — excellence, moderation, obedience to law — were those which his younger contemporary Pindar celebrated in the victory odes composed in honor of his aristocratic patrons. But Pindar, writing for such an audience, could take for granted the aristocratic conception of human life; Heraclitus, sensible of the fate of Hermodorus, who was best among the Ephesians, could not. He sought, therefore, to justify these values in terms of a larger framework of ideas, and in doing so brought into being, half-formed but recognizable, a moral philosophy: a theory of conduct grounded, however insecurely, upon reason.

SIX

Parmenides

To the question "Is reality one or many?" we have seen Heraclitus' answer: it is both one and many. From the point of view of the senses, to be sure, reality is simply a many. For it is made up of the opposites which we see about us — the hot, the cold, the wet, and the dry — which undergo a constant process of transformation. But the evidence of the senses is corrected by reason, for reason shows us that in changing it remains the same. Though we cannot step into the same waters twice, we can step into the same rivers, for fresh waters are always flowing on and they replace the old in the same measure as the old pass away. To all this the reply of Parmenides was uncompromising. It is true that what is is one, and true also that it is reason that tells us this. But reason tells us more than this; it tells us that if what is is one, it cannot also be a many.

Parmenides was a native of Elea, a Greek city in southern Italy. Plato says in his *Parmenides* that he once came to Athens on a visit with his famous pupil Zeno (Chapter Seven):

> **6.1** Parmenides was already quite elderly — gray-haired, very distinguished looking, perhaps sixty-five years of age. Zeno was at that time nearing forty — a tall, good-looking man. It was said that he had been Parmenides' favorite.

Socrates, Plato adds, was at this time quite young. If we suppose that he was about twenty, the visit would have taken place around 450 B.C. Parmenides would then have been born around 515 B.C.

There seem to have been at least three different traditions regarding Parmenides:

6.2   Parmenides . . . was a pupil of Xenophanes. Theophrastus, in his *Epitome*, says that he was a pupil of Anaximander. At any rate, though he was a pupil of Xenophanes as well, he did not follow him. He also associated, according to Sotion, with Ameinias the Pythagorean who, though a poor man, was noble and good. It was Ameinias whom he followed, and on his death Parmenides (who was himself of a good family and very wealthy) built a shrine to him. And it was by Ameinias, not Xenophanes, that Parmenides was converted to the contemplative life.

Even in this passage there seems to be some doubt as to the influence of Xenophanes; but the influence of Anaximander and of Pythagoreanism is amply borne out by the fragments of Parmenides' book.

Parmenides' Prologue

This book, written in hexameters, is divided into two parts, preceded by a kind of prologue. The prologue seems to have come down to us in its entirety:

6.3   The mares that draw me wherever my heart would go escorted me, when the goddesses who were driving set me on the renowned road that leads through all cities the man who knows. Along this I was borne; for along it the wise horses drew at full stretch the chariot, and maidens led the way. The axle, urged round by the whirling wheels at either end, shrilled in its sockets and glowed, as the daughters of the sun, leaving the house of night and pushing the veils from their heads with their hands, hastened to escort me towards the light.

There are the gates of the ways of night and day, enclosed by a lintel and a threshold of stone; and these, high in the ether, are fitted with great doors, and avenging Justice holds the keys which control these ways. The maidens entreated her with gentle words, and wisely persuaded her to thrust back quickly the bolts of the gate. The leaves of the door, swinging back, made a yawning gap as the brazen pins on either side turned in their sockets. Straight through them, along the broad way, the maidens guided mares and chariot; and the goddess received me kindly, and taking my right hand in hers spoke these words to me:

"Welcome, youth, who come attended by immortal charioteers and mares which bear you on your journey to our dwelling. For it is no evil fate that has set you to travel on this road, far from the beaten paths of men, but right and justice. It is meet that you learn all things — both the unshakable heart of well-rounded truth and the opinions of mortals in which there is no true belief. But these, too, you must learn completely, seeing that appearances have to be acceptable, since they pervade everything."

The tone of this prologue is quite unlike anything we have met with in the early philosophers. To find its like we must look further back — to Hesiod's *Theogony*, which also opens with a kind of prologue. In this prologue Hesiod tells us how he received instruction from the Muses:

6.4   They taught their lovely song
to Hesiod one day,
tending his flocks on Helicon,
the holy hill.
This was the tale they told me first,
the Muses of Olympus,
born of Zeus who bears the aegis:
"Wild shepherds, wretched things of shame,
like bellies of mankind,
we have the power to make the false
seem true in stories;
we have the power, if so we wish,
to utter truth as well."
Thus spoke the maidens, glib of tongue,
born of Zeus, the aegis bearer.
To me they gave a scepter,
a shoot of sturdy laurel,
a marvel they had plucked.
They breathed a voice divine
into my mouth, that I might tell
of what the future holds
and what the past.
And they bade me sing
the blessed race of gods
who live forever.

Parmenides, too, claims to have been instructed by a goddess, and the journey which he describes in 6.3 takes place against the background of the *Theogony*; for it originates in "the dreadful house of black-robed Night," and leads upward into the light, high into the upper air where stand the gates of night and day described by Hesiod in 1.7. Beyond them lies the realm of light and the goddess who is to instruct him in the truth.

But the goddess is to instruct him not only in the truth but also in "the opinions of mortals in which there is no true belief," and this, too, finds a parallel in Hesiod. For the Muses, though they know how to speak the truth when they wish, also know how to say many false things that seem like truth. Hesiod says nothing more of these false things, but Parmenides divides his poem into two parts, the first of which contains the truth, the second the opinions of mortals which, though they are false, *seem* like truth.

THE WAY OF TRUTH

The words that follow must have been very nearly continuous with **6.3**:

> **6.5** Come now, and I will tell you (and you, when you have heard my speech shall bear it away with you) the ways of inquiry which alone exist for thought. The one is the way of how it is, and how it is not possible for it not to be; this is the way of persuasion, for it attends Truth. The other is the way of how it is not, and how it is necessary for it not to be; this, I tell you, is a way wholly un-knowable. For you could not know what is not — that is impossible — nor could you express it.

> **6.6** For thought and being are the same.

> **6.7** Thinking and the thought that it is are the same; for you will not find thought apart from what is, in relation to which it is uttered.

In all thinking we seem at first sight to be confronted with a choice: we can think about what is, or we can think about what is not. But in fact this choice is illusory; we cannot think about what is not, for it is impossible to think about nothing. You cannot think at all without thinking of something — something which exists as an object *for* thought. Parmenides expresses this idea somewhat awkwardly by saying that thinking and being are "the same," but he does not mean by this that they are identical. They are "the same" in the sense in which, for Heraclitus, day and night are "the same." They are not identical, for they are clearly distinguishable, but they are inseparable; you cannot have one without the other. And this is what Parmenides means when he says that thought and being are "the same." He means, as he goes on to explain, that "you will not find thinking apart from what is"; for thought is *of* what is.

This does not mean that since we are able to think of mermaids, it follows that they exist. But thinking, even about mermaids, involves thinking about *something*, namely, about what is, though it involves thinking something false about what is, namely, that it contains mermaids. The existence of *something* is the presupposition of all thinking whatever. But precisely because it is, we cannot think its nonexistence; it not only is but, as Parmenides puts it, "it is impossible for it not to be."

Nor is not-being a possible object of thought. For to think it would be to make it an object of thought and thus give it an existence which by definition it cannot have. We cannot therefore think what is not; and since we can give utterance only to what passes in thought, it follows also that we cannot say anything about it.

The proposition that all thought is of what is seems harmless enough. But Parmenides immediately proceeds to deduce an important corollary from it:

> **6.8** It is necessary to speak and to think what is; for being is, but nothing is not. These things I bid you consider. For I hold you back from this first way of inquiry; but also from that way on which mortals knowing nothing wander, of two minds. For helplessness guides the wandering thought in their breasts; they are carried along deaf and blind alike, dazed, beasts without judgment, convinced that to be and not to be are the same and not the same, and that the road of all things is a backward-turning one.

> **6.9** For never shall this prevail: that things that are not, are. But hold back your thought from this way of inquiry, nor let habit born of long experience force you to ply an aimless eye and droning ear along this road; but judge by reasoning the much-contested argument that I have spoken.

Of the ways of inquiry which exist for thought, then, we must reject the first; for nothing is not. But by the same token we must reject any view which involves the denial of this, and the view which Parmenides attacks in **6.8** clearly does deny it, though what it asserts is much less clear.

The language in which this view is expressed has a familiar ring to it. To say "the same and not the same" — to assert and deny in the same breath — is Heraclitean. To say, for example, that day and night are "the same" is to say that they are inseparable from one another; to say that they are "not the same" is to say (with a shift of sense characteristic of Heraclitus) that they are distinct. They are "the same" and "not the same" both at once. But in "being" and "not-being" we have a similar pair of opposites. Insofar as they are distinct they are "not the same"; but in another sense they *are* "the same," for they are inseparable. They are inseparable because both are involved in all coming into being and passing away.

Wherever we look we are confronted with coming into being and passing away, for this is the essence of process. What is not comes into being, exists for a time, then passes away and exists no longer. In this sense "the road of all things" is indeed a "backward-turning one." But for Parmenides this alternation cannot possibly take place. For all talk of coming into being and passing away rests on the mistaken assumption that it is possible to think not-being. If the argument of **6.5** is sound, we cannot say of a thing that "it no longer exists"; for if it no longer exists it is nothing, and nothing is not a possible object of thought. "Not-being" is not the opposite of "being," as "day" is of "night"; it does not stand for anything at all. But in this case it does not make sense to speak of coming into being and passing away, for if "to pass away" means "to become non-existent," it is obvious that passing away is impossible. But by the same token, if "to come to be" means "to come out of not-being," this too is impossible.

It is useless to protest that both coming into being and passing away are matters of common experience, for Parmenides does not accept the arbitration of experience. He puts this very clearly in **6.9**. The question is not one, he says, which is settled by an appeal to sense — the evidence of eyes and ears. It is not "experience" which passes on such questions, but "argument." It is *reason* that shows us, by arguments of inescapable force, that what is not is not a possible object of thought, and therefore that coming into being and passing away cannot take place. If experience teaches us otherwise, so much the worse for experience. We have here the first statement of that uncompromising rationalism which has left its mark on so much of Western philosophy.

That it represented a radical break with the past is obvious enough. The whole Ionian philosophy of nature was based upon observation — not, to be sure, upon the controlled observation which characterizes modern science, but on "experience" in the ordinary sense. The appeal to the senses is so fundamental in the Milesians that it never occurs to them to mention it; but it is quite explicit in Heraclitus. "Those things of which there is sight, hearing, understanding, I esteem most," he says (**5.42**); the "eyes and ears are bad witnesses to men" only "if they have souls that do not understand their language" (**5.43**), that is, only if they are unable to grasp the significance of what they see and hear. Parmenides exploits the principle implicit in this unguarded admission. If it is intelligence alone that can make sense of experience, then intelligence is superior to experience. And if it should prove, as in the present case, that the deliverances of sense actually come into conflict with those of intelligence, it is clear which must give way. Whatever experience may have to say to the contrary, there can be neither any coming into being nor passing away.

Parmenides proceeds to develop this point in detail:

> **6.10** One way remains to be spoken of: the way how it is. Along this road there are very many indications that what is is unbegotten and imperishable; for it is whole and immovable and complete. Nor was it at any time, nor will it be, since it is now, all at once, one and continuous.
>
>   For what begetting of it would you search for? How and whence did it grow? I shall not let you say or think "from what is not"; for it is not possible either to say or to think how it is not. Again, what need would have driven it, if it began from nothing, to grow later rather than sooner? Thus it must exist fully or not at all. Nor will the force of conviction ever allow anything over and above itself to arise out of what is not; wherefore Justice does not loosen her fetters so as to allow it to come into being or pass away, but holds it fast.
>
>   Concerning these things the decision lies here: either it is, or it is not. But it has been decided, as was necessary, that the one way is unknowable and unnamable (for it is no true road) and that the other is real and true. How could what is perish? How could it have come to be? For if it came into being, it is not; nor is it if ever it is going to be. Thus coming into being is extinguished, and destruction unknown.

What is is unbegotten and imperishable; for if it had come into being it would have to have come from not-being, and this is impossible. For not-being has not that in it which could enable it to give rise to anything. It is nothing, and something cannot come from nothing; "nor will the force of conviction ever allow anything over and above itself to arise out of what is not." By the same token, it is impossible for what is to pass away and become nothing; for it would have to come to *be* nothing — would have to exchange its existence for non-existence. It is, then, as impossible for what is to cease to be as it is for it to come into being.

It would be better, therefore, if we did not speak of what is in terms having temporal reference. For to say of a thing that it was is to suggest that it no longer is, while to say of something that it will be suggests that it is not yet. This mode of speech is misleading when applied to what is, for what is "is now, all at once." The phrase is awkward only because, strictly speaking, "now" no longer has its ordinary meaning. The now ceases to be a time — the present; for the mode of existence of what is is nontemporal.

THE NATURE OF WHAT IS

Parmenides now turns to the task of deducing those characteristics which must of necessity belong to what is:

> **6.11** Nor is it divisible, since it is all alike; nor is there any more or less of it in one place which might prevent it from holding together, but all is full of what is.

> **6.12** Look steadfastly at those things which, though absent, are firmly present to the mind. For it cannot cut off what is from clinging to what is, either scattering it in every direction in order or bringing it together.

What is, says Parmenides, cleaves to what is; and it is easy to see why this must be so. For what is could be separated from what is only by what is not, and what is not has no existence. It has no power to prevent what is from "holding together" so as to be continuous. But if what is is continuous, it follows that "all is full of what is," so that it is impossible for there to be more or less of it in one place than another.

It will be obvious that as Parmenides proceeds he tends to speak of what is in more and more physical terms. In **6.11**, for example, being is pictured as everywhere in contact with being, whereas strictly speaking only bodies can be in contact with one another. But in **6.12** this tendency is even more pronounced; for the closing words of this fragment clearly refer to some sort of physical process, and one which is in fact perfectly familiar to us. It is, as the words "in order" indicate, the process of world formation and dissolution.

This double process is implicit from the first in Anaximander's conception of the world-order as coming into being and passing away through the separation of earth, air, fire, and water by the vortex motion and their reunion through its cessation. This conception was central to the Ionian philosophy of nature, and in questioning it Parmenides was questioning the work of his predecessors from Anaximander onwards. Yet his doing so was the inevitable consequence of his calling into question that still more fundamental assumption of the Ionian tradition, the reliability of the senses as sources of information concerning what is.

Parmenides proceeds to drive his point home:

6.13 But motionless in the limits of mighty bonds, it is without beginning or end, since coming into being and passing away have been driven far off, cast out by true belief. Remaining the same, and in the same place, it lies in itself, and so abides firmly where it is. For strong Necessity holds it in the bonds of the limit which shuts it in on every side, because it is not right for what is to be incomplete. For it is not in need of anything, but not-being would stand in need of everything.

All process is change, and all change involves coming into being and passing away. In a world from which these have been cast out there can be no process. What is lies motionless, abiding in itself, for "strong Necessity holds it in the bonds of the limit which shuts it in on every side." Parmenides, it will be observed, does not distinguish between logical and physical necessity. For us the necessity that renders being immovable is a logical one. If what is is everywhere in contact with what is, it *follows* (according to Parmenides) that it can neither scatter nor come together. But Parmenides thinks of Necessity as a kind of *force* which *prevents* being from scattering or coming together, and this mode of thought is typical of the early Greek philosophers. We have seen it already in Heraclitus, who thinks of the *logos* not merely as the order of events but as somehow enforcing that order, much as justice is enforced in the cosmology of Anaximander.

There is a further point to be observed in connection with **6.13**. It will be obvious that in certain respects Parmenides' conception of being resembles Anaximander's conception of the infinite. His description of it as unbegotten and imperishable answers to Anaximander's description of the infinite in **2.4**. But the infinite is, as the name implies, without limit, whereas Parmenides, as if in deliberate correction of Anaximander, describes the unbegotten and imperishable as "held in the bonds of the limit." Being, then, is limited, and the proof follows immediately. If it were without limit, it would stand in need of one. But if it stood in need of anything, it would be incomplete, which is not the case, for being is complete (**6.10**) and therefore cannot be without a limit.

Parmenides proceeds to draw certain consequences from this:

6.14 But since there is a furthest limit, it is complete on every side, like the body of a well-rounded sphere, evenly balanced in every direction from the middle; for it cannot be any greater or any less in one place than in another. For neither is there what is not, which would stop it from reaching its like, nor could what is possibly be more in one place and less than another, since it is all inviolable. For being equal to itself in every direction it nevertheless meets with its limits.

Shakespeare speaks of our little life as "rounded" in a sleep. He means, of course, "terminated"; but to set a term to something is to set a limit to it — to bring it to completion. All of these notions are bound up together, and the image of a sphere is well adapted to express them. But it is impossible to draw a sharp line in early Greek philosophy between the metaphorical and the literal. To be sure, Parmenides does not say that what is *is* a well-rounded sphere; he only says that it is *like* one. But he goes on to use language which irresistibly suggests something extended in space, to which the limit stands as a circumference. To this circumference being tends equally from the center, to form a motionless sphere.

The motionlessness of being is asserted again and again, and in the strongest possible terms:

> **6.15** For there is not, nor will there be, anything other than what is, since indeed Destiny has fettered it to remain whole and immovable. Therefore those things which mortals have established, believing them to be true, will be mere names: "coming into being and passing away," "being and not-being," "change of place and alteration of bright color."

We can see immediately why it would have to be motionless. In order for a thing to move, it must have a place to move to. But clearly there is no place into which being could move. For as Parmenides has already explained, "all is full of what is" (**6.11**). There is nothing outside what is, capable of containing it; for what could be outside it? Only nothingness, and the existence of nothingness is inconceivable. It follows that we must not think of being as having location at all. This is not easy to do; Parmenides himself lapses into saying that it remains "in the same place" (**6.13**). But he immediately adds that "it lies in itself." It "abides firmly where it is" because there is no place for it to go.

So far we have dealt only with local motion or change of place. In **6.15** this is set over against "alteration of bright color," or qualitative change. But the proof that this sort of change, too, is impossible is merely a corollary of the proof of the impossibility of coming into being or passing away. To say of a leaf that it has changed color is to say that something now exists, *i.e.*, a red leaf, which did not exist formerly; for what existed formerly was a green leaf. This would clearly involve a process of becoming, since if it did not exist formerly but does now it must, at some time in between, have come into being. Similarly, before the change took place something existed, *i.e.*, a green leaf, which no longer exists; hence at some time in between it must have passed away. But we have ruled out as impossible both coming into being and passing away; they have been "driven far off, cast out by true belief" (**6.13**). The alleged change, therefore, cannot have taken place.

Parmenides, then, rejects change as such, whether it takes the form of coming into being, passing away, local motion, or qualitative transformation; all these are "mere names" which mortals, "beasts without judgment," make use of, thinking them to be true (**6.8**). In denying reality to change, Parmenides was to all intents and purposes cutting the ground out from under all his predecessors. For to study nature is to study process, and no one can set out to investigate nature who does not assume its existence as process. Just as geometers, says Aristotle, must assume the existence of continuous quantity,

> **6.16** We physicists on the other hand must assume as "given" that the things that exist by nature are, either all or some of them, in motion — which indeed is evident from induction.

Unfortunately, the appeal to induction is useless in this case, for to appeal to induction is to appeal to experience, and in particular to our experience of particulars by means of sense perception. But it is precisely this appeal that Parmenides rejects. Do not, he says, "let habit born of long experience" direct your mind, "but judge by argument the much-contested argument that I have spoken" (**6.9**). It is a reasonable demand, and Aristotle, with some grumbling, breaks off his analysis of change long enough to submit Parmenides' logic to some shrewd criticism. But Parmenides' immediate successors were not capable of this sort of criticism. His logic seemed to them unanswerable. Their energies went instead into the attempt to save the Ionian philosophy of nature by adjusting it to the requirements of that logic. Indeed, the subsequent history of early Greek philosophy *is* the history of this attempt.

THE WAY OF OPINION

The goddess has promised to instruct Parmenides in "all things — both the unshakable heart of well-rounded truth and the opinions of mortals in which there is no true belief" (**6.3**). Of this task the first half is now complete. The truth has been revealed, and it may be seen to bear the marks of being itself. For as being is held fast by the bonds of the limit so as to be "complete on every side like the body of a well-rounded sphere" (**6.14**), so is the "unshakable heart of well-rounded truth" unchanging and self-contained. Hence the goddess can say:

6.17 It is all one to me where I begin, for I shall come back there again.

The truth possesses a unity which is a reflex of the unity of being itself.

The opinions of mortals are another matter, and to these the goddess now turns somewhat abruptly:

> **6.18** Here I end my trustworthy account and thought concerning truth. Learn henceforth the beliefs of mortals, harkening to the deceitful ordering of my words. For they have made up their minds to name two forms, one of which it is not right to name — here is where they have gone astray — and have distinguished them as opposite in bodily form and have assigned to them marks distinguishing them from one another: to one ethereal flame of fire, which is gentle, very light, the same with itself in every direction but not the same with the other. That other too, in itself, is opposite: dark night, dense in bodily form and heavy. The whole arrangement of these I tell to you as it seems likely, so that no thought of mortals shall ever outstrip you.

To this passage a scholiast has added:

> **6.19** There is further a passage in prose inserted between the verses, as though by Parmenides himself, which runs as follows: "In addition to this fire is called the rare, the hot, the 'illumining,' the 'soft,' and the light, while the dense is called the cold, 'darkness,' 'harsh,' and 'heavy.'"

Where mortals go astray is in breaking up the unity of being, in thinking of it as made up of opposites. That this is true of the Milesians is clear. Anaximander accounted for the diversity of experience in terms of the hot, the cold, the wet, the dry and the other opposites, and in this he was followed by his successors. Down to the time of the Pythagoreans, however, no attempt was made to produce a list of these opposites:

> **6.20** Alcmaeon . . . says that most things human go in pairs — meaning "by opposites." But his examples — white and black, sweet and bitter, good and bad, large and small — are chosen at random, and about the rest he is indefinite. But the Pythagoreans stated how many the opposites were and what they were.

Aristotle has preserved for us a table showing how many the opposites are, according to the Pythagoreans, and what they are. There are ten pairs:

6.21 limit and absence of limit
odd and even
one and many
right and left
male and female
rest and motion
straight and curved
light and dark
good and bad
square and oblong

Four of these pairs stand out sharply as having a peculiar relevance for Parmenides' thought: limit and absence of limit, one and many, rest and motion, light and dark. In the first part of his poem Parmenides argues that being is one, limited and at rest, and that motion, plurality, and want of limit are not predicable of what is. The first part of his poem, then, is an attack upon the dualism of Pythagorean thought. In **6.18** this attack is extended to the fourth pair of opposites mentioned above: light and dark. Mortals have decided to name both forms of being, and this is where they have gone astray. For being is "all alike" (**6.11**); there cannot be two forms of it.

So much seems clear. Yet the goddess announces that she will describe to Parmenides "the whole arrangement of these [light and night] as it seems likely," and the few fragments of the second part of the poem which have come down to us indicate that it covered essentially the same ground as that covered by earlier thinkers:

6.22 You shall know the nature of the ether and all the signs in the ether, and the unseen works of the pure torch of the bright sun and whence they came into being. And you shall know the wandering works of the round-faced moon and its nature, and you shall know, too, the heaven which surrounds all, whence it grew, and how Necessity, guiding it, fettered it to keep the limits of the stars.

6.23 [And you shall learn] how sun and moon, the ether which is common to all, the Milky Way and outermost Olympos, and the burning might of the stars, began to arise.

It is in fact a cosmogony that is announced — an account of the coming into being of the world-order. Yet we have just been told that coming into being is a mere name, signifying nothing real. Moreover, this cosmogony is based (as we shall see) on the very dualism which Parmenides rejects in **6.18** with the words "here is where they have gone astray." Indeed, the goddess herself states that the ordering of her words is deceitful, and that there is in them no true belief. Why, then, does the goddess require Parmenides to learn them?

The goddess herself answers this question in the concluding words of **6.18**: ". . . so that no thought of mortals shall ever outstrip you." What, precisely, would be required of any thinker who set out to "outstrip" Parmenides? He would, clearly, have to cover the ground already covered by Parmenides. But in order to outstrip him he would have to go further, and it is hard to see how he could do this without going on to account for the world of experience, using Parmenides' own principles. And this, to all intents and purposes, is what Parmenides himself does.

It is obvious that in the nature of the case no such attempt could be wholly successful. For change can only be dealt with in terms of an opposition between that which effects and that which suffers change. This is why, as early as Hesiod, it is necessary to assume *within* the primordial unity the opposition of male and female. For without the impregnation of the latter by the former the children of Earth could not come into existence. And so with Hesiod's successors: in one form or another all are obliged to assume the existence of opposites. No account of change, therefore, can avoid dualism; and no account of change, therefore, can be true, for being is one. Moreover, the unity of being is reflected in the unity of truth itself, so that no account of change can be *partly* true; it must, if it is false, be altogether false. The goddess herself insists that her words are deceitful, and that there is in them no true belief.

But as Xenophanes had already pointed out, an account which is not true may yet resemble truth (**3.48**), and one account may resemble it more closely than another. "The whole arrangement of these [light and night] I tell to you as it seems likely," the goddess says, and adds immediately, "so that no thought of mortals shall ever outstrip you" (**6.18**). The account which she gives, then, is to bear not only a likeness to the truth but the closest likeness which any account short of the truth *could* have to it.

We cannot avoid dualism if we are to give an account of experience at all. We must therefore allow the existence of a minimum of two "forms" of being. But we can insist upon requiring of each of these forms of being that it conform to the requirements which have been laid down as applying to being as such, and this Parmenides proceeds to do:

> **6.24** But now that all things have been named light and night, and their powers have been assigned to each, everything is full at once of light and obscure night, both equally, since neither has a share in nothingness.

Light and night are equal because, given dualism as a starting point, both of them *are*; and therefore what is true of one, so far as it *is*, is true of the other. The fact that everything is full equally of night and light is merely a corollary of this. For "all is full of what is" (**6.11**), and if night and light are to have an equal share in being they must play an equal part in filling the whole.

The concluding words of **6.24** may also mean "for neither has a share of the other." While this would not be sufficient to explain why night and light are "equal," it is in fact true. For what is is "all alike," and consequently this must be true of light and night. Each must be "all alike"; hence neither can have any share in the other's nature. This in turn implies the unchanging nature of both. For change requires opposition, and within light as within night there can be no opposition. Each is all alike; neither partakes of the other. Each is unchanging, and therefore meets the requirement which all that is must meet if it is to be at all.

Thus each has, so far as possible, the character of the one being of the way of truth. And to this extent the account of the visible world which follows, while it is not true, partakes indirectly of the truth insofar as it is patterned after it. It is only a likeness of the truth, but it supplies the standpoint from which alone appearances may be made "acceptable" (**6.3**).

The World-Order

Neither light nor night is subject to change, and consequently neither can come into being or pass away. But by their mingling and separation they bring about the coming into being and passing away of other things: "earth and sun and moon, the ether which is common to all, the Milky Way and outermost Olympus, and the burning might of the stars" (**6.23**).

Of the goddess' account of these things we know almost nothing, for of this part of Parmenides' poem scarcely anything has come down to us. But later authors have left us a fairly full, if somewhat confused, picture of the world-order as Parmenides conceived it:

> **6.25** Parmenides says that there are rings encircling one another: one sort formed of the rare, another of the dense, and between these are others compounded of light and darkness. What surrounds them all is solid like a wall, and beneath this is a fiery ring. And the midmost of all the rings is solid; and around this again is a fiery ring. The midmost of the mixed rings is the source and cause of movement and generation to them all, and he calls it the goddess who steers, holder of the keys, Justice and Necessity.

Air is separated from the earth, rising as a vapor due to the earth's greater force of compression. The sun is an exhalation of the fire, as is the Milky Way. The moon is a mixture of both elements, air and fire. Ether stands outermost, surrounding all; under it the fiery thing we call the heaven is arranged, and under this the region about the earth.

6.26 Parmenides places first in the ether the morning star (which he recognized as being the same as the evening star). After this he puts the sun, below which he places the stars in the region of the fiery which he calls the "heaven."

The account given in **6.25** tallies, in a rough way, with a single fragment which has come down to us from this part of the poem:

6.27 The narrower rings are filled with unmixed fire, those next to them with night; and into the midst of these a portion of fire is discharged. In the middle of these is the goddess who steers all things; for she is the beginner of all hateful birth and all begetting, sending the female to mix with the male and the male in turn to the female.

The description of the heavenly bodies as "rings," and as "filled with unmixed fire" indicates that in this part of his poem at least, Parmenides depended heavily upon Anaximander. But the details are unclear, and we hear little of how the whole system of rings came into being:

6.28 Parmenides says that the sun and moon were separated off from the Milky Way — the one from the rarer part of the mixture, which is hot; the other from the dense, which is cold.

6.29 For these are separated off each a different way.

That is, the fiery travels outwards to form the heavens, the dense inwards to form the earth and the region around it. Once again the distribution is by weight; night is a form of body dense and heavy, and what is heavy travels to the center in the formation of the world-order, while what is "gentle and very light" goes to the periphery. The result is the creation of a series of concentric rings with earth at the center, the whole being enclosed by something "solid like a wall"; for Necessity "fettered it to keep the limits of the stars" (**6.22**). In this as in other respects the world-order is a likeness of true being, "complete on every side like the body of a well-rounded sphere, evenly balanced in every direction from the middle" (**6.14**). For "it is not right for what is to be incomplete"; therefore "strong Necessity holds it in the bonds of the limit which shuts it in on every side" (**6.13**). But neither is it right for the sum of light and night to be incomplete; and therefore "outermost Olympus," like the crystalline sphere of Anaximenes, surrounds the world-order and contains it (**3.10**).

In the midst of these rings, says Parmenides, is the goddess who is "the beginner of all hateful birth and all begetting, sending the female to mix with the male and the male in turn to the female" (**6.27**). For the prototype of all begetting is the union of male and female, fifth of the pairs of opposites (**6.22**); and the force which brings them together is desire. Hence for Parmenides as for Hesiod, desire is the firstborn of the gods:

6.30   First of all the gods she devised Eros.

By this means she brings about that mingling of the opposites without which becoming cannot begin. Nor does the goddess merely initiate this process; she controls it. For in displacing the infinite as the source of being and passing away she has assumed its function as that which steers all things through all things (**6.27**).

Thought and Being

In his account of the generation of men, too, Parmenides follows in the Ionian tradition:

6.31   The rise of men came about in the first instance from the sun.

That is, it came about from the warmth engendered in the primeval mud. Afterwards men were begotten in the ordinary way, by the pairing of male and female:

6.32   When woman and man mix the seeds of love, the power which forms them in the veins from different blood fashions well-formed bodies if it keeps proportion. For if the powers fight with one another when the seeds are mixed, and do not form a unity in the body in which the mixture has taken place, then terribly will they harass the nascent sex which is born of the twofold seed.

The growth of the embryo depends upon the maintenance of due proportion among the elements which combine to form it. These are light and night, with their opposed "powers," and upon their right mixture the bodily constitution depends. But upon the bodily constitution depends, in turn, how men think:

> **6.33** For as at any time the mixture of their much-wandering limbs is, so thought comes to men. For to all men and to each the nature of the bodily frame is the same as that which it thinks. For what predominates in it is the thought.

> **6.34** For according as the hot or the cold predominates, the understanding varies, that being better and purer which derives from the hot . . . . But that he also attributes sensation to the opposite element in its own right is clear from his saying that a dead man will not perceive light and heat and sound because of the loss of fire, but that he will perceive cold and silence and the other opposites. And in general, all being has some share of thought.

Men's thought is a function of the ratio of light and night in their bodies. But this ratio is always changing, and as it changes men's thoughts change, whether they desire it or not, for they have no say in the matter: "helplessness guides the wandering thought in their breasts" as they are borne passively along (**6.8**). The mark of ordinary experience is that it fluctuates constantly, and can never remain the same. But in **6.3** the opinions of mortals are sharply contrasted with "the unshakable heart of well-rounded truth." The truth, like being, is not subject to change, but remains one and the same. And that this is so we know by a kind of thought which is expressly contrasted with "experience" in **6.9**, and which cannot, therefore, be accounted for in terms of the theory of knowledge advanced in **6.33**. How, then, did Parmenides account for it?

Knowledge is "better and purer," according to Theophrastus, when it derives from the hot (**6.34**). Everything depends upon the amount of heat in the body, and this varies with age, sex, state of health, and so on:

> **6.35** Aging, he says, comes about through the diminution of the hot.

> **6.36** Sleep is a chilling.

The end result of the process of aging, or cooling, is death, sleep's brother. And as birth involves the mingling of light and night, so death involves their separation. Light departs, leaving only darkness, silence and cold. Yet perception does not come to an end; the dead man continues to perceive darkness, silence, and cold, for all being has some share of thought (**6.34**).

Though Theophrastus calls this "thought," it is clearly thought of a very low order. It falls below even the confused "experience" of **6.9**; for "experience" involves memory and inference, but the dead do not remember or infer. On the other hand, Parmenides speaks more than once of a kind of knowing which is as far above "experience" as the "thought" of the dead is below it, and this knowledge he describes as being as stable and unchanging as opinion, founded upon "experience," is shifting and inconstant. But the instability of opinion arises from the fact that two elements are involved in it — light and night — the proportions of which are constantly changing. The kind of knowing which Parmenides contrasts with it must therefore be one in which this duality is not present. In this respect it will resemble the "knowing" of the dead; but whereas the dead are deprived of light, and their knowledge is a knowledge of darkness, the knowledge of "the man who knows" (**6.3**) will be of light "pure and unmixed."

Mortals wander "of two minds"; and this is a necessary consequence of the presence in them of light and night. But the road which Parmenides travels lies "far from the beaten paths of men," and the knowledge that is revealed to him at the end of it is a more than mortal knowledge. It is the knowledge of a god, and Parmenides, so far as he shares in this knowledge and possesses the "unshakable heart of well-rounded truth," is himself immortal and a god. The attempt which we saw in Pythagoreanism to bridge the gap between the human and the divine is complete.

PARMENIDES AND HERACLITUS

The closing of this gap, the union of thought and being, involves a knowing which differs not merely in degree but in kind from ordinary knowing; and in his insistence upon this Parmenides is at one with the great mystics who were to follow him in the history of Western thought. But in Parmenides this religious vision is joined with a passion for logic that distinguishes him at once from his successors, and is the chief source of his interest for philosophers. As the imagery of the prologue indicates, the revelation which Parmenides receives is a religious one. Yet the words of the goddess are addressed to the reason. "Judge by reasoning the much-contested argument that I have spoken," she urges, and the proofs which follow are linked together to form a chain of inferences more strict than anything we have yet met with in the history of Greek thought. In the fragments we are presented with a continuous argument in which the characteristics that must be possessed by what is — unity, indivisibility, fullness, rest — are deduced one by one in a series of indirect proofs.

Because of the logical form it took, Parmenides' vision of the unity of being was fruitful in a way in which Heraclitus' vision of it — though it was no less intense — was not. For in Heraclitus the sense of isolation which so often characterizes those whose way lies "far from the beaten paths of men" combined with a certain temperamental aloofness to cut him off from his fellow men. He had his followers, but they were imitators, not constructive thinkers, and Plato described them well when he wrote of the Heracliteans of his own day:

> **6.37** True to their own treatises, they are in perpetual motion. But their ability to keep to an argument or a question, quietly answering and asking in turn, amounts to less than nothing. Indeed, "less than nothing" fails to do justice to the absence of even the smallest particle of repose in these people. If you ask them a question, they pull from their quivers little oracular phrases and let fly at you with them. And if you ask for an explanation, you are transfixed with another garbled metaphor. You never get anywhere with them — nor do they get anywhere with one another, for that matter; for they take very good care to see that nothing gets settled, either in argument or in their own souls — thinking, I suppose, that this would constitute something stationary; and whatever is stationary they wage war on, and so far as they can banish it altogether from the universe!

Plato's attitude toward Parmenides ("Father Parmenides," Socrates calls him) is in marked contrast to this. He is treated with a respect which Plato seldom accords his predecessors, and the reason for it is clear. Parmenides offered something his successors could get their teeth into, something that would stand still long enough to be tested by those criteria to which all argument is subject. And to this task his successors grimly set themselves.

SEVEN

Zeno and Melissus

When Parmenides visited Athens in 450 B.C., he was accompanied by a pupil named Zeno, a favorite of his. "Zeno was at that time nearing forty," Plato says, "a tall, good-looking man" (**6.1**). He already had a reputation, based on a work which, on the occasion described by Plato, was read aloud by Zeno himself:

7.1 When Zeno had finished, Socrates asked that the first hypothesis of the first argument be read once more; and when this had been done he said, "Zeno, what do you mean by this? If existing things are a many, you say, then they must be both like and unlike. But this is impossible, since unlike things cannot be like or like things unlike. That's what you are saying, isn't it?"

"Just so," Zeno replied.

"Then if it is impossible for unlike things to be like, and for like things to be unlike, then it is impossible for things to be a many; for if there were a many, impossible consequences would follow. Is that the purpose of your argument — to maintain against all comers that there cannot be a many? And do you regard each of your arguments as proof of this, so that in your view the arguments put forward in your treatise are just so many proofs that there is not a many? Is that right, or have I misunderstood you?"

"No," said Zeno, "you have grasped admirably the whole purpose of the work."

"I see, Parmenides," said Socrates, "that Zeno here wishes to be related to you not only in friendship but in what he has written. For he has written much the same thing as you, except that by turning it round he tries to delude us into thinking that he is saying something different. For you, in your poem, say that the whole is one, and you furnish admirable proofs of this, while he for his part says that it is not a many; and he also furnishes proofs — very numerous and weighty ones. So one of you says that it is one and the other says that it is not many, and each expresses himself in such a way that in spite of the fact that what you say amounts to the same thing, you seem not to have said the same thing at all — a feat quite beyond the powers of the rest of us."

"Yes, Socrates," said Zeno; "but you have not seen the whole truth about my book. You pick up the trail of the arguments and follow it like a Spartan hound, but you fail to see that my treatise is by no means a display piece, written with the intention you ascribe to it of passing itself off as something great in men's eyes. That feature of it is merely accidental. The truth is that these writings were meant as a kind of support to the arguments of Parmenides against those who try to ridicule him by saying that if the whole is one, many absurdities and contradictions follow. This treatise of mine is a reply to those who say that there is a many, and it pays them back with interest; for it shows that consequences still more ridiculous follow if what is is a many than if it is a one, if you pursue the matter far enough. It was in this spirit of controversy that I wrote the book as a young man; and when it was written someone stole it, so that I had no opportunity of deciding whether it ought to see the light or not. But of course you did not know this, Socrates, so you thought it was written not from the love of controversy of a young man but from the love of display of an old one — though as to the rest, as I said, you were not too far off."

It is clear from this passage what Zeno's motives were in arguing as he did. Parmenides' opponents had argued from the absurdity of his conclusions to the falsity of his starting point. If the thesis that what is is one implies that motion is impossible, then it is patently false; for we can *see* that motion takes place. To this Zeno's answer was that still more ridiculous consequences follow if you assume that what is is a many. For while the consequences of supposing it to be one are in conflict with sense perception, the consequences of supposing it to be many conflict with logic itself — which is a far more serious matter. As we can see from the first hypothesis of the first argument of Zeno's treatise, the thesis that things are a many give rise to consequences that are inconsistent even with one another; for if things are a many they must be "both like and unlike," and this is impossible not because it violates sense perception (which is, after all, fallible), but because it violates the law of contradiction, which lies at the basis of all thought.

AN ARGUMENT AGAINST PLURALITY

We do not know how Zeno proved that if there were a many they would be both like and unlike; but Simplicius has preserved for us, largely in Zeno's own words, an argument to prove that if there were a many they would have to be both small and large — "so small as to have no size at all; so large as to be infinite" (**7.5**).

The first part of the proof is missing, but Simplicius says that in it

> **7.2** Zeno showed . . . that nothing has size, because each of the many is identical with itself, and one.

This, by itself, is not very helpful; but there is an argument to much the same effect in the writings of another follower of Parmenides, Melissus of Samos, which indicates the line Zeno might have taken:

> **7.3** If it existed, it would have to be one. But if it were one, it could have no body. If it had thickness, it would have parts, and then it would no longer be one.

The argument is fairly straightforward. That which is one, Melissus argues, cannot be a body; for bodies take up space, and within anything which takes up space (*i.e.*, which has magnitude) it must in principle be possible to distinguish between one part and another. But if it has parts it cannot be a true one, as Parmenides has shown.

If we use this fragment to fill in the bare outline provided by **7.2**, we get an argument to the following effect. If there were a many, each of the many would have to be one. But no one of them could have magnitude; for if it did it would have parts, and therefore would no longer be truly one. Consequently, if there were a many, they could not have any magnitude. As Zeno puts it, they would be "so small as to have no size at all."

In that case, however, they would not exist; for a thing that has no size at all is nothing:

> **7.4** For if it were added to another thing, it would not make it any larger. For, having no size, it could not contribute anything to the size of that to which it was added. And thus the thing added would be nothing. If, when it is taken away, the thing from which it is taken is no smaller; and if, when it is added to a thing, the thing to which it is added is not increased, then it is obvious that what is added or subtracted is nothing.

The clarity of the argument suffers from the fact that the definition on which it turns is stated last. Zeno's point is that if a thing were such that when added to another thing it made it no larger, and when subtracted from it left it no smaller, we should say that it was nothing at all. Yet if it had no size at all, this would clearly be true of it. In that case the many, if they exist, must have size. But if they have size, they must be "so large as to be infinite," as Zeno proves by the following argument:

> **7.5** If they exist, each must have some size and thickness, and one part of it must project beyond the other. And the same argument applies to the projecting part; for this too will have size, and some part of it will project. Now to say this once is the same as saying it forever. For no such part of it will be the last; that is, there is no part that will not stand in relation to another part. Thus, if there are a many, they must be both small and large; so small as to have no size, so large as to be infinite.

The reasoning will, perhaps, be made clearer by a diagram. If something has size, *i.e.*, magnitude, it must be possible to distinguish within it at least two different regions, one of which "projects beyond the other" as B "projects beyond" A in the accompanying figure:

But we can distinguish within B, since it too has magnitude, further regions, C and D:

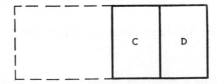

And within D, since it too has magnitude, we can distinguish regions E and F:

There is plainly no limit to this process. As Zeno puts it, "to say this once is the same as saying it forever"; for within any region, however small, we shall be able in principle to distinguish further regions. But if so, the original rectangle must consist of an infinite number of rectangles, all having *some* size; hence it must be infinitely large. The proof is complete; if there were a many, they would have to be "both small and large; so small as to have no size, so large as to be infinite."

A FURTHER ARGUMENT AGAINST PLURALITY

Simplicius has preserved a further argument against plurality, in which the number rather than the size of the many is in question:

> **7.6** If there is a many, there must be just *so* many — neither more nor less. But if there are just so many, they must be limited in number. [On the other hand,] if there is a many, there must be an infinite number of them. For between existing things there are always others, and between these others still. Thus existing things are infinite [in number].

If there are a number of things, Zeno argues, then there must be some number which is the number of things that there are; and this number, whatever it is, must be determinate and hence finite. For however large the number we assign to them, the fact that we have assigned a number to them at all indicates that there are just so many of them, and hence that there is some limit to their number.

But it is just as easy to prove that there *cannot* be any limit to their number. For between any two things there will always be a third. If they are two, they must be distinct; and if they are distinct, they must be separate. If they are separate, something must separate them, and this will be a third thing, distinct from either of those which we began. But if this third thing is distinct, it too must be separated from its neighbors by something further; and since there is no stopping point to this process, the number of things that are will obviously be infinite.

THE DICHOTOMY

Plato implies that all of the arguments in Zeno's book were directed against the hypothesis that what is is a many. This may have been true of the book to which he refers; but we know that Zeno composed a number of other arguments, some of which were concerned with motion, and this is not surprising. For Parmenides held not only that what is is one, but also that it is motionless (**6.13**). This conclusion is as abhorrent to common sense as the conclusion that what is is one, if not more so; and we should therefore expect to find Zeno arguing in support of it in his usual way, *i.e.*, by attacking the hypothesis that motion exists.

Aristotle mentions four such arguments:

> **7.7** Zeno has four arguments concerning motion which present difficulties to those who would solve them. The first says that there is no motion because the moving object must reach the halfway point before it reaches the end.

> **7.8** The argument of Zeno . . . was as follows. If there is motion, there will be something which has traversed an infinite series of distances in a finite time. For since the process of dichotomy has no limit, in any continuum there will be an infinite number of halves, since every part of it has a half. A body, therefore, which has traversed a finite distance will have traversed an infinite number of halves in a finite time, *i.e.*, in the time which it actually took to traverse the finite distance in question. He assumes . . . that it is impossible to traverse an infinite distance in a finite time (because it is impossible to complete an infinite series), and thus does away with the existence of motion.

Once more a diagram may help to make the reasoning clearer:

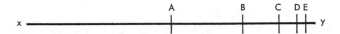

To get from x to y the moving object must first traverse xA, which is half the distance. But the distance which remains to be traversed, namely Ay, is also divisible into halves, so that in order to get from A to y the moving object must first traverse AB, which is half that distance. But By is also divisible into halves, and so on without limit; for every portion of the continuum, no matter how small, is in principle divisible into halves. This means that in order to get from x to y a moving object must traverse an infinite number of these half-distances, which is impossible. For it takes *some* time to traverse *any* distance, however short. Consequently, if the object is to travel an infinite number of distances, it will require an infinite amount of time in which to do so; and this is contrary to our initial assumption, namely, that the distance xy has *already* been traversed, *i.e.*, that motion exists.

THE ACHILLES

7.9   The second [argument] is the so-called Achilles. This is, that the slowest runner will never be overtaken by the swiftest. For the pursuer must first reach the point from which the pursued started, so that the slower must always be some distance ahead.

7.10   This argument too is based on infinite divisibility, but is set up differently. It would run as follows. If there is motion, the slowest will never be overtaken by the swiftest. But this is impossible, therefore there is no motion . . . .

The argument is called the "Achilles" because of the introduction into it of Achilles who, the argument says, cannot overtake the tortoise he is chasing. For the pursuer, before he overtakes the pursued, must first arrive at the point from which the latter started. But during the time which it takes the pursuer to get to this point, the pursued has advanced some distance. Even though the pursued, being the slower of the two, covers less ground, he still advances, for he is not at rest . . . . Thus, assuming the distances to be successively less without limit, on the principle of the infinite divisibility of magnitudes, it turns out that Achilles will fail not only to overtake Hector but even the tortoise.

The form of this argument, like that of the first, is borrowed from Parmenides: if p implies q, and q is false, then p is false. In the present case p is the proposition that there is motion, and q the proposition that Achilles cannot overtake the tortoise. In other respects, too, this argument resembles the first, as Simplicius points out:

No matter how quickly Achilles, starting from A, arrives at T, the point from which the tortoise starts, *some* time will have elapsed; and the tortoise will, during that time, have made *some* progress, however slight. By the time Achilles reaches t_1 — the point reached by the tortoise during the time it took Achilles to reach T — the tortoise will have reached t_2. And so on: the tortoise will always maintain its lead, no matter how close Achilles gets to it, and consequently Achilles, though admittedly the faster of the two, will never overtake the tortoise. But the conclusion is absurd, and therefore the hypothesis from which it follows, namely, that motion exists, is absurd.

THE ARROW

The third argument purports to prove that a moving object is actually at rest:

> **7.11** If, he says, everything is at rest when it is in a place equal to itself, and if the moving object is always in the present [and therefore in a place equal to itself], then the moving arrow is motionless.

This is the heart of an argument which appears to have been stated originally in the form of a dilemma:

> **7.12** Zeno argues thus. Either the moving object moves in the place where it is, or in the place where it is not. And it does not move in the place where it is, nor in the place where it is not; therefore nothing moves.

The arrow cannot move where it is not; so much is obvious. But it cannot move where it is, either. For when it is in the place where it is, it is in a place equal to its own length. But a thing that occupies a place equal to its own length is at rest. Hence at any moment the arrow will be at rest. But the time spent in traversing a given distance is made up of just such moments, and therefore the flying arrow is in fact at rest during the whole of the time that it is supposedly in motion, which is absurd.

THE STADIUM

> **7.13** The fourth argument is the one about the equal bodies which move in a stadium past equal bodies in opposite directions at equal velocities — some moving from the end of the stadium, some from the midpoint. This, he thinks, involves the conclusion that half the time is equal to its double . . . .
>
> For example, let the *A*'s be stationary bodies of equal size; let the *B*'s, starting from the midpoint, be bodies equal in number and size to the *A*'s; and let the *C*'s, starting from the end, be bodies equal in number and size to the *A*'s, and move with a velocity equal to that of the *B*'s. What happens, as the *B*'s and *C*'s move past each other, is that the first *B* reaches its goal at the same moment that the first *C* reaches its. But the first *C* has passed all the *B*'s, whereas the first *B* has passed only half that number of bodies, so that it has taken only half the time. For each takes an equal time to pass each body. Further, at the same moment the first *B* has passed all the *C*'s; for the first *C* and the first *B* arrive at opposite ends at the same time, since both take an equal time to pass the *A*'s.

It is not difficult to reconstruct the diagram which Aristotle presumably had in mind. In a stadium the "midpoint" is the turning post at which the runners reverse direction; it is therefore at the opposite end from the starting point, thus:

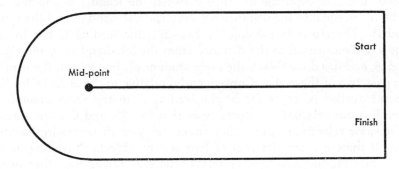

Now we are to imagine three sets of bodies — one stationary and two in motion, the first from the midpoint of the stadium, the second from the end of it, as follows:

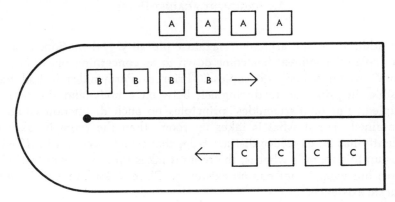

We are to imagine, further, that the *B's* and *C's* move past each other with equal velocity until the *A's*, *B's* and *C's* are in line with one another, thus:

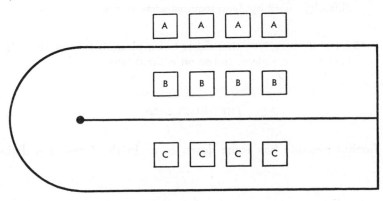

It is obvious that the leading B and leading C will reach their terminal positions opposite the first and last A's respectively at one and the same time. They will, in short, have traversed equal distances in equal times. But the leading B has passed only two A's, whereas the leading C has passed four B's. And the distance between the leading B and the last of the B's is equal to the distance between the left-hand A and the right-hand A. Therefore, in passing the four B's, the leading C has in fact gone a distance equal to the distance from the left-hand A to the right-hand A, and has done this in the same amount of time it took the leading B to pass two of these A's. Consequently, relative to the A's, the leading C has travelled twice as far as the leading B in the same amount of time. But our original hypothesis was that the B's and C's are moving at the same velocity, *i.e.*, that they cover the *same* distances in the *same* time. It therefore appears that of two sets of objects, travelling at the same velocity, one nevertheless travels twice as far as the other in the same time, which is absurd.

An Argument against Place

In addition to the arguments against plurality and motion, a somewhat isolated argument has come down to us concerning place, *i.e.*, the "room" which a body "occupies." Prior to Parmenides it had been possible, in principle, to distinguish between a body and the room it occupied. But on Parmenides' principles no such distinction could be maintained. For if what is takes up room, then the room it takes up evidently has an existence distinct from that which occupies it. If what takes up this room is what is, the room it takes up must consist of what is not; but what is not has no existence. Place, therefore, can have no separate existence.

Zeno's argument reinforces this line of thought:

> **7.14** If place is something that exists, where will it be? The difficulty raised by Zeno requires some answer.

> **7.15** For if *everything* that exists has a place, it is clear that place too will have a place, and so on without limit.

The Millet Seed

A further paradox has come down to us in the form of a dialogue between Zeno and the sophist Protagoras, whose views are discussed in Chapter Twelve:

> **7.16** "Tell me, Protagoras," he said, "does a single millet seed, or the ten-thousandth part of one, make a noise when it falls?"
>
> Protagoras replied that it did not.
>
> "What about a bushel of millet?" said Zeno. "Does that make a noise when it falls?"
>
> Protagoras replied that it did.
>
> "Well," said Zeno, "but is there no ratio between the bushel and a single seed, or the ten-thousandth part of it?"
>
> Protagoras admitted that there was.
>
> "Then," said Zeno, "will not the sounds made in the two cases stand in the same ratio? For if the things making the sounds stand in a certain ratio to one another, so must the sounds that they make. And if the bushel of millet makes a noise, then a single millet seed, or the ten-thousandth part of one, will also make a noise."
>
> This was the way Zeno used to put his questions.

This argument is aimed directly at the senses. For it is they that tell us that the millet seed does not make a noise when it falls. Reason shows that it must; if, therefore, the senses do not hear it, that only proves that the senses are inadequate instruments for determining what is.

DIALECTIC

We think of Zeno, nowadays, as the inventor of these puzzles. But Aristotle, who did not have a very high opinion of them, thought otherwise:

> **7.17** According to Aristotle, Zeno was the founder of dialectic.

In this he was clearly right; for Zeno's method of doing philosophy was to color deeply the whole European tradition.

In its simplest form dialectic involves two people: a questioner and an answerer. The questioner invites the answerer to take up a position which he thinks he can defend, and proceeds by a series of well-placed questions to drive him from it. He does this by getting the answerer to agree to a series of further propositions which, taken together, imply the contradictory of the original thesis. The method employed is exactly that of **7.16**, where Protagoras, having taken the position that a single millet seed does not make a noise when it falls, is forced to abandon it. "This was the way," says Simplicius, "Zeno used to put his questions."

The method is plainly destructive; the aim of the questioner is to unseat his opponent. It was, therefore, particularly well-suited to Zeno's purposes. For Zeno was not a constructive thinker. Unlike his predecessors, he conceived of his task as limited to the defense of certain views against criticism; and perceiving clearly that the advantage lay, in such cases, with the attacking party, he carried the war to the enemy. From first to last his approach was polemical; with him "dialectic" was the verbal counterpart of war. The weapons are words; skill, the ability to secure the desired admissions; success, the defeat of one's opponent. Zeno himself confesses (in **7.1**) to having written his book in precisely this spirit.

The influence of Zeno in this respect was very great. We can see it at work in the early dialogues of Plato. In all or most of them we find Socrates putting to someone a question of the form "What is X?". In the *Euthyphro* the question is "What is piety?"; in the *Laches* it is "What is courage?"; in Book One of the *Republic* it is "What is justice?". In each case the answerer responds by making an assertion of the form "X is Y" — "Piety is doing what is pleasing to the gods"; "Courage is staying at your post and facing the enemy and not running away"; "Justice is the interest of the stronger." And in each case Socrates proceeds to elicit from the answerer, by cross-examining him, admissions which, taken together, commit the answerer to a view quite inconsistent with that which he began by adopting. Thus the claim that justice is the interest of the stronger (*i.e.*, of the ruler) is met by securing the agreement of Thrasymachus, Socrates' opponent, to only two premises: that no science seeks its own advantage, and that all forms of rule are sciences.

Not all of Socrates' arguments have the same logical form, but all have the same aim: the refutation of the answerer. It is true that Socrates does not aim at refutation for its own sake; philosophy is not a game, to be entered into in a youthful "spirit of controversy." But there are different ways of being serious, and there is no disguising the pleasure which Socrates takes in reducing his opponents to silence. As the young Meno, caught out in a contradiction, says ruefully:

> **7.18** Socrates, I used to hear before ever I met you that you do nothing but perplex yourself and other people. And now, it seems, you are bewitching *me* — and drugging me and binding me completely with your spells, so that I have become saturated with perplexity. And if you will allow me to speak facetiously, you seem to me to resemble to a striking degree, both in appearance and in other respects, the flat electric ray that lives in the sea.

For it numbs anyone who comes in contact with it, and you seem to have done something of the sort to me. For in truth, I feel a numbness both in my mind and on my lips, and I do not know what answer to make to you.

The opponents of Zeno must have experienced a similar paralysis in the face of arguments such as **7.16**.

The art of Socrates is the art of Zeno put to a different purpose. To the end it gave shape and form to the philosophy of Plato; and through Plato it entered into the very structure of European philosophy. For it was Plato's pupil Aristotle who gave to logic the form which it was to bear for the next two thousand years; and to an extent which we are only beginning to realize this logic was a rationalization of the techniques of debate. It was for this reason that the founders of modern science, when they rebelled against the logic of Aristotle, did so on the ground that it was concerned not with discovery but with proof. Through Aristotle the spirit of Zeno passed into the thought of the late middle ages. The clashes of the schoolmen, flushed with their reading of Aristotle, over doctrinal points so fine that it is difficult now for us to determine precisely what they were, were the intellectual counterpart of the great tourneys in which men and horses measured themselves against one another in the shock of combat. Nor has this spirit disappeared from contemporary philosophy; for to the extent that European philosophy is Greek, it is inherently polemical. It is a reflex of that quality of Greek thought which finds classical expression in Heraclitus' assertion that "war is the father and king of all" (**5.24**). Because it seems to have no essential connection with that calm, dispassionate search for truth which we find elsewhere in Greek philosophy, it tends to be overlooked. Yet it too is Greek. For the mode of Greek thought is contentious; the *agon* or contest for the prize of victory is central to it; and this spirit has entered into the very texture of the philosophical tradition which is the creature of that impulse.

Melissus, like Zeno, was a follower of Parmenides. In this sense he was an Eleatic. But he was not a native of Elea; he was a native of Samos, the island from which Pythagoras had gone into voluntary exile many years earlier. Plutarch, in his life of Pericles, says that Melissus was in command of the Samian forces in a sea battle which took place in 441/440 B.C.; but we do not know whether he wrote his book on the nature of things before or after this date.

SUMMARY OF MELISSUS' BOOK

In addition to the fragments of this book which have come down to us, we have what purports to be a summary of it, attributed in ancient times to Aristotle, but now believed to be of a much later date. It does not tell us a great deal that the fragments themselves do not tell us. But it has the appearance of having been written by someone who had the original, or a good paraphrase of it, before him, and therefore has a certain value as indicating the order in which the extant fragments may have stood in the original.

7.19 Melissus says that if anything is, it is eternal, since it is impossible for anything to come into being out of nothing. For whether all things have come to be, or not all, in either case they are eternal. For if they came into being, they would have to come to be out of nothing. For if all things have come into existence, then nothing existed previously. If [on the other hand] some things [already] existed, and others were continually added to them, then what is would have become more and greater; and if it did grow more and greater, the addition would come into being out of nothing. For the more cannot exist in the less, nor the greater in the smaller.

Being eternal, it is infinite, because it has no beginning from which it began to come into being, nor an end to which it might come and so terminate at some time, for it exists entire.

Being infinite, it is one. For if it were two or more, these would limit one another.

Being one, it is the same in every direction. For if it were not the same, but were more, it would no longer be one but many.

Being eternal, infinite, and the same in every direction, the one is motionless. For it could not move unless it moved into something. Now if it moves, it must move either into a place which is full, or into one which is empty. But the first of these could not receive it, and the second does not exist.

This being the nature of what is, the one is insensible to pain and sorrow, and is healthy and free from sickness, undergoing neither change of position nor alteration of form, or mingling with anything else. For in all these cases the one would become many, and what is not would be born, and what is would perish, of necessity. And these things are impossible.

For if it is said that the one is a mixture of many, and that there are a many, and that things move into one another, then the mixture is either a composite of the many in one, or else a hiding of the things that were mixed would take place by layering. But in the first case the things that were mixed, being separate, would be distinguishable; whereas, if they were hidden, each ought to be revealed in turn by the process of wearing away, as the layers under which each is hidden are removed. In fact, neither of these things happens. Yet these are the only ways in which there could be a many, and yet at the same time appear to us as they are. So that, since neither is possible, what is cannot be a many, and to suppose that it is is an error. For many other things, too, that appear to the senses are deceptive.

What Is Is Eternal

The original, to judge from this summary of it, was arranged in the form of a chain of inferences: if *a*, then *b*; but if *b*, then *c*; and if *c*, then *d*; and so on. The starting point for this series was the eternity of what is:

7.20 What was always was and always will be. For if it had come into being, it necessarily follows that before it came into being nothing was. But if nothing was, nothing could in any way come to be out of nothing.

The proof is indirect, in the manner of Parmenides. Suppose that what is had come into being. In that case, before it came into being nothing existed, and what is would have to have come out of nothing. But this is impossible; nothing can come out of nothing. What is, therefore, must always have been.

But despite the resemblance to **6.10**, the conclusions of the two arguments are very different. For Parmenides argues, in effect, that what is is not in time at all, "nor was it at any time, nor will it be; since it is now, all at once," whereas Melissus argues that what is "always was and always will be." It is hard to resist the impression, borne out by other fragments, that the temporal aspect of the real has an importance for Melissus that it does not have for Parmenides.

This impression is enhanced when we turn to the following fragments:

7.21 Since, therefore, it did not come into being, it is and always was and always will be, and has no beginning or end, but is infinite. For if it had come into being, it would have a beginning (for it would have begun to come into being at some time) and an end (for it would have ceased to come into being at some time). But since it neither began nor ceased, it is and was and always will be, and has neither beginning nor end. For it is impossible for anything to be forever, unless it exists entire.

7.22 Nothing which has a beginning or an end is either eternal or infinite.

7.23 But as it always is, so too its greatness must always be infinite.

If we neglect for a moment the opening sentence of **7.21**, we have what appears to be a perfectly straightforward argument to prove that what is cannot have come into being. For if it had come into being, it would have had a beginning; but it did not have a beginning, and therefore it did not come into being, but is and always was and always will be. This, however, has already been proved in **7.20**, and if we look more intently at the opening sentence, we see that it does not sound as though what was to be proved is that what is did not come into being but something else, namely, that it is infinite. Certainly this is the intention of **7.22**.

On the other hand, it is difficult to know what to make of **7.22**, for as it stands, it does not at all imply the infinity of what does not have a beginning. We cannot conclude from the fact that what has a beginning is not infinite that therefore what does *not* have a beginning *is* infinite, for that does not follow. It is possible, however, that Melissus was only trying to make clear what we *mean* when we use certain terms. To say (Melissus might argue) that a thing is finite, is to say that it is limited. Again, to say of a process that it has a beginning and an end, is to say that it is limited. In saying, then, that a thing has neither beginning nor end, we are saying that it is infinite.

Here too, in asserting that what is is infinite, Melissus is departing from Parmenides. For Parmenides it is "not right" for what is to be infinite, and therefore "incomplete"; for "it is not in need of anything" (**6.13**). If what is were to lack being in any way, it would lack it entirely; for being is something which a thing either has entirely or not at all. Now it is clear that Melissus has no quarrel with this. He argues himself that "it is impossible for anything to be forever unless it exists entire" (**7.21**). His objection is rather to Parmenides' peculiar use of the term "infinite." For Melissus, as an Ionian, the term has first and foremost a temporal reference; and since what is is everlasting, and always was and always will be, without beginning or end, it *is* "infinite" in the traditional sense of that word.

What, then, are we to make of **7.22**? For here Melissus himself appears to be using the term in a nontemporal sense, and indeed to be asserting in the clearest possible way the spatial infinity of what is. There is, however, a serious obstacle to taking the fragment in this, its natural, sense. Simplicius, who had the text of Melissus in front of him, goes out of his way to point out that Melissus could not have been thinking in terms of size here; for in **7.29**, as we shall see, he argues that what is is incorporeal; and it is obvious that if it is incorporeal, it cannot take up space at all. We should expect, too, that if Melissus had wished to assert the spatial infinity of what is, he would have offered some proof of it, since he is so careful to prove everything else. But we do not have any such argument, and the summary does not refer to any. On the other hand, we need not assume, as Simplicius did, that if Melissus did not mean size, he must have meant duration. There is a third possibility: "greatness" can refer to the degree to which a thing is capable of manifesting its peculiar quality or power, and it is just possible that that is its sense here. For Melissus thinks of being in terms of power. In being, what is puts forth its strength, and "nothing is stronger than true being" (**7.32**). In a similar way, when Diogenes of Apollonia speaks of the infinite as "great and strong and eternal and deathless and much-knowing" (**3.22**), it is plain from the context that it is the might, not the size, of being that is in question. It is because being is great in this sense that Parmenides calls it "inviolable" (**6.14**). So too, Melissus may be insisting, in **7.22**, on the power of being, which is infinite.

WHAT IS INFINITE IS ONE

Melissus now proceeds to argue from the infinity of what is to its unity:

> **7.24** If it were not one, it would be limited by another.

> **7.25** For if it were infinite, it would be one. For if it were two, they could not be infinite, but would be limited by one another.

The argument, as usual, is indirect. If what is is infinite, it is one; for if it were not one, it would be two or more, and each would limit the other. But in that case, neither would be infinite, contrary to what has already been proved in **7.21**. Therefore, what is is one. Here, too, we must beware of assuming that Melissus is thinking in spatial terms. For the argument turns upon what has already been proved, and what has been proved so far is not that what is is spatially infinite, but that it is temporally infinite.

DEDUCTIONS FROM THE UNITY OF WHAT IS

Melissus proceeds, like Parmenides, to deduce certain consequences from the unity of what is:

> **7.26** Thus it is eternal and infinite and one and all alike. Nor can it perish, or grow greater, or undergo rearrangement, or suffer pain or sorrow. For if it underwent any of these, it would no longer be one.
>
> For if it altered, then of necessity what is would not be the same, but what was would be destroyed, while what was not would come into being. If it were to become different by a single hair in ten thousand years, then in the whole of time it would perish utterly.
>
> But it is not possible, either, for it to be rearranged. For the order which already exists is not destroyed, nor does one which does not exist come into being. But since nothing is added to it, and it is not destroyed or altered, how can there be any rearrangement of existing things?

The summary with which this fragment begins reveals a gap in the argument, the existence of which is confirmed by **7.19**. At some point between **7.25** and **7.26** there was an argument to prove that what is is "all alike." The impression of this argument given by **7.19** is very sketchy, but the general sense is clear enough; if the one were *not* "all alike," there would be more than one of a kind, and hence a many, contrary to what has already been proved in **7.24**.

But from this it follows immediately that what is cannot change. For if it did, it would not be the same; but being *is* the same, and therefore it cannot become different by so much as a single hair. Neither can rearrangement of it take place; for this, too, would cause it to be different.

In all of this Melissus follows Parmenides closely. For the former, as for the latter, "coming into being and passing away" and "change of place and alteration of bright color" belong solely to what appears; they are "mere names," which mortals have established, believing them to be true (**6.15**).

THE IMPOSSIBILITY OF MOTION

But while Parmenides specifically relegates change of place to the realm of appearance, when he comes to describe the motionlessness of what is, he does so in very general terms. "Remaining the same, and in the same place," he says, "it lies in itself, and so abides firmly where it is. For strong Necessity holds it in the bonds of the limit" (6.13). But the thought is not altogether clear, and we are left with the impression that change of place is impossible, not because it involves some physical impossibility, but merely because it is a kind of change. Melissus deals with change of place in a much more concrete way:

> **7.27** Nor is anything empty; for what is empty is nothing, and what is nothing cannot be.
>
> Nor does it move; for it is unable to make room, but is full. For there to be any emptiness, what is would have to retire into the void; and since there is no void, it will not be able to retire anywhere.
>
> It cannot be either dense or rare; for what is rare cannot be as full as what is dense, but on the contrary is emptier than what is dense. It is necessary to distinguish what is full from what is not full in the following way. If a thing has room in it for something, or receives it, then it is not full; if it neither has room for anything nor receives it, then it is full. It must, therefore, be full if it is not empty; and if it is full, it does not move.

To the Pythagoreans the void was real: "It is the void which keeps things distinct, being a kind of separation and division of things that are next to each other" (4.35). But to Melissus the void is "nothing," and nothing cannot exist; for to call it "nothing" is to admit that it has no share in being. Hence the void cannot exist. But if so, motion is impossible. For what is is full; consequently, if any part of it were to move, room would have to be made for it to move into. But this could hardly be done without displacing some part of the whole into the surrounding void; and as we have just seen, there is no surrounding void, and therefore motion is physically impossible.

Melissus next considers the objection that room might be made in what is through compression, as a space is cleared in the center of a room by causing the persons in it to stand closer together around the walls. The objection, Melissus holds, is based on a misunderstanding. What is dense is not full; it merely has less of the empty in it than in what is dilated. What is, on the contrary, *is* full; it contains no emptiness at all, nor is there, in the words of Parmenides, "any more or less of it in one place which might prevent it from holding together, but all is full of what is" (6.11).

Melissus, too, insists on the contact of what is with what is:

> **7.28** For if what is is divided, it moves; but if it moved, it would not be.

It is easy to see why this is so from the accompanying diagram. Suppose we have a rubber ball, *AB*, and that we cut it in half along line *xy*.

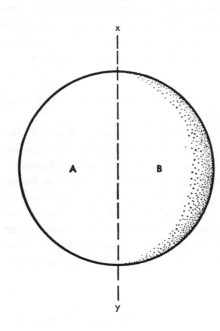

If we have divided it in *two*, then *A* will have to be separated from *B* by some distance, however small; for otherwise we would not have *two* things, but one. But this separation clearly involves motion on the part of *A* or *B* or both, and as we have just seen, motion belongs to the realm of appearance. If either moved, it would no longer *be*. It is impossible, therefore, to "cut off what is from clinging to what is" (**6.12**).

Language such as this inevitably conjures up a mental picture of what is. We are apt to think of it, in fact, as resembling *AB*: a figure "complete on every side, like the body of a well-rounded sphere, evenly balanced in every direction from the middle" (**6.14**). We are left with the impression that for Parmenides being is still thought of as corporeal — perhaps because it has not yet occurred to anyone that anything can have existence *except* what is corporeal. Even "opportunity" and "justice" are corporeal for the Pythagoreans; for they are numbers, and numbers are corporeal (**4.25**). From this point of view the work of Melissus represents a striking advance; for he argues that what is is not, and indeed cannot be, corporeal:

> **7.29** If being is, it must be one. On the other hand, if it is one, it cannot have body. If it had thickness, it would have parts, and would no longer be one.

Once more the argument is indirect: if what is were a body, it would have thickness; but if it had thickness, it would have parts; and if it had parts, it would not be truly one, but a mere collection of ones. But the unity of what is has already been proved; therefore what is cannot be a body.

It is hard to say whether this represents a radical break with the thought of Parmenides or not; for the appearance of corporeality which the one has in the fragments of Parmenides may be due solely to the use of metaphor. It is clear, nevertheless, that this language had laid Parmenides open to the very objection which Zeno had brought against the opponents of Parmenides: that if a thing has thickness, it must also have parts, and therefore be no true one (**7.3**). If this was to be avoided, it was necessary to make explicit what was implicit from the first in Eleatic thought, namely, that to say that a thing *is* is not to say that it has a body. To have grasped this clearly is to have taken a long step forward toward the final solution of motion.

What Is Is Insensible to Pain

We must now consider the oddest of all the descriptions which Melissus gives of the one, namely, that it is insensible to pain or sorrow:

> **7.30** Neither does it suffer pain. For if it suffered pain, it would not be completely; for a thing that suffered would not be able to exist forever. Nor would it have equal power with what is healthy. Nor would it be the same, if it were to suffer pain; for it would suffer pain through the addition or subtraction of something, and would no longer be the same.
>
> Nor would what is healthy be able to suffer pain; for in that case what was healthy and in being would pass away, and what was not would come into being.
>
> And the same reasoning applies to sorrow as to pain.

The opening words of this fragment resemble the closing words of **7.21**: "It is impossible for anything to be forever unless it exists entire." But what *is* is forever; therefore it must exist entire. And this would not be possible if it were capable of hurt; for the capacity to feel pain implies a deficiency of being. Consequently, it cannot feel pain.

The logic is sound, but the language is puzzling. What has suffering to do with being? The answer is not far to seek. The infinite, being "deathless" and "imperishable," is a god:

> **7.31** Both Melissus and Zeno assert that the one or whole is a god, and that the one alone is eternal and infinite.

Being a god, it lives; but its life is not subject to the accidents of pain, old age, and death. For it exists, as it were, full strength; there is no imperfection of being in it, and hence it does not know sickness or sorrow. Here, as elsewhere, Melissus is only making explicit what is implicit in the thought of his predecessors.

AN ARGUMENT AGAINST THE SENSES

The chief obstacle to the Eleatic doctrines was the testimony of the senses. Parmenides had been forced to reject it, and Melissus followed suit:

> **7.32**   This argument, then, is the greatest proof that it is one only; but the following also are proofs of it.
>
> For if there were a many, they would have to be of the same sort as I say that the one is. For if there is earth and water and air and fire and iron and gold, and one thing lives and another dies; and if things are black and white, and all the other things that men say are true — if, I say, these are so, and if we see and hear rightly, then each must be such as we first decided, and may not change or come to be different, but each of them must always be what it is.
>
> Now we say that we see and hear and perceive rightly. Yet it appears to us that what is hot becomes cold, and that what is cold becomes hot, that what is hard becomes soft, and the soft hard, and that what is alive dies and comes to be out of what is not living, and that all these change, and that what they were and what they are now is not the same. We suppose that iron, which is hard, is rubbed away by contact with our finger, along with gold and stone and everything else that appears to us to be strong, and that earth and stone come into being from water. So, as it turns out, we neither see nor perceive the things which are.
>
> Now these things do not agree with one another. For we said that existing things were a many and eternal, having forms and strength. Yet all seem to change and alter from what we see them to be at one moment to what we see them to be at another. It is evident, therefore, that we do not see rightly after all, and that existing things do not rightly appear to be a many. For they would not change if they were real, but each would be just what it seemed to be. For nothing is stronger than true being. If it has changed, what is has passed away and what is not has come into being.
>
> So, then, if there were a many, they would have to be such as the one is.

The argument is directed against those who maintain that the senses do not deceive us, that they reveal to us a plurality of existing things, and that therefore what is is not one but many. The premise on which this argument turns, Melissus replies, is false, and can be shown to be false. For what do the senses actually show us? They show us a world in which hot things become cold, the living perish, and earth comes into being from what is not earth. They show us, in short, a many, but a many in flux, unstable, and therefore deficient in being. For "nothing is stronger than true being"; whatever is endures and does not change. But the many that the senses show us change continually; therefore they cannot be real.

The conclusion is not new, but Melissus' proof of it sets the problem of the one and the many in a new light. It does this by stating the terms which must be met by any solution to the problem: "If there *were* a many, they would have to be such as the one is." Whoever asserts that the many exist must meet this requirement. To Melissus belongs the credit for stating it clearly.

Aristotle did not think highly of Melissus:

> **7.33** The reasoning of Melissus is crude, and presents no difficulty; accept one absurdity and the rest follow — there is nothing difficult in this.

But Aristotle had little patience with *any* of the Eleatics. "Their premises," he says in another place, "are false, and their conclusions do not follow." The modern reader may be forgiven if he feels a similar impatience. But Plato, with deeper insight, realized that the Eleatics were trying — perhaps fumblingly — to say something of the greatest importance. In the *Theaetetus* he makes Socrates say:

> **7.34** A feeling of respect keeps me from treating in a boorish spirit Melissus and the others who say that the universe is one and at rest. But there is one being whom I respect above all, and that is Parmenides himself. Parmenides appears to me, in Homer's words, a "reverend and aweful" figure. For I met him when I was very young and he quite old, and he appeared to me to have a kind of depth that was altogether noble.

The respect of Plato might well give us pause, especially since it was shared by the formidable group of thinkers with whom we shall be concerned in Part Three. Each of them had read and digested the Eleatic argument, and each was sufficiently impressed by it to set himself the task of meeting the challenge which, as each clearly perceived, Parmenides and his followers had thrown down to the Ionian philosophy of nature.

PART THREE

THREE SOLUTIONS

EIGHT

Empedocles

In setting out to give a coherent account of the world about them, the Ionians had proceeded on certain assumptions. They had assumed, first and foremost, the reliability of the senses; and the senses revealed to them a world which, though it was in some respects one, was made up of opposites which, by interacting with one another, produced change. Parmenides had called all this into question. It is impossible, he argued, to maintain that the world is in any real sense one and at the same time many. If it is one at all, the very possibility of a many is ruled out, and in such a world motion and change simply cannot take place. The arguments by which these conclusions were reached seemed to Parmenides' contemporaries and immediate successors to be compelling, and it was obviously impossible to proceed with the program of the Ionians until Parmenides was answered. To answer him, therefore, became the immediate task of all those who were committed to carrying out this program.

The first to attempt it, about the middle of the fifth century B.C., was Empedocles, a citizen of Acragas, one of the Greek colonies in Sicily. A tradition going back at least to the fourth century B.C. asserts that Empedocles was a Pythagorean, and that he was censured by the members of the order for revealing the teachings of Pythagoras in his published writings. This tradition is certainly borne out by the many fragments which have come down to us. These fragments belong to two distinct works: *On the Nature of Things* and *Purifications*, both of them verse imitations of Parmenides.

THE PURIFICATIONS

The *Purifications* is a religious work concerned with the fallen estate of man:

8.1   There is an oracle of Necessity, an ancient decree of the gods, eternal, sealed with broad oaths, that whenever one of the divine spirits whose lot is long life has sinfully defiled his own limbs with murder, or in strife has sinned and sworn a false oath, for thrice ten thousand seasons he wanders, far from the blessed gods, being born throughout that period in all kinds of mortal shapes, exchanging one painful path of life for another. For the mighty ether drives him into the sea, the sea spews him forth upon the dry land, earth casts him into the rays of the blazing sun, and the sun casts him into the eddies of ether. One receives him from the other, and all hate him.

I, too, now am one of these — a fugitive from the gods and a wanderer — because I put my trust in raging Strife.

8.2   From what honor, from how great a happiness [am I exiled]!

8.3   Alas that the pitiless day of death did not destroy me before I devised that abominable act the eating of flesh!

In Hesiod's *Theogony*, too, we find the notion of exile from the company of the gods. It occurs in connection with his account of the river Styx, by whose icy waters the oaths of the gods are sworn:

8.4   If one of the immortal gods
who hold Olympus' snowy peaks
should pour forth water from this stream
and by his oath forswear himself,
breathless he lies for one whole year,
cut off from nectar and ambrosia,
which are the food of gods.
Bereft of spirit and of voice he lies
on covered couches, veiled in a deep trance.
Yet, when a year's long illness has been spent,
a still more dreadful trouble will ensue.
For nine whole years he lives his life
apart from the immortal gods.
He must not join the councils of the gods
nor share their feasts for nine whole years.

> But in the tenth again he joins the company
> of those who dwell, immortal, on Olympus' height.

There are, however, profound differences between these two conceptions. In Hesiod's, the exiled god remains a god; he is of a race set apart from men, and the gap which separates him from them remains the same even in exile. In Empedocles', the exiled god falls from his estate; he enters the cycle of birth and death, assuming one mortal form after another.

The reason for banishment is different too. In Hesiod it is a punishment for oath-breaking; in Empedocles an echo of this remains in the reference to swearing false oaths, but it is only fleeting. The primal sin of **8.1** is murder, the shedding of blood. It is for this (and, as **8.3** shows, the eating of what is killed) that the fallen divinity is exiled from the company of the gods.

Moreover, his place of exile is specified: it is this world — the world of mortal forms into which he is thrust, himself a mortal:

8.5　I wept and wailed when I saw the unfamiliar land.

8.6　. . . a joyless place, where Murder and Vengeance dwell, and swarms of other Fates — wasting Diseases, Putrefactions and Fluxes — roam in darkness over the meadow of Doom.

8.7　Here were the goddess of earth and the far-seeing goddess of the sun, bloody Discord and grave-eyed Harmony, Beauty and Ugliness, Swiftness and Delay, lovely Truth and dark-haired Uncertainty.

8.8　Growth and Decay, Repose and Waking, Movement and Immobility, crownéd Majesty and Defilement, Silence and Voice.

This is the world of the senses. Birth and Decay, Movement and Immobility, Discord and Harmony are the opposites whose warring powers generate the world-order of the Ionians. But that world-order is seen, in these fragments, from a point of view peculiar to Pythagoreanism. It is a "joyless place," dark and full of corruption — "a roofed-in cave," as Empedocles calls it, in an image which Plato was to make famous in his *Republic*. Here the exiled spirit wanders, clothed in

8.9　. . . an unfamiliar garment of flesh . . .

8.10　. . . that earth which envelops mortals.

This is Shakespeare's "muddy vesture of decay" **(4.29)**, the body conceived not as beautiful — as we see it in the bronze athletes of the Greek sculptors — but as corrupt, one with the world in which it comes to be and passes away, a burden to the soul.

The body is mortal, but the soul is not; hence at the death of the body the soul must enter into a new body, plant or animal:

> **8.11** For by now I have been born as a boy, a girl, a plant, a bird, and a dumb fish in the sea.

So the soul changes one path of life for another: the air pursues him into the sea, the sea spews him forth upon the dry land, earth casts him into the rays of the burning sun, and the sun into the eddies of air; one takes him from another and all alike abhor him.

The cycle is endless because the exiled spirit commits again and again the primal sin for which it fell. By a terrible irony the blood sacrifices by means of which men seek to appease the gods only plunge them further into guilt:

> **8.12** The father lifts up his own dear son in a changed form, and with a prayer slays him in his great folly. Some of those sacrificing hesitate, hearing the entreaties [of the victim]; but he, deaf to its outcries, slaughters it and makes ready in his halls the evil feast. In like manner the son seizes upon his father and the children their mother, and tearing their lives from them, devour the flesh of their own kin.

> **8.13** Will you not cease from this slaughter, terrible to hear? Do you not see that you are devouring one another in your folly?

> **8.14** Alas, wretched breed of mortals, sore unblessed; such are the strifes and groanings from which you have been born!

> **8.15** For this reason are you distraught with dire evils, and shall never ease your heart of grievous sorrows.

Like Hesiod before him, Empedocles heightens the darkness of the present age by contrast with a former time, when men lived without bloodshed:

> **8.16** They did not have Ares for a god, or Battle Cry, or Zeus the king, or Cronus or Poseidon, but Cypris the queen. They sought to please

her with pious gifts — with painted figures and cunningly blended perfumes, with offerings of pure myrrh and sweet-smelling frankincense, casting upon the ground libations of yellow honey. And the altar was not drenched with the pure blood of bulls, but it was the greatest defilement among men to tear the life from the goodly limbs and devour them.

8.17 And all creatures were tame and gentle towards man, wild animals and birds alike, and friendliness was kindled between them.

But Empedocles looks back to a golden age more remote than that of Hesiod. For in Hesiod the men of the golden age lived under the rule of Cronus, who achieved the kingship by violence, castrating his father the sky with an iron sickle (**1.4**). Empedocles has in mind an age before the Olympian gods were, when blood sacrifices were not made but the Cyprian, Aphrodite, goddess of love, prevailed everywhere, and there was no strife between man and man or man and beast. It is a vision of life lived according to the teachings of Pythagoras, a life of friendship, of mutual forbearance and of peace.

To this vision human life as it is presents the greatest possible contrast. Yet men can approach nearer to it by refraining from bloodshed and from the eating of certain foods:

8.18 Wretches, utter wretches, keep your hands from beans!

8.19 Abstain wholly from laurel leaves!

For the soul, by purifying itself, may rise by degrees to higher forms of existence:

8.20 Among beasts they are born as lions, having their lairs in the hills, and among lovely-haired trees as laurels.

8.21 And in the end they live among men on earth as prophets, poets, physicians, and princes. Thence they rise up as gods, exalted in honor.

8.22 Sharing the hearth with the other gods, and sharing the same table with them, they have no part in the griefs of men, indestructible.

To this blessed state Empedocles himself has attained:

> **8.23** Friends who inhabit the great town looking down on golden
> Acragas and the citadel, mindful of good deeds, compassionate
> haven for strangers, unacquainted with wickedness, greeting! I
> go about among you an immortal god, no longer mortal, honored
> by all as is my due, crowned with fillets and flowing garlands. When
> I enter the prosperous towns with these men and women, I am
> revered. They follow me in countless numbers asking, "Where is the
> path to gain?" — some seeking prophecies, others, long racked by
> grievous pains, begging to hear the word that heals all manner
> of sickness.

Prophet, healer, poet, holder of high office in the city, Empedocles has
reached the end of his long exile. He has become a god among men,
recognized as such by the crowds who attend him seeking to be cured
and to know the future.

THE WORK ON NATURE

The *Purifications* not only gives a far richer impression of Pythagorean religious teaching than the meager scraps of information on which
we had to rely in Chapter Four; it exhibits fully the depth of Empedocles'
own commitment to that teaching. The work on nature, too, reflects
this commitment; but, unlike the *Purifications*, it is strongly marked by
the influence of Parmenides.

It is addressed to one Pausanias, a member of the Pythagorean order,
and begins with a defense of knowledge based upon sense perception:

> **8.24** For narrow are the ways that are scattered throughout the limbs,
> and many the troubles that press upon them, blunting the edge of
> their careful thoughts. And having perceived but a small part of
> life while they live, doomed to perish, they rise up and are dis-
> sipated like smoke, each persuaded only of what he has chanced
> upon as he is driven this way and that, vainly supposing that he
> has discovered the whole.
>
> So hard is it for these things to be seen or heard by men, or
> comprehended by the mind. And you, who have come here into
> retirement, shall learn no more than mortal mind has power to know.
>
> **8.25** Turn aside from my tongue, you gods, the madness of those men;
> make flow from lips that are holy a pure stream! And you also,
> much-wooed, white-armed virgin Muse, send, I entreat you, such

wisdom as is right for mortal creatures of a day to hear, driving your well-yoked chariot from the halls of piety; nor let the flowers of glorious honor force you to be revered by mortals on condition that you speak in rashness more than is holy. Then indeed will you sit upon the heights of wisdom.

But come, consider now with all the means at your disposal, in whatever way each thing is clear, not putting more trust in sight than in hearing, nor in clamorous hearing than in the evidence of the tongue; nor should you withhold your trust from any of the other limbs in which there is a passageway for perception, but perceive each thing in the way in which it is clear.

8.26 For intelligence increases in men according to what is present in them.

Parmenides had denied flatly that there is any truth in the opinions of mortals; for the opinions of mortals are based upon the fluctuating evidence of the senses, and upon this no reliance can be placed. In part Empedocles admits the charge. Our means of grasping the truth are indeed limited, and the miserable state of man described in the *Purifications* cannot fail to blunt the edge of his thought. Moreover, we live but a short time at best, and come in contact with but a small portion of the whole. So much must be admitted; our knowledge is but a mortal knowledge. But such as it is, it rests upon a weighing of the testimony of the senses. Hence we ought not to withhold our confidence from any of the organs of sense, "but perceive each thing in the way in which it is clear."

The Four Elements

Now the senses show us a world made up of four great masses — earth, air, fire, and water:

8.27 Hear first the four roots of all things: shining Zeus, life-bearing Hera, Aidoneus, and Nestis, who with her tears waters the mortal spring.

They are called the roots of things because from them all other things arise. But the things that arise from them do not come into being. It is here that men have fallen into error:

8.28 When these [the elements] have been mingled in the form of a man, or some kind of wild animal or plant or bird, men call this "coming into being"; and when they separate men call it "evil destiny" [passing away]. This is established usage, and I myself assent to the custom.

8.29 Fools! they have no far-reaching thoughts who imagine that what was not before can come into being, or that anything can perish and be utterly destroyed.

8.30 For to come to be out of what is utterly nonexistent is inconceivable, and it is impossible and unheard of that what is should pass away. For it will always *be*, wherever you put it.

8.31 . . . there is no real coming into being of any mortal creature, nor any end in wretched death, but only mingling and separation of what has been mingled, and "coming into being" is merely a name given to them by men.

The influence of Parmenides is unmistakable. Nothing can come into being; nothing can be utterly destroyed. The mortal forms which arise through the mingling of the elements do not come to be in any true sense; only the elements *are*:

8.32 These alone exist; but running through one another they become men and the tribes of other animals — at one time coming together into a single order through Love, at another time each being borne apart again through the hostility of Strife until, grown together once more, they are wholly subdued.

Thus insofar as they have learned to grow into one from many and, when the one grows apart, to become many again, to this extent they come into being and have no lasting life; but insofar as they never cease changing places continually, they remain inviolate throughout the cycle.

LOVE AND STRIFE

As **8.32** shows, the mixture and separation of the elements is effected by two forces which Empedocles calls Love and Strife. These rule the world-process in turn:

8.33 I shall tell a twofold tale. For at one time it grew to be one only from many, while at another it dispersed again to be many from one. And there is a twofold generation of mortal creatures, and a twofold passing away; for one [generation] is begotten and brought to ruin at the coming together of all things, and the other grows up and is dispersed as these are scattered again. And these never cease changing places continually — at one time all coming together into one through Love, at another each being borne apart again through the hostility of Strife.

8.34 But come, harken to my words; for learning will increase your understanding. As I said before, in declaring the limits of my story, I shall tell a twofold tale.

At one time it grew to be one only from many; at another it dispersed again, to be many from one: fire and water and earth and the boundless height of air; dread Strife too, apart from these, evenly balanced in every direction, and Love in their midst, equal in length and breadth. Observe her with your mind; do not sit with dazed eyes. She it is who is known as inborn in mortal limbs, through whom they think friendly thoughts and do well-fitted deeds, calling her Joy and Aphrodite. No mortal man has perceived her as she circles among them; but do you attend to the undeceitful progress of my argument.

Love is the force that unites, bringing together unlikes and binding them,

8.35 Even as the juice of figs binds together white milk . . . .

She is, in fact, the divinity which Parmenides describes as "the beginner of all hateful birth and all begetting, sending the female to mix with the male and the male in turn to the female" (6.28). Strife is the force that disrupts and disunites, separating what Love has joined and sending each thing to its like, earth to earth and fire to fire.

Empedocles often speaks of Love and Strife as though they were things rather than forces; they seem to behave like fluids, which alternately fill the cosmos and retire from it (8.39). But he writes, after all, as a poet, and the language he uses is the language proper to poetry — vivid and concrete. That Love is not a thing in the sense in which fire is a thing is indicated by the fact that "no mortal man has perceived her as she circles among them." Only the elements are given to the senses; the existence of the forces which move them are inferred from their effects.

Similarly, when Empedocles speaks of Strife as "evenly balanced in every direction," and of Love as "equal in length and breadth," he means not that they are extended and have weight, but that they are on the same footing with the elements:

8.36 For all these are equal and of like age, but each has its own office and its own way of behaving, and they prevail in turn as time goes by. And besides these nothing comes into being or perishes; for if they were continually passing away, they would not be any longer. What could increase the whole? Where could it have come from? And where could it pass away, since no place is empty of these things? No, there are these things alone; but running through each other they become at one time this, at another that, while remaining ever the same.

The lack of any sharp distinction here between the elements and the forces that move them shows that Empedocles conceives Love and Strife as having the same kind of ultimate reality as the elements. Like the elements, therefore, they are eternal:

8.37 For as they were before, so also will they be; nor ever, I think, shall endless time ever be emptied of these two.

THE RULE OF LOVE

These forces, as we have seen, work in opposite directions. Strife, when it achieves mastery, separates out what Love has united; Love, when it achieves mastery in its turn, unites what Strife has separated:

8.38 This is manifest in the mass of mortal limbs. At one time all the limbs that are the body's lot come together into one through Love, in the prime of flourishing life; at another, sundered by cruel strifes, each wanders apart by the breakers of life's sea. So it is with plants and water-dwelling fish, the beasts that lie up in the hills and winged sea birds.

Love, when it enters the world-order created by Strife, joins together the limbs sundered by Strife:

8.39 I will return to the path of song which I followed before, driving my chariot from one argument to another.

When Strife had reached the lowest depth of the vortex, and Love was in the midst of the eddy, then all things came together in it to be one — not all at once, but they came willingly from this side and that. And as they came together Strife began to move out to the furthest limit.

Many things remained unmixed side by side with the things that were being mixed, namely, those which Strife, still ascendant, yet retained; for it had not withdrawn entirely from them, blamelessly, to the outermost bounds of the circle, but some parts of it had passed out from the limbs [of the whole] while some still remained within. And in proportion as it kept on running out, a gentle immortal stream of blameless Love kept entering in; and forthwith those things came to be mortal which before were wont to be immortal. Things which were before unmixed changed their paths, and as they mingled there poured forth countless tribes of mortal creatures, endowed with all manner of forms, a wonder to behold.

For at the close of the rule of Strife

8.40   Single limbs wandered alone.

8.41   Many heads sprang up without necks; arms wandered unattached, without shoulders; and eyes wandered alone, bereft of foreheads.

8.42   But as divinity mingled with divinity more and more, these things fell together as each chanced, and many other things besides these were continually produced.

Since, however, these combinations were purely fortuitous, and they "fell together as each chanced," the results were monstrous:

8.43   [Creatures with] rolling gait and countless hands.

8.44   Many came into being with faces and breasts on both sides, offspring of oxen with the faces of men; others again sprang up that were offspring of men with the heads of oxen — creatures in whom male and female were mingled, furnished with sterile parts.

Most of these creatures perished immediately, for they were not fitted to live. But in time even those who were able to defend themselves and to reproduce their kind perished; for they fell victim to the more and more complete mingling of those elements which Strife had separated — a process which could only end in the fusion of these into a single, compact mass:

8.45   There is no discord or unseemly strife in its limbs.

8.46 Therein are distinguished neither the swift limbs of the sun, nor the shaggy might of earth, nor the sea; thus does it stand fast in the close covering of Harmony, a rounded sphere, rejoicing in its circular rest.

8.47 Two branches do not spring from its back; it has no feet, no swift knees, no organs of reproduction, but is a sphere, equal in every direction to itself.

The language of these fragments echoes that of Parmenides. The "one" of Empedocles, "equal in every direction to itself," is clearly modeled after the "one" of Parmenides, "like the body of a well-rounded sphere, evenly balanced in every direction from the middle" (**6.14**). Like the "one" of Parmenides it is at rest. But there are echoes, too, of earlier thought; for the undifferentiated mass in which "are distinguished neither the swift limbs of the sun, nor the shaggy might of earth, nor the sea" finds a more ancient counterpart in the distinctionless mixture from which Anaximander generates the visible world-order. Moreover, it is these older connections of thought which in the long run prevail. For the "one" of Parmenides is static, frozen in the bonds of its own existence, whereas the primordial unity of Anaximander is instinct with life, for out of it world-orders ceaselessly arise. It is to this conception that Empedocles reverts.

THE RULE OF STRIFE

For though the sphere is a god, it is a mortal god; the forces which created it must give way, at the appointed time, to Strife, and its unity must be destroyed:

8.48 But when Strife was grown great in the limbs [of the sphere], and sprang forth to claim his own when the time was fulfilled which is appointed for them in turn by a broad oath . . . .

8.49 All the limbs of the god trembled in succession.

Motion begins in the undifferentiated mass, and, as it spreads, the elements begin to separate out from the mixture, each to its own kind:

8.50 For when the whole is separated into the elements by Strife, fire is aggregated into one, and so with each of the other elements.

8.51 Earth increases its own bulk, ether increases ether.

This process leads to the formation of the world-order which we know:

> **8.52**   Come now, and I will tell you first of the beginning — of all the things which now we see, and how they came to be manifest: earth and billowy sea, damp air and the Titan ether, binding his circle around everything.

Empedocles' account of this process has not been preserved, but later reports afford us a glimpse of its general character:

> **8.53**   Empedocles says that ether was separated off first, fire second, and after that earth. From the earth, as it was sharply constricted by the force of the rotation, water gushed forth, and from this in turn air ascended in the form of vapor. The heaven arose from the ether, the sun from the fire, terrestrial things being compressed from the other elements.

> **8.54**   He says that air, having separated off from the mixture of the elements, poured around in a circle; and after the air fire ran outwards, and having nowhere else to go ran up under the solid surrounding the air.

> **8.55**   Empedocles says that the heaven is solidified air, compacted by the fire like crystal.

In Empedocles' case it is unnecessary to infer the nature of the motion which rules the whole from its effects; he refers to it explicitly as one of rotation (**8.39**). And the effect of rotation upon the mixture is, as in earlier thinkers, the separation of the elements concentrically by weight. Earth, being heavy, goes to the center, where it is compressed into a solid mass by the force of the rotation. The lighter elements move out to the periphery, where they are contained by a crystalline substance similar to that which surrounds the world-order of Parmenides and Anaximenes (**6.26, 3.10**).

The necessity of fixing a limit to the world-order created its own problems, however, for the outermost heaven, being denser and more compact than air, must also be heavier. What, then, prevents it from falling in upon the center under the influence of the forces exerted by the rotation? To explain this Empedocles had recourse to a new analogy:

> **8.56**   Empedocles maintains that it has been kept up all this time by the vortex, that is, by having a swifter motion imparted to it than that to which its own weight inclines it.

8.57 Similarly, water in a cup which is swung round in a circle, is for the same reason prevented from moving with the downward motion which is natural to it, though it is frequently below the bronze.

The outer heaven, then, is subject to two forces — one operating at right angles to the direction of rotation, the other in the direction of the rotation itself. But there is no composition of forces; the second, being greater, simply cancels out the first.

PLANTS AND ANIMALS

The reign of Strife is marked by the rise of new forms of life:

8.58 Come now, hear how fire, as it was separated out, led up the night-born shoots of men and tearful women; for my tale is not wide of the mark or uninformed. First of all, undifferentiated forms sprang up from the earth, having a share both of water and fire. These fire sent up, wishing to reach its like, exhibiting as yet neither a form lovely of limb nor the voice or organ proper to men.

That the separation of fire from earth is not complete even in our own time is evident from volcanic activity. For this shows that

8.59 Many fires burn beneath its surface.

But in the beginning earth contained much more fire, even, than it does now, and this fire, as it moved outwards towards the periphery, penetrated the earth in many places, warming the primordial mud and generating in it "undifferentiated forms."

A much later account of this process, which preserves many echoes of Empedocles' thought, will perhaps help to make its nature clearer:

8.60 When in the beginning, as their account runs, the universe was being formed, both heaven and earth were indistinguishable in appearance, since their elements were intermingled: then, when their bodies separated from one another, the universe took on in all its parts the ordered form in which it is now seen; the air set up a continual motion, and the fiery element in it gathered into the highest regions, since anything of such a nature moves upward by reason of its lightness (and it is for this reason that the sun and the multitude of other stars became involved in the universal whirl); while all that was mud-like and thick and contained an admixture of moisture sank because of its weight into one place; and as this continually turned about upon itself and became compressed, out of the wet it formed the sea, and out of what was firmer, the land, which was like potter's clay and entirely soft. But as the sun's fire shone upon the land, it first of all became firm, and then, since its surface was in a ferment because of the warmth, portions of the wet swelled up in masses in many places, and in these pustules covered with delicate membranes made their appearance. Such a phenomenon can be seen even yet in swamps and marshy places whenever, the ground having become cold, the air suddenly and without any gradual change becomes intensely warm. And while the wet was being impregnated with life by reason of the warmth in the manner described, by night the living things forthwith received their nourishment from the mist that fell from the enveloping air, and by day were made solid by the intense heat; and finally, when the embryos had attained their full development and the membranes had been thoroughly heated and broken open, there was produced every form of animal life. Of these, such as had partaken of the most warmth set off to the higher regions, having become winged, and such as retained an earthy consistency came to be numbered in the class of creeping things and of the other land animals, while those whose composition partook the most of the wet element gathered into the region congenial to them, receiving the name of water animals. And since the earth constantly grew more solid through the action of the sun's fire and of the winds, it was finally no longer able to generate any of the larger animals, but each kind of living creatures was now begotten by breeding with one another.

Empedocles' own account of the process is more highly colored:

8.61 Then did Cypris, busying herself about the forms, moisten earth with water and give it to fire to harden.

8.62 The grateful earth received in its broad crucibles two parts of gleaming Nestis [water] out of the eight, and four of Hephaistos [fire]; and white bones were produced, divinely begotten by the bonding of Harmony.

8.63 And earth, coming to anchor in the perfect harbors of Cypris, came together with Hephaistos, with moisture and with bright-shining ether in almost equal proportions — a little more of it to their less or less to their more. And from them came blood and forms of other flesh.

What distinguishes blood from bone is the ratio of the mixture; for Empedocles as for Pythagoras "number is the essence of all things."

From blood and bone in turn the bodies of animals were formed, and the sexes were distinguished. But because they were once one, they seek to be reunited with one another. For the male does not merely recognize the female:

8.64 Upon him comes longing also, reminding him through sight.

From such unions arise the creatures we know, each kind being distinguished by the ratio of the mixture in them.

THE SURVIVAL OF THE FITTEST

Aristotle was justly puzzled by certain features of this theory — the mingling of the elements in a certain proportion, for example:

8.65 What is the cause of this? Not fire or earth, surely. But neither is it Love or Strife, for the former is simply the cause of coming together, the latter of separation . . . . "Chance," not "proportion," is the name one applies in such cases; for things can be mingled at random.

Aristotle's point is this: it is not the mere presence of water and fire and earth in it that makes bone bone; it is their presence in a certain ratio. But what brings them together in this particular ratio rather than another? Is it not mere chance?

Empedocles' answer to this question is not altogether clear. Sometimes he seems to regard Love as something more than a cause of association only — as where he speaks of her as "busying herself about the forms" (**8.61**). Yet during the reign of Love, when we should most expect to see a guiding intelligence at work, things seem to come together as chance directs (**8.42**). Aristotle fastened on this point unerringly:

8.66 Why should not nature work, not for some end, or because it is better so, but just as the sky rains — not in order to make the grain grow but of necessity? For the vapor that is drawn up must cool, and when it is cooled become water and descend; and when this occurs the grain grows. Similarly, if the grain is spoiled on the threshing floor, it did not rain for the sake of this, *i.e.*, in order that the grain might be spoiled, but this simply happened. Why should it not be the same, then, with the bodily parts in nature — that our teeth, for example, should come up of necessity, the front ones sharp and fitted for tearing, the molars broad and useful for grinding the food, not because they are formed for this end but simply by chance? And so with the other parts in which it appears that there is purpose. Whenever all the parts turned out as they would if they had come into being for a purpose, these creatures survived, being organized spontaneously in a fitting way; and those that were so organized perished — and still do perish — just as Empedocles says his offspring of oxen with the faces of men did.

There is, on this view, no need to invoke design to account for the origin of plants and animals; we may think of them as having come into being by a process similar to that which we can see taking place around us at the present time — the progressive elimination of the unfit by natural selection. In the beginning blood and bone could have been formed by chance, and from these in turn animals and plants could have arisen of every sort, some of which would perish, some of which would live to reproduce themselves, according as they were "organized spontaneously in a fitting way." This conception, which appears to have originated with Empedocles, finds its classical expression in the ancient world in Lucretius' great poem *On the Nature of Things:*

8.67 At that time, many generations of living things must have perished and have been unable to reproduce their species.

For whatsoever you see feeding on the breath of life, some craft or strength or fleetness has kept preserved from the beginning of its life. There are also many creatures which survive because their usefulness has commended them to us, and they have been entrusted to our care.

In the first case, the savage species of lions in all their ferocity has been preserved by strength, the wolves by cunning, and the deer by flight. On the other hand, dogs, with their trusty hearts alert even in sleep, and every sort of pack animal, and woolly sheep and horned cattle have all been entrusted to the care of men, Memmius. For eagerly they have fled from beasts of prey and pursued a life of peace and the lavish feasts they are given without toil on their part, which are their reward for usefulness.

But those to whom nature gave none of these gifts, unable to survive by themselves or to offer us any useful service in return for which we might let them feed and live safely under our care — they all lay trapped in their fateful bonds as prey and plunder for others, until nature brought that species to an end.

But even the swift and the strong must pass away; for as the creatures which arose during the reign of Love perished as that reign drew to a close, so the creatures which arise during the reign of Strife must perish. Their destruction is but a consequence of the process by which earth, air, water, and fire — already far advanced in their separation into distinct masses — will become completely separated, and mortal forms, which depend upon the mingling of the elements, will cease to exist. The cycle will have completed itself. Strife will begin once more to pass out to the outermost limit of the rotation, and as it passes out "a gentle immortal stream of blameless Love" will run in to take its place. A kind of compromise is thus effected between the demands of Parmenidean logic and the witness of the senses. For being is both one and many; the sphere and the world-order in which the separation of the elements has proceeded to its furthest limit represent its two poles. Only through change can this double aspect of being be maintained; for change alone prevents the absorption of the one in the many, or the many in the one.

The Microcosm

The reciprocal ebb and flow of opposing forces in the whole is mirrored in man. It is evident, for example, in the process of respiration:

> **8.68** All creatures inhale and exhale in the following way. All have pallid tubes of flesh extending over the surface of the body. And at the mouths of these the outermost surface of the skin is pierced through and through with channels, constricted so as to keep in the blood while easy access is provided for the air. When the smooth blood recedes from the surface, the bubbling air rushes in with a violent surge; and when the blood leaps up the air is exhaled again, as when a girl plays with a klepsydra of shining brass. For when she places the mouth of the stem against her shapely hand and immerses it in the smooth mass of silvery water, no liquid enters the vessel, but the bulk of the air within, pressing on the close-packed holes, holds it back until she uncovers the dense current [of air]; but then, as the air escapes, an equal volume of water enters. In the same way, when water occupies the depths of the brazen vessel and the mouth of the passage is blocked by the human hand, the air outside, striving to get in, holds back the water, prevailing at the entrance of the noisy strainer until she lets it go with her hand. Then once more, but in reverse, as the air rushes in the water flows out in equal volume. In just the same way, when the smooth blood, surging through the limbs, rushes backwards into the interior [of the body], immediately a stream of ether enters in a quick surge; but when the blood leaps up, again an equal volume of air is exhaled.

There is a particular reason for Empedocles' insistence on the equality, volume for volume, of the exchanges of air and blood. If the air withdrew faster than the blood could take its place, a void would be created; and according to Parmenides no void can exist, for "all is full of what is" (6.11). With this Empedocles agrees:

8.69   No part of the whole is empty . . . .

The clepsydra is a funnel-shaped device for taking up wine from a mixing bowl too large to decant. It is hollow and pierced with holes at either end — many small ones at the lower end, which is broad, and a single one at the upper end, which is narrow:

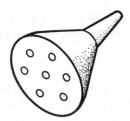

When the larger end is dipped into wine with the upper hole uncovered, the air inside the clepsydra is displaced as the wine enters. When the hole at the upper end is closed, the wine can be transferred to a smaller vessel. But as soon as air is allowed to enter through the hole at the upper end, the wine will run out through the holes in the lower end. There is, thus, a reciprocal displacement of air and wine, and Empedocles' point is that this is also what happens in the body. As the clepsydra is pierced with many holes through which air and wine pass, so the body is pierced with passages through which the flux and reflux of air and blood pass in respiration. As air is drawn in, the blood retreats before it towards the heart; from there it is thrust outward again, and the air retires before its advance as far as the periphery of the body. In such fashion do Love and Strife alternately advance and retreat in the whole (8.39).

THOUGHT AND SENSATION

Upon the mechanism of respiration thought also depends, for it is through the channels that everywhere pierce the body that the materials of thought enter. This comes about in the following way:

8.70   Know that effluences are given off from everything that comes into being.

8.71 Not only animals and plants and earth and sea, but even stones and brass and iron continually emit streams [of them].

A running hare, for example, leaves behind it in the grass minute bits of its body, which are picked up by the dog which follows its trail,

8.72 . . . searching out with its nostrils the fragments of the wild limbs [of the hunted thing] — the living parts which it shed from its feet in the soft grass.

Through the nostrils these reach the heart,

8.73 . . . reared in seas of blood which leap back and forth. There is what most men call thought; for the blood about men's hearts is thought.

Not all of the effluences enter the body by the same channels; for the channels of sight and hearing differ from those of smell as they do from one another, and the effluences received by each must be fitted to them:

8.74 This is why one sense cannot judge of the objects of another; for the passages of some are too wide and of others too narrow for the object perceived, so that some [effluences] go straight through without touching whereas others are unable to enter at all.

Sensation takes place when the particles of earth, air, fire, and water that enter through these passages meet with their own kind in the region about the heart, where thought takes place:

8.75 For by means of earth we see earth; by means of water, water; by means of ether, divine ether; by means of fire, destroying fire. With Love we see Love, and with Strife baneful Strife.

8.76 For out of these all things are fitted together and joined, and by means of these men think and feel pleasure and pain.

What happens to these effluences, once they have entered into the body, depends upon the state of the thinker himself:

8.77 If you fix them deep in a mind that is not in a whirl, meditating on them sympathetically and with an attention that is pure, all of these will remain with you throughout your life, and you will obtain, by means of them, many others. For each increases in the usual way, according to the nature which belongs to each.

But if your thought is for other things — the countless wretchednesses which arise among men and blunt the edge of their careful thought — these will desert you quickly when the time comes round; for they long to return to their own kind. For be assured that all things have intelligence and a share of thought.

If the blood about the heart is calm and steady, the effluences remain and are increased by the continual arrival of new ones, each going to swell its own kind. When this happens, experience accumulates in us; "for intelligence increases in men according to what is present in them" (**8.26**). But if the mind is turbulent and unstable, the effluences pass, as it were, in one ear and out the other, and so are lost.

Certain implications of this view had already been recognized by Parmenides (**6.35**). If perception depends upon the presence in us of those things which we perceive, then what is perceived will vary with the ratio of these elements in us. For though the blood about the heart, which is thought, contains these "in almost equal proportions" (**8.63**), the proportions are never *exactly* equal, and from this fact arise the differences in temperament and ability which men exhibit:

8.78 Those in whom the elements are mingled in equal or almost equal proportions, and are neither too dispersed nor too small nor too large as to size, are the most intelligent and have the most exact perceptions; and those that come next in these respects are intelligent in proportion. But those who are in the opposite condition are the least intelligent.

The Problem of Parmenides

More than any of his predecessors Empedocles applied himself to the study of plants and animals — an interest which he inherited from Parmenides. His theory of vision led him to speculate on the structure of the eye, why it varies in different animals so that some see better at night than others, and why it is that though we see with both eyes at the same time we do not see double. To the solution of these problems he applied his theory of effluences and the fitting of these to passages of different sizes.

But these speculations, important as they were for the subsequent development of biology, presupposed the solution of more fundamental problems, and it is at this more fundamental level that the success of the whole enterprise must finally be judged. The problem that Parmenides had set was: how is it possible to reconcile change with the unity of what is? For change implies multiplicity, and this is incompatible with any genuine unity. Empedocles answered this question by following up the clue which Parmenides himself had supplied in the Way of Opinion. If change were to be accounted for, at least two principles would have to be admitted. On the other hand, each of these principles would have to answer to Parmenides' description of the "one"; each, that is, would have to be homogeneous, internally changeless, and subject to neither coming to be nor passing away. By their mingling and separation the coming to be and passing away of all other things might then be accounted for.

These ideas Empedocles modified scarcely at all. Where Parmenides had admitted only two principles, Empedocles admitted four. More important, he added to Parmenides' principle of attraction a principle of repulsion, the alternating rule of which permits the cyclic process which we have studied. But in principle Empedocles did not alter the scheme of things described in the second part of Parmenides' poem, and this was fatal. It was fatal because Parmenides had made it very clear that the account given in this part of his poem fell short of truth. It was, he thought, the best that could be given, short of the truth. But it was not the truth; and it was not the truth because the premises on which it proceeded were derived from the testimony of the senses. Between such testimony and knowledge proper, Parmenides drew a sharp line.

Empedocles recognized the existence of this line. In **8.34**, for example, he urges Pausanias to observe Love with his mind rather than with his eyes. But in other fragments the line becomes blurred:

> **8.79** Come now, look at the things which bear witness to what I said earlier, lest anything in my previous account be defective in form. Behold the sun, bright and warm everywhere, and the immortals bathed in its bright radiance; rain, everywhere dark and chill; and from the earth pour forth things compact and solid. During the reign of Strife all these are different in form and separated; but during the reign of Love they come together and long for one another. For from these spring all the things that were and are and will be: trees and men and women and beasts and birds and fishes who dwell in the sea — even the long-lived gods who are highest in honor. For there are these alone, but running through one another they assume different forms, so much do they change through mingling.

8.80 Just as two painters — men skilled by wisdom in their art — make votive offerings, and take in their hands colorful pigments and blend them in greater or less proportions, and from these fashion likenesses of all things, and make trees and men and women and beasts and birds and fishes who dwell in the sea and also the gods who are highest in honor, so let not deceptions beguile you into thinking that the countless manifestations of mortal things have any different source. But know these things for certain, having heard the story from a goddess.

These two fragments constitute a kind of summary of Empedocles' teaching. It is, as we have seen, based at least in part on sense perception. Yet Empedocles claims for it a certainty which, in Parmenides' view, it cannot possibly have. Parmenides' goddess offers certainty only with respect to what is; concerning the world of the senses there is no certainty, for all such knowledge must rest upon the fluctuating and unreliable testimony of the senses.

Empedocles lays great stress upon the usefulness of such knowledge, and the rewards which he holds out to Pausanias are great indeed:

8.81 You shall learn all the drugs that are a defense against sickness and old age, since for you alone I will do all this. You shall check the force of the untiring winds that rush upon the earth with their blasts and lay waste the fields; and if you wish you shall call up counterwinds. You shall make a dry spell out of a dark storm just when men need it, and streams that nourish trees as they pour from the sky out of summer drought. And you shall bring back out of Hades the strength of a dying man.

But as impressive as these claims are, they are beside the point. The question at issue is not whether the teachings of Empedocles are useful but whether they are true. Empedocles clearly supposes that they are. "Listen," he says to Pausanias, "to the undeceitful progress of my argument" (**8.34**); and at the close of it he adds, "Know these things for certain, having heard the story from a goddess" (**8.80**). Parmenides would have to reject any such claim. For him no account of the nature of things based upon sense perception could be either true or certain. Here indeed lay the crux of the matter. Parmenides had refused certainty to all knowledge derived from the senses; and no answer to Parmenides could succeed which did not make greater concessions to this claim than Empedocles was disposed to make. The problem had not been solved.

NINE

Anaxagoras

Anaxagoras was a native of Clazomenae, a Greek city on the Ionian seacoast north of Miletus. Born about 500 B.C., he came to Athens not long after the battle of Salamis in 480 B.C., and there became a member of the circle of intellectuals which gathered around Pericles. As a result he attracted the attention of Pericles' political opponents and was brought to trial on a charge of impiety because of his teachings. He was acquitted, with some difficulty, through Pericles' influence, and left Athens (apparently about 450 B.C.) for the Hellespontine region, where he died at Lampsacus in 428 B.C. Anaxagoras was thus roughly contemporary with Empedocles. Aristotle says that he was "older than Empedocles but later in his philosophical activity." It is therefore quite possible that he was influenced by Empedocles, and the evidence rather strongly suggests that he was.

The two men had in common an awareness of the difficulties raised by Parmenides for any philosophy of nature, and a willingness to accept his conclusions as their starting point. The most momentous of these was Parmenides' condemnation of coming into being and passing away. This condemnation Anaxagoras, like Empedocles, accepts:

> **9.1**   The Greeks are accustomed to speak of "coming into being" and "passing away" — but mistakenly; for nothing comes to be or passes away. There is only a mingling and separation of what is. It would be more correct, therefore, to call coming into being "mingling" and passing away "separation."

But his response to the challenge offered by Parmenides was very different from that of Empedocles:

9.2   Anaxagoras and Empedocles hold opposing views concerning the elements. For Empedocles says that fire and its fellow elements are the elements of bodies, and everything else is constituted from these. But Anaxagoras says just the opposite; he holds that the elements are the bodies which are made up of parts like themselves — such as flesh and bone and things of that sort.

9.3   He says that nearly all the things that are made up of parts like themselves, such as water or fire, come into being and pass away through coming together and separation only, and do not in any other sense come to be or pass away, but remain eternal.

THE HOMOIOMERAI

According to Empedocles, bone is made up of earth, air, fire, and water, blended in a certain proportion (**8.62**). It should be possible, therefore, to break it down again into these elements. The difficulty is that when this is done the bone ceases to be bone any longer; and if Parmenides is right, this is impossible. If bone *is*, it cannot cease to be.

Anaxagoras sought to evade this difficulty by insisting that bone is *homoiomerous*, i.e., made up of parts having the same nature as the whole. No matter how far it is broken down, what remains is bone.

9.4   When Anaxagoras speaks of the *homoiomerai* of things he means that bones are made up of tiny, miniature bones; flesh, of tiny, miniature bits of flesh; blood, through the coming together of many droplets of blood. Gold, he thinks, is made up of grains of gold, earth is a concretion of tiny earths, fire of fires, moisture of moistures. And he fashions and conceives of everything else in the same way.

Bone and flesh, then, are as much natural kinds as air and fire; all are made up alike of parts having the same nature as the whole.

Now these, according to **9.3**, do not come into being or pass away but "remain eternal"; that is why they are called by Aristotle (though not by Anaxagoras) the "elements" of existing things. How, then, are we to account for what happens in the growing child where, to all appearances, flesh and bone are actually formed where there was none before? Clearly, the growth of the child is due to the nourishment that it receives. Bone, hair, blood, muscles — all these must be augmented from the water the child drinks and the bread it eats. But bread is bread, not bone, or hair, or blood; if flesh and blood do actually arise from the bread eaten, therefore, what is must come to be from what is not. And this is impossible:

9.5   How could hair come from what is not hair, and flesh from what is not flesh?

There seemed to Anaxagoras to be but one way out of this dilemma. Since flesh and blood obviously *do* come out of bread and water, they must be contained *in* them, though in the form of particles too small to be seen:

9.6   We take in nourishment that is simple and of one kind, such as bread and water, and by this hair, veins, arteries, flesh, sinews, bones, and the other parts of the body are nourished. This being so, we must agree that all existing things are in the nourishment that is taken in, and that by these everything is increased. There exist in the nourishment "portions," of which some are productive of blood, others of sinews, others of bones, and so on — these "portions" being perceptible to reason [alone].

The particles of bone and flesh in the bread are separated out from it during the process of digestion, bone going to augment bone, blood to blood, and so on — like going to like in the body exactly as it does in that greater process of growth which, as we shall see, the world-order as a whole undergoes. This is what Aristotle means when he says that flesh and bone and the like come into being through coming together (**9.3**).

ALL THINGS IN ALL THINGS

Of all of these, then, there are portions in bread and water. But this cannot be the end of the matter; for the child, grown a man, dies, and other changes follow, "as thus: Alexander died; Alexander was buried; Alexander returneth into dust; the dust is earth, of earth we make loam, and why of that loam (whereto he was converted) might they not stop a beer barrel?" There must, therefore, be portions not only of blood and bone and the rest in the water, but also of earth and loam as well; and if the process is to continue indefinitely, bread must contain portions of *every* sort of thing.

This consequence Anaxagoras accepts:

9.7   In everything there is a portion of everything . . . .

But how is this possible? For Anaxagoras also asserts that there is no limit fixed to the number of natural kinds:

> **9.8**   He makes the number of things having parts of the same nature
> as the whole . . . infinite, whereas Empedocles assumes only the
> [four] so-called elements.

If a piece of bread were to contain portions of all of these, would it not
have to be infinitely large?

Anaxagoras maintained that it would not:

> **9.9**   For of the small there is no smallest, but there is always a smaller;
> for it is not possible for what is not to be. But of the great there
> is always a greater also. And it is equal in number to the small,
> each thing being with respect to itself both great and small.

Zeno had argued that "if there are a many, they must be both small
and great; so small as to have no size, so large as to be infinite" (**7.5**).
For suppose we cut one of the many in half, and this in half again, and
so on. One of two things must happen: either we must reach a point
at which there is nothing left to cut (in which case the whole will have
no size at all, since it is composed of parts having no size), or else we
go on dividing forever (in which case the whole will be infinitely large,
since it is made up of an infinite number of parts each of which has
some size). In **9.9** Anaxagoras replies to this dilemma. It is, he admits,
impossible to suppose that nothing is left as a result of the division;
for that would contradict Parmenides' contention that it is not possible
for what is not to be. The process of division, therefore, must go on
forever: "of the small there is no smallest, but there is always a smaller."
Moreover, Zeno is right in insisting that the further we carry the division, the greater the whole will be; so that if there is no limit to the
process of division, there can be no limit to the greatness of the whole:
"of the great there is always a greater also." But this whole will be
infinitely great only in the sense that "it is equal in number to the small."
There is nothing to prevent its being small in another sense; on the
contrary, each thing is "with respect to itself both great and small."

Anaxagoras' assertion that there is a portion of everything in everything is thus bound up in the most intimate way with his doctrine of
the infinitely small:

> **9.10**   Since the portions of the great and the small are equal in
> number, so too would all things be in everything. Nor is it possible
> for any to exist apart, but all things have a portion of all. Since it
> is impossible that there should be a smallest part, it is unable to be
> separated or come to be by itself, but as it was in the beginning,

now too all things are together. In all things there are many things, and they are equal in number in the smaller and in the greater of the things which are being separated off.

9.11 The things in the one world-order are not separated from one another, or cut off with an axe — neither the hot from the cold nor the cold from the hot.

The corollary which Anaxagoras draws from his principle in these fragments is of the utmost importance, for it guarantees the continuance of change. Consider, for example, what happens when water evaporates. The vapor which rises from the surface of the sea does not come into being; it pre-exists in the water and is merely separated off from it by the sun. But if there were a limit to the amount of air contained in the water, a time would come when evaporation would fail. And so with all the other processes in nature; becoming in general would fail — as Empedocles saw that it must, given the continued operation of Strife. Empedocles had had to introduce Love in order to bring the opposites together once more; Anaxagoras simply denies that the separation can ever be complete, and he does so on the basis of his principle that there is a portion of everything in everything.

But although there is a portion of everything in everything, there will be more of certain portions in a given thing than of others; and this will determine the name which we give to that thing:

9.12 Things appear different from one another and receive different names depending upon which of the innumerable constituents of the mixture are present in the greatest numbers. For nothing is purely or simply black or white or sweet or flesh or bone, but the nature of each thing is taken to be that of which it contains the most.

There are in corn, then, portions of blood and bone and many other things, but they are swamped and overlaid by the greater number of portions of corn, after which the whole is named.

But why is it that we never see these other portions?

9.13 He asserts that in everything there is a hidden mixture of everything, but that one thing is apparent whose particles are the most numerous and most conspicuous and are placed nearest the surface. However, this is very far from the truth. For it would follow that corn ears, when they are crushed by the dreadful weight of a millstone, would show some sign of blood; or, when we crush between stones anything which nourishes our body, blood would flow forth. Similarly, grass and liquid ought also to produce sweet drops of the same savor as the milk in the udders of sheep. And when clods of earth have been crumbled, divided particles of grasses and grains and leaves ought to be seen hiding in tiny quantities among the soil. And lastly, ashes and smoke should be seen in logs when they have been split, and tiny fires should lie hidden. Since it is clear that none of these things happens, obviously things are not mingled with one another in this way . . . .

Lucretius hardly does justice to the subtlety of Anaxagoras' theory. Blood does not exist in the corn in the form of droplets visible to the eye; many portions of blood would have to come together to form even a single droplet of this size. And in the corn these are scattered far from one another and mingled with countless portions of other kinds which prevent them from being visible. The state of things envisaged here is in fact identical with that which prevailed before there was any corn or any grass or water or indeed any of the other things which we see now, including the world-order itself:

> 9.14 Before these were separated out, when all things were together, not even color was visible. For the mixture of all things — of the wet and the dry and the hot and the cold and the bright and the dark — prevented it, there being in it much earth and an infinite number of seeds in no way resembling one another. For none of the other things in any way resemble one another, either. And this being so, we must suppose that all things are present in the whole.

> 9.15 All things were together, infinite both in number and in smallness; for the small, too, was infinite. And all things being together, nothing was visible because of smallness. For air and ether dominated all things, both of them being infinite. For these are greatest in the whole, both in number and size.

At that time the mixture of many things prevented any one of them from being visible. But as in the case of the corn, certain portions dominated the mixture numerically, namely air and ether, so that these gave their appearance to the whole.

Each thing, therefore, is a microcosm of the whole, having in it whatever in the course of time may be separated out of it. Nor is there any limit to the number of things which may be separated out; for in everything there are "an infinite number of seeds in no way resembling one another,"

9.16 So that the number of the things which are separated off cannot be known either in word or deed.

MIND

The principle that there is a portion of everything in everything is clearly central to Anaxagoras' thought. Nevertheless there is an important exception to that principle:

9.17 In everything there is a portion of everything except mind; and in some things there is mind too.

9.18 Other things have a share of everything, but mind is infinite and self-ruled and not mixed with anything, but is alone by itself. For if it were not by itself, but were mixed with anything else, it would, by virtue of being mixed with this, have a share of all things; for there is a portion of everything in everything, as I said before. And the things that were mixed in it would hinder it, so that it could control nothing as it does now, being alone by itself. For it is the finest of all things and the purest, and it has all knowledge concerning all things and the greatest power; and over everything that has soul, large or small, mind rules.

And mind controlled the whole rotation, so that it rotated in the beginning. And at first it began to rotate from a small beginning, but now it rotates over a larger area, and it will rotate over a still larger area. And mind knows all the things that are mingled and separated out and distinguished. And what sort of things were to be, and what sort of things were (which now no longer are), and what now is, and what sort of things will be — all these mind arranged, and the rotation in which now rotate the stars and the sun and the moon and the air and the ether that are being separated off. The rotation caused them to separate off. And the dense was separated from the rare, and the hot from the cold, and the bright from the dark, and the dry from the moist.

There exist many portions of many things. Nothing is separated entirely, or distinguished one from another, except mind. Mind is all alike, both the greater and the smaller; but nothing else is like anything else, but each individual thing is and was most manifestly whatever that of which it has the most [portions].

There is a certain similarity in the way Anaxagoras speaks of mind in these fragments and the way Empedocles speaks of Love and Strife.

Empedocles thinks of Love and Strife as actually setting the elements in motion; therefore he tends to conceive of them as fluids, *i.e.*, as having a nature not so wholly unlike that of the elements that they cannot act upon them. It is the same with Anaxagoras. Since mind sets the mixture in motion, it must have a nature sufficiently like that of the mixture to make this possible. True, it is "the finest of all things"; but it dominates the mixture physically, and it does so because there is as yet no other way of conceiving its mode of action.

It is not only the finest of all things; it is the "purest." Otherwise, it would not be able to dominate the mixture. If it were mixed with other things, it would no longer have power over them. The principle involved here is well-known to us from Greek medical theory. If the health of the body is to be preserved, a balance must be maintained between the opposing powers in it: the hot and the cold, the wet and the dry. This balance is more easily maintained if the opposites are blended with one another; for then the presence of the other powers will prevent any one of them from exerting its full force. If one of these powers, however, should become separated, so that it is no longer hemmed in and hindered from putting forth its full strength, it will dominate the other powers. Since, therefore, in the system of Anaxagoras mind must dominate and control all things, it must be separate from them and unmixed in order that it may not be hindered in any way.

Empedocles, to judge by what Aristotle says of him (**8.66**), did not attribute the formation of the first animals to intelligence or design but to chance. Anaxagoras, in making mind the active agent in the formation of the world-order, seemed to set himself squarely against any such view of nature, and Socrates, in Plato's *Phaedo*, tells how as a young man, disappointed by the merely mechanical explanations of natural phenomena which he heard from his teachers, his hopes were raised by his discovery of the writings of Anaxagoras:

> **9.19** Then one day I heard someone reading from a book which he said was by Anaxagoras, saying that mind is the disposer of all things and the cause of them. I was delighted with this; it seemed somehow right that mind should be the cause of all things, and I thought that if this were the case then mind, in arranging all things, would arrange each in the way that was best for it. So that if anyone wished to discover the cause of the generation or destruction or existence of each thing, the question to ask was: how is it best for it to be or to be acted on or to act? On this reasoning all that a man need consider, whether in regard to himself or anything else, is what is best. And he would have to know what is worst, too; for the knowledge of good involves the knowledge of bad.

Considering this, I was delighted to think that I had found in Anaxagoras a teacher of the causes of existing things that was to *my* mind, and I thought that he would tell me first whether the earth is flat or round, and then go on to explain the cause and the necessity for it in terms of the better — showing how it is better for it to be as it is. If he said it was in the center, he would go on to say why it was better for it to be in the center; and if he could make these things clear to me I would ask for no other sort of cause. I was determined to find out about the sun, too, and the moon and the other heavenly bodies — their relative speeds and turnings and so on, and how it is best for them to act or be acted upon as they are. For I never supposed that, having said that these things were arranged by mind, he would bring in any other cause for them than that it was best for them to be as they are. I assumed that, having assigned the cause of each thing and of things in general, he would go on to state what is best in each case and what is good for the whole. I would not have sold my hopes for a great deal, but in great haste secured the book and read it as quickly as I could, so as to know as soon as possible the better and the worse.

My fine hopes, my friend, were quickly dashed. As I went on with my reading I found that the man made no use of his mind, and that he did not credit it with any real responsibility for the arrangement of things, but mentioned as causes air and ether and water and many other absurdities.

It is not quite true to say that Anaxagoras made *no* use of mind; Aristotle gives a somewhat more moderate account of the matter:

> **9.20** Anaxagoras uses reason as a fairy godmother for producing the world-order, and when he is at a loss to know from what cause something necessarily is, *then* he drags mind in. But as for the rest, he attributes what happens to anything rather than mind.

Yet it is obvious that Socrates' hopes were ill-founded, and that in fact Anaxagoras made very little use of mind. Why was this so?

THE VORTEX

The similarity between the thought of Anaxagoras and that of Anaximander was noticed even in ancient times. Anaxagoras was closer than Empedocles not only geographically but in other ways to the source of the Ionian tradition, and this is quite evident from **9.18**. The mind that controls the rotation and arranges all things in Anaxagoras' system is the

intelligence that steers all things in that of Anaximander. Even in Anaximander this principle remains shadowy and indefinite. It is not appealed
to in explaining such phenomena as rainbows and earthquakes, and in
his successor little has changed in this respect. Mind has taken on a
more definite form as the "finest" and "purest" of all things; and it
serves at least one perfectly definite function: it sets the mixture in
motion. But its more general function of steering or controlling all
things seems to have been left as vague by Anaxagoras as it was by
Anaximander. When it came to the detailed explanation of natural
phenomena, such as the earth's position at the center, he mentions as
causes "air and ether and water and many other absurdities."

There was, in fact, a good reason for this: the vortex motion was
doing more and more of the work. Anaximander had used it only to
account for the large-scale features of the world-order — the massing
of the elements in concentric circles. Anaximenes had extended its use
to account for the orbiting of the heavenly bodies, borne like leaves in
the cosmic eddy. Empedocles had extended it still further; for it is the
vortex motion, sending like to like, that first sends up the fire from the
earth and hence gives rise to the first living creatures. In Anaxagoras
it has come to dominate the whole world-process; for the whole process
is essentially one of separating off, and "the rotation caused them to
separate off" (**9.18**):

> **9.21** And when mind began to set things in motion, from all that was
> moved a separating off began; and all that mind set in motion
> was separated. And as things were moving and separating off, the
> rotation caused them to separate out much more.

> **9.22** The dense and the moist and the cold and the dark came together
> here, where they are now; but the rare and the hot and the dry
> traveled outwards to the farthest part of the ether.

> **9.23** From these, as they are separating off, earth is compacted; for
> water is separated off from the clouds, but earth [is compacted]
> from water, and stones are compacted from earth by the cold, and
> these travel outwards more than water.

By this means the opposites are separated out from the mixture described in **9.14** and **9.15**, and the world-order we know is brought into
being with earth at the center, surrounded by concentric masses of
increasingly lighter elements (**9.22**).

But the process of separation does not stop there:

9.24 These things being so, one must believe that there would be many things of every sort in all the things that were being aggregated, and seeds of all things having all sorts of shapes and colors and tastes. And men, too, would be compacted, and the other creatures that have soul. And the men would possess inhabited cities and artifacts, just as we do, and have a sun and a moon, just as we do; and the earth would produce for them many things of all sorts, of which they would gather the best into their dwellings and make use of them. This, then, I have said concerning the separation: that it would have taken place not only with us but anywhere.

Socrates assumes that mind always acts for the best. But in men, too, there is mind, and certainly men do not always act for the best. Yet "mind is all alike, both the greater and the smaller" (**9.18**); what reason, therefore, have we to assume that the mind which began the rotation will act any more uniformly than the mind of man? Here lay the superiority of the vortex motion as an explanatory principle; since the forces which it brought into play were purely mechanical, they could be counted upon to be absolutely uniform. This is nowhere more apparent than in **9.24**. Given the initial conditions — a mixture containing portions of all things that are to be, and a rotation capable of effecting their separation — then not only plants and animals but men and cultivated fields and cities, and with them the whole apparatus of civilized life, must come into being.

It is only in the latter stages of this process, after men have been "separated out," that mind comes to play a significant role in it, teaching men to gather the fruits of the earth and to cultivate it and to build cities. Yet even here it is not clear how much credit is to be given to mind:

9.25 Anaxagoras asserts that men are the wisest of the animals because they have hands.

The sole function of mind, so far as we can tell from the evidence at our disposal, is to start the process, to set in motion the forces which actually effect the separating out of all things.

THE HEAVENLY BODIES

In his views of the nature of the heavenly bodies Anaxagoras was greatly influenced by Anaximenes. But Anaximenes had imagined these bodies to be flat, leaflike structures, composed of some fiery substance and hence capable of being supported by the rotating upper air like leaves in an eddy. Anaxagoras was led to abandon this view by the fall of a large meteorite at the Hellespont in 467 B.C. To account for this extraordinary phenomenon Anaxagoras was obliged to elaborate a different theory of the nature and origin of the heavenly bodies:

> **9.26** Anaxagoras is said to have predicted that if any displacement or wavering were to occur among the bodies held fast in the heavens, there would be a hurtling-off and a fall as one broke away. And he says that each of the stars, too, is not in its natural place; for being stony and heavy, they shine by the resistance and breaking upon them of the ether, and are dragged along by force, being embraced by the spin and intensity of the revolution — for which reason, I take it, they were prevented from falling here at the start also, when the cold and the heavy were separated out from the whole.

From this somewhat confused account certain features emerge clearly. The heavenly bodies are glowing masses of red-hot stone, held aloft by the force of the rotation, which overcomes their natural tendency to travel to the center. The friction created by their passage through the upper air ignites them, and they glow with a heat which we feel in proportion as their distances from us are greater or less:

> **9.27** We do not feel the warmth of the stars because of their great distance from the earth; besides which they are not as hot as the sun because the region they occupy is colder. The moon is below the sun and closer to us.

But how did these great stones come to be at the outside of the rotation in the first place?

> **9.28** Anaxagoras says that the surrounding ether is fiery in its essence, and that by the vigor of its rotation stones are snatched up from the earth, set on fire, and become heavenly bodies.

This, then, is what lies behind the otherwise inexplicable assertion in **9.23** that stones "travel outwards more than water." Despite their density, which is greater than that of water, they are flung outward by the rotation and, once aloft, are maintained there by the speed of their passage:

> **9.29** . . . these things going around and being separated off by force and speed in this way. The speed creates the force. Their speed is

not like the speed of any of the things now existing among men, but altogether many times as fast.

These passages betray a certain ambiguity in the appeal to "what happens in liquids and in air" (**2.8**). The Milesians had based their theory of the formation of the world-order on what they had observed of the behavior of twigs and leaves in eddies of water. When Empedocles pointed to what happens when a pail of water is swung round at the end of a rope (**8.57**), he was appealing to a quite different principle. But there is no evidence that he was aware of this, or that Anaxagoras, in appealing to the same principle, perceived the impossibility of combining it with the principle appealed to in **9.22**.

THE TRIAL OF ANAXAGORAS

Anaxagoras lavished upon the heavenly bodies the same attention Empedocles had given to biological phenomena:

9.30   He was the first to set forth the facts concerning eclipses and illuminations.

9.31   He maintained that the sun is a molten mass or red-hot stone.

9.32   According to him, it is many times larger than the Peloponnese.

9.33   The moon is of an earthy nature, and has in it plains and ravines.

9.34   It has a light which is not its own, but comes from the sun.

Or, as Anaxagoras himself puts it:

9.35   It is the sun that gives the moon its brilliance.

Hence,

9.36   The moon is eclipsed when the earth comes between them.

Anaxagoras also offered an ingenious explanation of the Milky Way:

9.37 The followers of Anaxagoras and Democritus hold that the Milky Way is the light of certain stars. For the sun, when it passes underneath the earth, does not shine on some of the stars. The light of those stars on which the sun does shine is not visible to us, for it is hindered by the rays of the sun; but those which are screened from the sun by the earth shine with their own proper light, and this is the Milky Way.

That is, the stars which lie in the shadow cast by the earth as the sun goes beneath it are seen to glow like coals and to shed a diffuse light, whereas those upon which the sun's rays fall are overpowered and are seen only as pinpoints of light.

In Athens, where the sun was regarded as divine and eclipses of the moon were taken to be portents of things to come, these opinions of Anaxagoras were not well received. In 450 b.c. they led to his arrest and trial for impiety:

9.38 Different accounts are given of his trial. Sotion, in his *Succession of Philosophers*, says that he was prosecuted by Cleon for impiety, because he maintained that the sun is a molten mass; and that after Pericles, his pupil, had made a speech in his defense, he was fined five talents and exiled. But Satyrus, in his *Lives*, says that the charge was brought by Thucydides the son of Melesias as part of a political campaign against Pericles, and that the charge was not only impiety but Medizing [*i.e.*, making common cause with the Persians] as well; and he was condemned to death *in absentia*.

Of the two accounts that of Satyrus is most likely to be true. It places the incident earlier in the career of Pericles, when feeling still ran high against the Persians, and when the fact that Anaxagoras was an alien and an Ionian could be exploited. It is unlikely that he was the teacher of Pericles in any formal sense, but the evidence suggests that his association with him was a close one. Plutarch, in his life of Pericles, says that

9.39 Pericles admired Anaxagoras extravagantly, and by drinking deep of the so-called higher philosophy he not only came to have a lofty spirit and an elevated mode of speech, free from the vulgar and knavish tricks of mob-orators, but also a composed countenance that never gave way to laughter, a dignity of carriage and restraint in the arrangement of his clothing which no emotion was allowed to disturb while he was speaking, a voice that was evenly controlled, and all the other characteristics of this sort which so impressed his hearers.

Plato, who had no love for Pericles, put it less charitably:

>**9.40** Greatness in all fields requires a certain amount of prating and high-flown talk about "the nature of things." For loftiness of mind and all-around perfection seem somehow to come from such pursuits. Pericles added these to his natural gifts, I gather, by falling in with Anaxagoras, who was just this sort of man. This filled him with high thoughts concerning the nature of mind and mindlessness (these being the chief subjects of Anaxagoras' conversation), and from these he extracted what he could use and applied it to the art of rhetoric.

It is very probable that the attack on Anaxagoras was inspired by political motives, that it was aimed at Pericles, and that it sought to draw attention to the sort of men with whom the latter surrounded himself. But it was the nature of Anaxagoras' teachings that made the attack possible, and there is no doubt that his prosecution for impiety had the most far-reaching effects. For it created in the minds of men among whom there was no native tradition of speculation concerning "things above and below the earth" the profoundest suspicion of all natural philosophy. It was this suspicion, more than anything else, which was to lead, more than fifty years later, to the trial and execution of Socrates.

EARTH AND THE RISE OF MAN

The influence of Parmenides may be detected even in Anaxagoras' speculations concerning the earth:

>**9.41** The earth, he says, is flat in shape, and remains suspended because of its size, and because there is no void, and because the air, which is very strong, bears up the earth which rides on it.

>**9.42** The air, not having enough room to change its place because of the air massed beneath it, stays still, like water in a klepsydra. And they adduce much evidence to prove that when air is confined and at rest it will bear considerable weight.

Anaximenes too had spoken of earth as riding on the air beneath it (**3.12**), but there is nothing in his account about the void. He could think of the earth as compressing the air beneath it by settling on it "like a lid." For Anaxagoras this was impossible; for compression involves the notion of empty space, and as Parmenides had shown there can be no such thing as empty space. Anaxagoras was therefore forced to shift ground; he appealed to a new analogy — the analogy of the clepsydra.

The nature of this device has already been explained (p. 169). It is easy to see that if the upper hole is covered *before* the clepsydra is plunged into the mixing bowl, the wine will not enter because of the resistance of the air which is shut up inside. The clepsydra does not admit a little of the wine, showing that the air inside has been compressed; it admits none at all, showing that it is *not* compressed. The experiment demonstrates that when air is confined it is capable of resisting considerable pressure; and by applying this principle to the earth we can see why it does not fall. The air directly below the earth is trapped between its lower surface and the mass of air beneath, and being confined is able to hold the earth up.

At first the earth was barren, for it was composed of "the dense and the cold and the moist and the dark" (**9.22**); but when the sun had warmed it, life arose from it:

> **9.43** Animals were produced from moisture and heat and an earthy substance. Later they were produced from one another . . . .

Among these man is pre-eminent. For though we are inferior to the other animals in strength and swiftness,

> **9.44** We make use of our own experience, memory, wisdom, and skill.

Because of these possessions man has become all that Sophocles, in his *Antigone*, portrays him as being:

> **9.45** Many the wonders that exist,
> and none more wonderful than man.
> He crosses the gray sea's wintry waves,
> traversing the roaring surge.
> The mightiest of the gods, immortal Earth,
> he stirs up with his plows from year to year,
> tilling with horses.
>
> The light-brained birds he snares and hunts,
> and the tribes of wild beasts;
> and those who live in the salt sea
> he takes in his nets, this thoughtful man.
> He conquers with cunning devices

the beasts who range the mountains,
and leads beneath the double yoke
the horse with his shaggy mane,
and the wild mountain bull.

Speech he has taught himself, and airy thought,
the social dispositions, and to take
refuge from bitter frost and stormy shafts,
this man of many devices.
Resourceful, he looks to the future;
contrives escape from every disease,
save only death.

"Save only death." Yet it would be a mistake to suppose that when a man dies he ceases to be; for "nothing comes to be or passes away. There is only a mingling and separation of what is" (**9.1**). The body, being a mixture of many things, is subject to dissolution, and in that sense it passes away. But mind is "not mixed with anything" (**9.18**), and because it is not mixed with anything it cannot suffer dissolution. Neither by death nor by death's image, sleep, is its nature for a moment obscured:

9.46 Sleep comes from weariness of the body. It is a thing undergone by the body, not the soul. And death is the separation of the soul from the body.

THE GOOD LIFE

Mind, then, is immortal; and being immortal, it finds its happiness in the detached contemplation of that undying order of things in which its own nature is reflected — the order of the cosmos:

9.47 They say that when Anaxagoras was asked why anyone should wish to have been born rather than not, he answered, "In order to contemplate the heaven and the structure of the world-order as a whole."

In this activity, and not in those which are conventionally thought to bring happiness, man finds his true end:

9.48 When he was asked who he thought was the happiest of men, he replied, "Not the person you think; on the contrary, he would seem to you strange indeed." He answered in this way because he saw that the man who asked the question assumed that it was impossible to call a man happy who was not either great or handsome or rich, while Anaxagoras himself thought, perhaps, that the man who lived a life without offense to others and conforming to justice or participating in some form of divine contemplation was, humanly speaking, happy.

The ideal of the contemplative life goes back at least to the Pythagoreans, and receives classical expression in the parable of the three lives. According to legend, Leon, ruler of Phlius, asked Pythagoras in what way philosophers differed from other people:

9.49 Pythagoras replied that to him the life of man seemed like that festival which was held [at Olympia] with magnificent games before an audience from the whole of Greece. For at that festival some sought the glorious nobility of a crown through bodily fitness, while others were led there in quest of the profit to be had from buying and selling. There was, however, another class of men — and that by far the best — who sought neither applause nor profit, but went to be spectators and watched closely what was happening and how it was being done. In the same way, we come to this life from another, and from a different nature, just like a throng of people going from some city to a festival, and some of us are slaves to glory, others to money; but there is a handful of men who count everything else as worthless and closely examine the nature of things, and these men call themselves "lovers of wisdom," for that is what "philosopher" means. Just as at the festival the mark of the best men was to watch, without self-seeking, so in life the contemplation and understanding of nature far surpass all other pursuits.

The ideal of the contemplative life may go back further even than this, judging from a story which Plato tells of Thales of Miletus:

9.50 It seems that while Thales was engaged in studying the stars and gazing upwards he fell into a cistern; whereupon he was jeered at (they say) by a witty and attractive serving-wench from Thrace for being so eager to know what was happening in the sky that he did not see what was under his nose.

To this story, moreover, there is a sequel:

9.51 When they reproached Thales for his poverty, saying that philosophy was of no use to anyone, he, having observed through his study of the heavenly bodies that there would be a bumper crop of olives the following summer, raised a little capital (though it was still winter) and put a deposit on every olive-press in Miletus and Chios, getting them cheaply because no one bid against him. When the time came, and everybody wanted the presses at once, he proceeded to hire them out on his own terms and so made a large profit — showing that it is easy for philosophers to get rich if they wish to, but that this is not what they are after.

It may be that both stories are apocryphal; but it is equally possible that the ideal of the philosophic life which they express so well had its roots deep in the Ionian tradition.

THE PROBLEM OF PARMENIDES

We have seen that Empedocles failed to solve the problem posed by Parmenides, and the question naturally arises whether Anaxagoras fared any better.

At first sight he seems to be willing to make greater concessions to Parmenides than his predecessor, for he rejects the senses as an independent source of knowledge:

9.52 Because of the weakness of the senses we are unable to determine the truth [by means of them].

It does not follow, however, that the senses play no role whatever in the pursuit of truth; for Anaxagoras also asserts that

9.53 Visible things are a sight of the unseen.

What this means will be evident from **9.6**. It is the senses that tell us that growth takes place; but it is reason that tells us that there must be minute portions of bone and muscle and hair and blood in bread and water, for certainly the senses do not show them to us. The role of the senses, then, is to provide the starting point for reasoning.

From Parmenides' point of view, of course, this was no more satisfactory than the position taken by Empedocles. It involves taking for true and certain the conclusions of thought processes for which the senses have provided the all-important premises, and on this Parmenides permitted no compromise; in the testimony of the senses there is possibility of certainty or truth. From Parmenides' point of view neither Empedocles nor Anaxagoras had faced up to the real problem at all.

This was that the senses and the processes of inference seemed to contradict each other flatly. The senses reveal a world of opposites — hot and cold, wet and dry, sweet and sour, dark and bright — infinite in their variety. Thought, on the other hand, reveals a "one" which is "all alike" and "the same as itself in every direction"; there is no room in it for the rich diversity of colors, tastes, and odors which characterize the Ionian world-order. Between these two worlds there could be no hesitation; the principle of the primacy of reason involved the abandonment of real qualities. To this principle Empedocles and Anaxagoras were in theory committed. Yet neither could bring himself to make so radical a break with common sense. Instead each tried to compromise and failed. A satisfactory solution had not yet been found.

TEN

Atomism: The Macrocosm

Where Empedocles and Anaxagoras had failed, Leucippus succeeded. Considering the magnitude of his achievement it is curious that we know so little of him. Of the two works ascribed to him by the ancients only a single sentence has come down to us; and even this sentence does not come from his *Great World-System*, the book in which he set forth his theory of the natural order, but from a lesser work on *Mind*. His ideas are known to us mainly in the form which they received at the hands of his successor Democritus.

Democritus, a native of Abdera, in Thrace, was born about 460 B.C. He lived to a very advanced age and was a prolific writer; the titles of more than fifty works have come down to us. But the evidence suggests that he did not add greatly to the hard core of basic ideas contributed by Leucippus. He seems rather to have set himself the task of applying these ideas to the solution of traditional problems. The result was a systematic and comprehensive theory of the nature and origin of things in which it was difficult even for the ancients to distinguish clearly between the work of Leucippus himself and that of his successor. In what follows no attempt will be made to keep them distinct.

THE EXISTENCE OF THE EMPTY

Aristotle, who admired Leucippus, grasped the significance of his achievement correctly:

10.1   It seemed to some of the early philosophers that what is must of necessity be one and immovable; for the void is not-being, and

196 / An Introduction to Early Greek Philosophy

motion would not be possible unless there were a void having separate existence, nor could there be a many without something to keep them apart . . . . Led by these arguments beyond sense perception, and disregarding it on the ground that "one ought to follow the argument," they declared the whole to be one and immovable and (some added) infinite — since any limit would be a limit against the void . . . .

Leucippus, however, thought he had arguments which, while consistent with sense perception, would not destroy coming into being or passing away or the multiplicity of existing things. These he conceded to be appearances, while to those who upheld the "one" he conceded that there can be no motion without a void, that the void is not-being, and that not-being is no part of being; for what is, in the strict sense, is completely full. But there is not one such being but infinitely many, and they are invisible owing to the smallness of their bulk. These move in the void (for void exists) and, by coming together and separating, effect coming into being and passing away.

10.2 Leucippus and his associate Democritus say that the elements are the full and the empty. They call the one being and the other not-being; being is full and solid, not-being is empty and rare. And since the void exists no less than body, not-being, they say, exists no less than being. And these are the material causes of existing things.

The oneness and immobility of being seemed to the Eleatics to follow directly from their denial of any sort of being to what is not. For being is all alike; consequently the separation of any part of being from any other part which is implied in plurality would at the same time involve the existence of gaps in being, that is to say, the existence of not-being. And this is impossible. The motion of any part of being is ruled out for the same reason; since it cannot enter where being already is, it must enter where nothing is, and this involves once more the existence of what is not. Neither motion nor plurality is real, then; and since their denial involves the denial of the world given to us in sense perception, sense perception is fatally undermined.

Leucippus met this line of reasoning by denying the principle on which the arguments against plurality and motion both rest, namely, the principle that being is identical with the full. This assertion contains an ambiguity. If it means that there is no part of what is that is not, it is clearly true. For to deny this assertion would be to involve ourselves in self-contradiction. But if it is taken to mean that there is no part of what is that is empty, the truth of the assertion is no longer so obvious. For there is no contradiction in asserting that some part of what is is empty. There would be a contradiction in asserting this only if we identified body with being; and it is evident that this is precisely what Parmenides had done. He speaks of the "one" as though it were extended in space, "complete on every side, like the body of a well-rounded sphere, evenly balanced in every direction from the middle" (**6.14**). The description is not intended to be taken literally, but it is not merely metaphorical either; it represents the struggle with language of a mind seeking, however imperfectly, to achieve a level of abstraction for which no adequate means of expression yet exists. We have observed this struggle in Empedocles and Anaxagoras, and it is reflected in the language of the atomists themselves:

> **10.3**   Democritus gives to space the names "void," "no-thing," and "the infinite." To each of his substances [*i.e.,* the atoms] he gives the name "thing," and "the compact," and "being." He supposes them to be so small that they elude our senses; but they have forms of all sorts and shapes of all sorts and differ in size. So that already he is able to create from these, as elements, by aggregation, the masses that are perceptible to sight and the other senses.

Democritus is sufficiently under the influence of Parmenides to reserve for the atoms, which are "full," the name "things." Space, which is not a thing in this sense, he calls "no-thing." Yet clearly this nothing *exists* for Democritus. It is fully as real as the things which occupy it:

> **10.4**   No-thing exists just as much as thing.

To have grasped this is to have seen that the real is not identical with the full — that empty space, too, is real. And to have seen this is to have broken the stranglehold of Parmenidean logic; for the existence of empty space makes possible both plurality and motion.

THE ATOMS

Melissus had anticipated this development by means of his distinction between "being" and "having body" (**7.29**); "to exist" does not mean "to occupy space." But in another way, too, he had anticipated the atomists. He had laid down the terms on which the existence of a many could alone be maintained: "If there were a many, they would have to be such as the one is" (**7.32**). The atomists now proceeded to show that these terms could be satisfactorily met.

Each, for example, must be indivisible:

10.5 [Leucippus, Democritus, and Epicurus] said that the first principles were infinite in number; and they supposed them to be uncuttable and indivisible and impassive because of their solidity, and without any share of the void. For division, they maintain, takes place because of the void which is in bodies.

10.6 Those who assert the existence of atoms say that the cutting does not proceed without limit, but stops at bodies having no parts.

A loaf of bread can be cut because the knife blade, in passing through it, encounters empty space. A slice of bread can be cut in half for the same reason, and that half can be cut in half again. But this cutting "does not proceed without limit"; eventually the knife encounters particles having no void in them. Because there is no void in them, the knife blade cannot pass through them; they are "uncuttable," and these "uncuttables" are the "atoms," infinite in number, which ultimately constitute the world-order. Leucippus seems to have called them "solids" using for this purpose a word meaning "well-kneaded," *i.e.,* "without air spaces."

The atoms are also "impassive," that is, incapable of undergoing change. For change involves motion, and motion implies empty space; but within an atom there is no empty space. Hence it is impossible for it to undergo any internal alteration:

10.7 Because of their solidity the atoms are not affected, nor do they change.

It follows from this that they are indestructible. For to be destroyed is to be acted upon, to suffer alteration, and this is impossible. In the language of Parmenides, it is impossible that what is should cease to be.

Nor can what is come into being; the atoms, like the "one" of Parmenides, exist eternally. Only compounds "come into being" and "pass away," and these are formed and dissolved by the coming together and separation of the atoms in the void (**10.1**):

10.8 They jostle and move in the void because of their unlikeness and the other differences mentioned above [**10.3**], and as they move they collide and become entangled so as to touch and make contact with one another — though not so as to come to have a single nature, for it would be silly to suppose that two or more things could ever become one. Their coherence with one another for a time he explains by the interlocking and clinging of the [primary] bodies; for some of them are angular, some are hooked, some concave, some convex, and they differ in countless other ways. And so, he thinks, they cling to one another and remain together until such time as some stronger necessity from outside shakes them loose and scatters them abroad.

In this way "the masses that are perceptible to sight and the other senses" (**10.3**) are formed.

COMPOUND BODIES

These compounds differ in many ways: some are hard, some soft; some are sweet, others bitter; some are light, others heavy; some are of one color, some of another. How are these differences to be accounted for? For the atoms constitute being, and being is "all alike" according to Parmenides.

The answer which the atomists gave to this question went to the very heart of the problem which Parmenides had raised:

10.9   Democritus does not give the same account of all the objects of sense, but distinguishes between some on the basis of size, some on the basis of shape, and others on the basis of arrangement and position . . . .

Heavy and light he distinguishes on the basis of size. For if each thing were divided up into units, even if these were to differ in shape their weight would depend on their size. Among compounds, however, the lighter is the one containing the most void, the heavier the one containing less. In some places he speaks thus; in others he says that the light is simply the fine.

He speaks of hard and soft in just the same way. The hard is the dense, the soft is the rare; and the differences in degree are accounted for accordingly. But because of differences in the amount of void enclosed in it, a hard body may be light or a heavy body soft. Thus, while iron is harder than lead, lead is heavier than iron. For iron is not uniformly put together; it has in it many void spaces of considerable extent, and though close-packed in some places it contains, generally speaking, much empty space. Lead, on the other hand, which contains less empty space, is uniformly put together throughout and therefore, though softer than iron, is heavier. This, then, is what he has determined concerning heavy and light and hard and soft.

Of the other objects of sense he says that they have no existence in nature, but that all are affects of our sense organs as they undergo the alteration which brings into being what appears to us. For neither hot nor cold has any reality, but the shape, "undergoing a change," works a change in us also. For whatever is present all at once prevails in each of us; but what is spread out over a long time is imperceptible.

An indication that the aforementioned qualities do not exist in nature is that things do not appear the same to all living creatures, but what is sweet to us is bitter to others, and to still others sour or pungent or astringent; and so with the rest.

Moreover, he says that men "alter in makeup" according to age and condition — from which it is clear that a man's bodily state is a cause of what appears to him.

There is much here that calls for comment. To begin with, it is clear that the atomists accounted for the differences between compounds in three ways:

> **10.10** They say that the differences are three in number: shape, arrangement, and position; or, as they put it, being differs only in "form," "disposition," and "turning" — "form" being shape, "disposition" arrangement, and "turning" position. For *A* differs from *N* in shape, *AN* from *NA* in arrangement, and ⊐ from *H* in position.

According to Theophrastus (**10.9**), Democritus was able to account for a large variety of differences on the basis of shape and size alone. Here, for example, is his account of differences in taste:

> **10.11** In assigning shapes to each taste, Democritus made what is sweet to consist of atoms that are round and of a good size. What is sour consists of atoms that are bulky, jagged, and many-angled, without curves. Sharp-tasting things, as the name implies, consist of atoms that are themselves sharp, angular, crooked, fine, and without curves. Pungent things are made of atoms that are round, fine, angular, and crooked. Salty things, of atoms that are angular, of a good size, twisted, and with two sides equal. Bitter, of atoms that are curved and smooth but very crooked and small in size. Oily-tasting things consist of atoms that are fine, round, and small.

> **10.12** In like manner he accounts for the other powers of each in terms of the shapes of the constituent atoms. Of all these shapes no one exists pure and unmixed with the others, but in each thing there are many shapes, and the same taste will have in it atoms that are smooth and rough, round and angular, and the rest. Whichever shape predominates in it will determine what

sense-impression we receive and its strength, depending upon the sort of state it finds us in. For this matters not a little in explaining how it is that the same thing produces opposite effects and opposite things the same effect on us at different times.

Other differences, such as those of heavy and light, Democritus accounted for on the basis of arrangement and position. For the amount of void in a compound body will clearly affect the disposition of the atoms in it, and in the same way the concentration of atoms in certain parts of the body will have an influence. The shapes of the atoms cannot change, but their disposition, *i.e.*, their spatial relations to one another, can; and by means of such groupings and regroupings Democritus is able to account for all aspects of change:

> 10.13 Democritus and Leucippus, postulating the "figures" [*i.e.*, the atoms], produce alteration and generation from these — generation and passing away by coming together and separation, alteration by configuration and position . . . so that, owing to changes in the compound, the same thing appears opposite at different times, and being altered by a small addition appears wholly different by virtue of this single alteration. For tragedy and comedy are made of the same letters.

The Illusions of Sense

The analogy with language is apt. The same letters are used indifferently in tragedy and comedy; the result depends upon their arrangement. But the similarity goes deeper than this. For when these letters are combined in words they have a power to move us which, taken separately, they lack. It is the same with the compounds which confront us in experience. As such, they are able to affect us through the infinite variety of colors, odors, and sounds which they emit. But in themselves they are neither colored nor odiferous:

> 10.14 Democritus says that color does not exist in nature; for the elements — both the solids and the void — are without qualities.

> 10.15 The primary bodies are impassive (some, like the associates of Epicurus, holding them to be unbreakable because of their hardness; others, like the associates of Leucippus, holding them to be indivisible because of their smallness), and are in no way able to undergo any of those changes which all men, having been

taught by their senses, believe to exist. They say, for example, that no one of these bodies becomes hot or cold or dry or moist, let alone white or black, or, in general, acquires any other quality through any change whatsoever.

It is not quite accurate to say that the atoms have *no* qualities, for they have shape and size and, as we shall see, weight. Moreover, they would not rebound from one another when they collide if they did not have what we call "mass." We must, therefore, distinguish between the real properties of bodies and the properties which only appear to belong to them:

> **10.16** Sweet exists by convention, bitter by convention, color by convention; but in reality atoms and the void alone exist.

> **10.17** So Democritus says, supposing that from the meeting of atoms arise all of the sensible qualities perceived by us, but that neither white nor black nor yellow nor red nor bitter nor sweet are anything in nature. For "by convention" means "by custom" or "for us," and not according to the nature of the things themselves, which he calls "reality" — deriving the word from "genuine," which means "true." And the full meaning of his statement would be as follows: a thing is customarily thought to be white or black or sweet or bitter (and so with the rest) apart from men, but in truth "thing" and "no-thing" are all there is.

It would be difficult to overestimate the importance of this distinction for the history of thought. Galileo, standing on the threshold of modern science, restates it in its classical form:

> **10.18** I feel myself impelled by the necessity, as soon as I conceive a piece of matter or corporeal substance, of conceiving that in its own nature it is bounded and figured in such and such a figure, that in relation to others it is large or small, that it is in this place or that place, in this or that time, that it is in motion or remains at rest, that it touches or does not touch another body, that it is single, few, or many; in short, by no imagination can a body be separated from such conditions: but that it must be white or red, bitter or sweet, sounding or mute, of a pleasant or unpleasant odor, I do not perceive my mind forced to acknowledge it necessarily accompanied by such conditions; so if the senses were not the escorts, perhaps the reason or imagination by itself would never have arrived at them. Hence I think that these tastes, odors, colors, etc., on the side of the object in which they seem to exist

are nothing else than mere names, but hold their residence solely in the sensitive body; so that if the animal were removed, every such quality would be abolished and annihilated.

"Nothing else than mere names . . . ." Parmenides had expressed the same thought in very nearly the same words: "Those things which mortals have established, believing them to be true, will be mere names: 'coming into being and passing away,' . . . 'change of place and alteration of bright color' " (**6.15**). The claim of Parmenides is far more radical, for it denies truth even to change of position or plurality; but Democritus was prepared to make concessions which went far beyond those which Empedocles and Anaxagoras were prepared to make. Neither of these thinkers had been willing to face as radical a break with the world of colors, sounds, and odors as Democritus was prepared to do.

For the consequences were great. It is, after all, sense perception which tells us that the world is full of odors, sounds, and colors. If these are not real, if they exist only "for us," then sense perception clearly does not give us knowledge of what is:

> **10.19** It is necessary to realize that by this principle man is cut off from the real.

> **10.20** And indeed it is evident that it is impossible to know what each thing really is.

> **10.21** In truth we know nothing of anything, but belief is a flowing in upon each of us.

The things which flow in upon us are the streams of atoms which bodies continually emit, and which enter our sense organs and give rise to impressions of color and smell. But the bodies which emit these "effluences" are not themselves colored or odiferous, and in supposing that they are we miss the truth entirely. It is in this sense that man is "cut off from the real" (**10.19**). But it is only with regard to sensation that "it is impossible to know what each thing really is" (**10.20**); through reason the real *can* be known:

> **10.22** There are two forms of knowledge: one legitimate, one bastard. To the bastard sort belong all of the following: sight, hearing, smell, taste, touch. The legitimate is quite distinct from this. When the bastard form cannot see more minutely, nor hear nor smell nor

taste nor perceive through touch, then another, finer form must be
employed.

An example of a situation in which a "finer" form of knowledge is
required may help. Aristotle says that Protagoras, the sophist whose
work is discussed in Chapter Twelve,

> **10.23** ... used to maintain, in his refutation of the geometers, that a
> hoop touches a straight edge not at one point [but at more than
> one].

From this Protagoras concluded that the geometers were mistaken in
thinking that a circle can touch a straight line at only one point. Democritus, who was opposed to Protagoras on a number of points, was
opposed to him on this one also. Of the work which he wrote on the
subject only the title has come down to us: *On Difference of Compre-
hension*, or, *On the Contact of Circle and Sphere*; but the title indicates
pretty clearly the line he took. Protagoras speaks of hoops and straightedges, and of these it is perfectly true to say that they cannot touch at
a point. But the geometer is not talking about hoops and straightedges.
He is talking about circles and straight lines, and these *can* touch at
one point, though the point at which they touch is not visible to the
eye. It is perceived by the mind, which sees that, given the nature of
these objects, they can touch *only* at a point.

We need not take **10.22** to mean that the senses have no place whatever in knowledge. Galen, who quotes it, says that Democritus makes
the senses reply to the reason:

> **10.24** Wretched mind, would you overthrow us, from whom you have
> received your evidence? Our overthrow would be the end of you!

The relation between the two is perhaps implicit in the wording of **10.22**:
sense perception takes us just so far; where it fails, because of the
smallness of the atoms, which renders them invisible, only reason can
penetrate. But for Democritus this means that reason alone can reach
the truth, for the atoms and the void *are* the truth (**10.17**). This is a
major concession to Parmenides. It represents that rationalism which is
but the obverse of the distinction between real properties and names,
and which, along with that distinction, has entered into the framework
of modern science.

Is there any proof that the distinction between real properties and
names is in fact sound? Only this: that it enables us to deal with the

long-standing problem of disagreements arising out of sense perception. Theophrastus stresses this in **10.9** and touches upon it again in **10.12**. The nature of the problem will be evident from the following passages:

> **10.25** They say that to many living creatures the same things appear opposite to the way in which they appear to us, and that even to the same person the same thing will not always appear the same. Which of these appearances is true and which is false is not obvious, for neither is more true than the other, but both are alike. Hence Democritus, at least, says that nothing is true — or that the truth is not evident to us at any rate.

> **10.26** It seems strange to insist that the same thing appears to all who perceive the same things and to question the truth of these appearances, when he has already said that to people in different states different things appear, and that neither is closer to the truth than the other. For it is likely that the better come closer than the worse and the well than the sick, since they are more in accord with reality.

Suppose that a sick man and a well man taste the same honey. To the sick man it appears bitter, to the well man it appears sweet. We are faced with two alternatives: either the honey is both sweet *and* bitter, or it is neither sweet *nor* bitter. But the first of these alternatives is ruled out for us by the law of contradiction; it is impossible that the same thing should be both sweet and not sweet at one and the same time. The second alternative, therefore, must be true:

> **10.27** From the fact that honey appears bitter to some and sweet to others Democritus concluded that it was neither sweet nor bitter in itself, whereas Heraclitus said it was both.

The law of contradiction, as we have seen, held no terrors for Heraclitus; but it is the fulcrum upon which the argument of Democritus turns. Sweet and bitter exist only for the perceiver; in reality there are only atoms and the void.

Still, the atoms which make things taste sweet are of a perfectly determinate sort. They are, in fact, "round and of a good size" (**10.11**). Why, then, do they not arouse the same perceptions in the well man and the sick? The answer is obvious: "men 'alter in make-up' according to age and condition" (**10.9**). This has an influence upon what we perceive; hence it is clear that what appears to a man will, at least in part, depend upon his bodily state. The sick man and the well man are, as these names signify, in different states, and therefore they perceive the same things differently.

There is a sense in which neither appearance is truer than the other, for each man is correctly describing what is happening to *him*; in this sense "both are alike" (10.25). But in another sense, too, they are "both alike"; for each appearance is false when taken for the truth about the object itself. The honey in itself is neither sweet nor bitter: *that* is the truth, though "to us at any rate" it is not evident. For in truth there are only atoms and the void.

THE MOTION OF THE ATOMS

Out of these unpromising materials — "thing" and "no-thing" — Leucippus and Democritus proceeded to construct the world order which they saw about them. According to Leucippus:

> 10.28 The world-orders arise in this way. Many bodies of all sorts of shapes "split off" from the infinite into a great void where, being gathered together, they give rise to a single vortex, in which, colliding and circling in all sorts of ways, they begin to separate apart, like to like. Being unable to circle in equilibrium any longer because of their congestion, the light bodies go off into the outer void like chaff, while the rest "remain together" and, becoming entangled, unite their motions and produce first a spherical structure.
>
> This stands apart like a "membrane," containing in itself all sorts of bodies; and, because of the resistance of the middle, as these revolve the surrounding membrane becomes thin as contiguous bodies continually flow together because of contact with the vortex. And in this way the earth arose, the bodies which were carried to the middle remaining together. Again, the surrounding membrane increases because of the acquisition of bodies from without; and as it moves with the vortex, whatever it touches it adds to itself. Certain of these, becoming entangled, form a structure at first very watery and muddy; but afterward they dry out, being carried about with the rotation of the whole, and ignite to form the substance of the heavenly bodies.

The opening lines of this passage carry us back to the beginnings of Greek thought. The "infinite" from which the atoms which are to form the world order are "split off" is the infinite of Anaximander, the womb of becoming. In this vastness innumerable atoms move perpetually:

> 10.29 Leucippus and Democritus say that the primary bodies move continually in the infinite void.

10.30 They say that there is always motion; but why, and what this motion is, and the cause of it, they do not say.

It is difficult to believe that neither Leucippus nor Democritus said anything about the kind of motion which the atoms have in the void. According to Simplicius,

10.31 They describe the atoms as "tossed about"; and this is not only the primary but the *only* motion they assign to the elements. The other sorts of motion they assign to those bodies which are made up of the elements.

"Tossed about" is ambiguous, but it suggests a back-and-forth, up-and-down motion of the sort familiar to us in the behavior of dust particles suspended in a shaft of sunlight. Anaxagoras had already noticed this phenomenon:

10.32 He says that the air is moved by the sun with a quivering, vibrating motion, as is evident in the tiny dust particles and fragments which are always dancing in the sunlight, which some call "motes."

Democritus too was impressed by it:

10.33 Democritus says that soul is a kind of fire or heat; for the shapes of atoms being infinite, he calls the spherical ones fire and soul, likening them to the so-called "motes" in the air which may be observed in the sunbeams which enter at windows.

Since we have no reason to believe that atoms of different shapes move in different ways, and good evidence for supposing that they do not (10.31), we shall not be far off in thinking of the atoms as moving in the void in the same way. The question *why* they move in this way is one which Aristotle, on the basis of his own philosophy, regards as requiring an answer; but it is unlikely to have occurred to Leucippus at all. Had it done so, he would have answered simply that it is the *nature* of atoms to move in this way.

According to 10.28 a vast swarm of these bodies "split off" from the infinite to form a vortex containing atoms of every sort. Democritus describes the process in very nearly the same words:

10.34 A vortex of all manner of forms is separated off from the whole.

How does this come about? Anaxagoras had answered this question by asserting that "mind controlled the whole rotation, so that it rotated in the beginning" (**9.18**). Democritus would have none of this; in his *Lesser World-System*

> **10.35** He tore to bits Anaxagoras' views on mind and the formation of the world-order.

In their place he offered an account of the creation of the vortex from which the last traces of anthropomorphism had been removed:

> **10.36** There are some who explain this heaven and all the world-orders by chance; for the vortex and the motion that separated and ordered the whole in its present arrangement arises by chance.

The atoms move at random in the void, their movements being combined in an infinite number of possible ways, until at last, in the course of time, they fall by chance into a vortex motion. All that is required is enough time, and Democritus meets this requirement by making time infinite:

> **10.37** Democritus is so convinced that time is everlasting, that when he wants to prove that not everything has come into being he employs as self-evident the principle that time has not come into being.

Sooner or later, then, the atoms must fall into a vortex motion. But the process is the same as that by which (so mathematicians assure us) a chimpanzee chained to a typewriter for a sufficient length of time would produce all the books in the British Museum simply by pounding on the keys at random.

Lucretius puts it very clearly:

> **10.38** Certainly the atoms did not arrange themselves in order by design or intelligence, nor did they propound what movements each should make. But rather myriad atoms, swept along through infinite time or myriad paths by blows and their own weight, have come together in every possible way and tried out every combination that they could possibly create. So it happens that, after roaming the world for aeons of time in making trial of every combination and movement, at length they come together — those atoms whose sudden coincidence often becomes the

origin of mighty things: of earth and sea and sky and the species
of living things.

Once begun, the rotation perpetuates itself, other atoms are drawn into
it, and that sorting process begins which leads eventually to the formation of a world-order.

Leucippus says that the atoms separate "like to like"; "the light bodies
go off into the outer void like chaff" (**10.28**). Democritus, too, compares
the action of the vortex to that of a sieve:

> **10.39** For living things consort with their own kind: doves with doves,
> cranes with cranes, and similarly with other irrational creatures. So
> it is with inanimate things also, as one can observe in the sifting
> of seeds and in pebbles on the beach. For in the one case, by the
> rotation of the sieve beans are ranged separately with beans,
> barley with barley, and wheat with wheat; in the other, by the
> motion of the waves the oval pebbles are driven to the same place
> as the oval, and the round to the round — as if the similarity among
> them exercised some kind of attractive force.

But inanimate things only behave *as if* such a force were at work; in
fact, the only forces at work are those which everywhere in the Ionian
tradition are brought into being by the vortex:

> **10.40** The atoms which were larger and heavier sank down altogether,
> while those which were small and round and smooth and slippery
> were squeezed out in the coming together of the atoms, and car-
> ried aloft.

In the void, of course, there is neither up nor down:

> **10.41** In the infinite void there is neither top, bottom, middle, center,
> or circumference.

But in a vortex "down" means "inwards," towards the center of the
rotation; "up" means "outwards," towards the periphery. In the vortex,
then, the larger and heavier atoms "sink down," impelled by the cen-
tripetal force generated by the rotation toward the center, while the
smaller and lighter bodies are "carried aloft" towards the periphery:

> **10.42** The followers of Democritus suppose that all bodies have
> weight, but that, having less weight, the fire, which is being
> squeezed out by the things going before, is carried upward, and

for this reason *appears* light. They suppose that nothing is without weight, and that this is continually carried towards the center.

Earlier thinkers had treated heavy and light as opposites. They had spoken of them as they spoke of hot and cold or wet and dry; just as some things are hot and others cold, so some are heavy and others light. The atomists appear to have broken with this way of speaking. Nothing is light; all of the atoms have weight; but some, being smaller, are less heavy than others, and so are displaced outwards by the heavier ones. Fire, for example, is not absolutely light; it is only lighter than earth. The atoms of which it is composed, being smaller, rounder, smoother, and more slippery, are "squeezed out" in the coming together of the atoms and "carried aloft" (**10.40**).

THE VORTEX MOTION

Judging from **10.28**, the atomists seem to have paid more attention to what actually happens "in liquids and in air" than their predecessors. In earlier thinkers the rotating mass is treated as though it were a rigid body in which points on the circumference and near the center complete their circuits in the same period. Leucippus, however, speaks of it as if it were a fluid the parts of which are in disequilibrium. The nature of this disequilibrium is unclear, but some light is thrown on it, perhaps, by a passage in which Theophrastus analyzes the causes of dizziness:

> **10.43** The head is by nature moist. When air gets into it and penetrates the moisture, forcing its way toward the blood-vessels, it thrusts the moisture around in a circle. This has the same effect as if one were to move one's head around in a circle deliberately; it makes no difference whether the motion originates from within or without. The motion being like that of a vortex, the moisture does not hold together uniformly but one part lags behind while the other goes ahead. That part which is forming a sediment settles, because it offers resistance, while that which is settling is dragged along by that in which it is sinking, because it is not in equilibrium with it. The result is dizziness and frequent falling down.

The lack of equilibrium between the parts of the fluid would appear to arise from the fact that they are revolving at unequal rates of speed, the heavier parts at the center moving more slowly by virtue of the greater resistance which larger and heavier objects offer to the vortex.

Now the heavenly bodies, which are borne by the vortex, do in fact revolve at different rates, depending upon their distance from the center:

> **10.44** The first explanation which presents itself is that which Democritus' revered authority proposed. He suggested that the nearer the heavenly bodies are to the earth, the less they are caught up in the vortex of the heavens; for the rushing strength of this fierce vortex fades and decreases at a lower level. It is for this reason that the sun gradually falls back to join the later constellations, for its course is much lower than that of the fervent constellations. This is even more true of the moon; for the lower its course falls from the heaven and the nearer it comes to the earth, the less it is able to keep up with the constellations. The more sluggish the vortex in which it is borne, beneath the sun, the more do all the stars overtake it as they are borne past in revolutions. This is why the moon seems to return more swiftly to each constellation — they in fact return to it.

It is because of the "resistance" of the center that the discrepancy arises between the motions of center and circumference.

If a good deal of attention has been given to the vortex it is because its importance for early Greek thought was very great. Its importance lay originally in its explanatory power. From the very beginning it provided an explanation of the large-scale features of the physical world as it appeared to the Ionians. But it proved capable of explaining small-scale phenomena as well. Nowhere is this more apparent than in the Greek medical writers. We have already seen how it was used to explain dizziness; still earlier writers used it to explain the formation of stones in the bladder:

> **10.45** Just as when impure water has been churned up in a cup or in a copper vessel and has settled a salt sediment is formed in the middle, in the same way a sediment is formed in the impure urine in the bladder. And it is not discharged because it lies in the hollow of the bladder and, becoming very compact under the action of the rotation, it does not pass out in making water.

Others used it to explain the formation of the child in the womb (**2.9**); Democritus was to use it to explain respiration (**11.7**). There seemed to be no limit to its usefulness as a principle of explanation, and Anaxagoras had claimed for it all that could possibly be claimed in treating the formation of the world-order and the rise of the arts and sciences as so many stages in a single process of separation in which the vortex was the active agent (**9.24**).

But the vortex came to serve a still more important function for the philosophers of the Ionian tradition. It symbolized for them the operation of impersonal law:

> **10.46** All things come into being by necessity, the cause of the coming into being of all things being the vortex, which Democritus calls "necessity."

What Democritus means by "necessity" is quite clear:

> **10.47** He means by it the resistance, motion, and impact of matter.

The vortex, therefore, exemplifies in the highest degree the working of the laws of motion and impact in the world-order.

To these laws there are no exceptions:

> **10.48** Nothing occurs at random, but everything occurs for a reason and by necessity.

When we ascribe an occurrence to chance we signify not that it has no cause but that we do not know what its cause is:

> **10.49** Some people question whether chance really exists. For nothing, they say, happens by chance, but there is a definite cause, other than chance, for everything which we say happens "spontaneously."

Commenting on this passage, Simplicius says:

> **10.50** This seems to refer to Democritus. For though Democritus appears to make use of chance in the formation of the world-order, when he comes to details he asserts that chance is the cause of nothing . . . .

In itself every event follows rigidly from the laws of motion and impact, and of these the vortex is the very symbol. It has become the guarantor of the natural order, playing in the new age the role formerly played by fate and the gods.

THE PLURALITY OF WORLD-ORDERS

The world-order-to-be is distinguished from the surrounding mass by a membrane similar to that which surrounds the child in the womb and distinguishes it from the mother:

10.51 Leucippus and Democritus envelop the world-order in a membrane or "caul," formed by the entangling of the hooked atoms.

Within this "caul" the sorting process proceeds. The larger and heavier atoms go to the center, where they form the earth — a flat, rotating drum; the lighter and finer atoms are squeezed outwards toward the periphery.

The details of the system need not concern us. There is one feature of it, however, which calls for notice: **10.28** speaks not of one world-order but of more than one.

10.52 The world-orders are infinite in number and of different sizes. In some there is neither sun nor moon; in others they are larger than in ours; and in others there are more of them. And there are some world-orders that are devoid of living creatures or plants or any moisture.

The intervals between the world-orders are unequal; in some places there are more world-orders, in others less. And some are increasing, some are at their height, and some are decreasing; and in some places they are just coming into being and in others failing. They are destroyed by colliding with one another.

The earlier Ionians too had spoken of a plurality of world-orders; but they had thought of them, apparently, as succeeding one another in time. The atomists enlarged upon this idea, and though we do not know what prompted them to do so, the reasoning behind it may perhaps be guessed at from an argument attributed to Democritus' pupil Metrodorus of Chios:

10.53 Metrodorus says that it would be as absurd to suppose that there was only one world-order in the infinite as it would be to suppose that a single cornstalk would grow in a vast plain.

If the whole is infinite in extent, and the atoms are everywhere in motion in it, there is no reason to expect that the chance combinations which lead to the formation of a vortex should not be repeated over and over again.

On the other hand, there is no reason to assume that the process of world-formation will follow exactly the same course in every instance. Anaxagoras had maintained that in *any* world-order there would be men like ourselves, living in cities like our own and practicing the selfsame arts. Democritus evidently thought this picture overdrawn. The general structure of each world-order will be the same: earth, air, fire, and water (if they are present) will occupy their present places in accordance with laws everywhere and always the same. But whether there are two suns or one in a given world-order is a matter of chance. Similarly, the presence of men in a world-order is not necessary. Man has no special claim to being. His existence is contingent upon the blind operation of mechanical forces, and the universe is as indifferent to his birth as to his death.

Indeed, the world-order itself has no greater claim to being:

> **10.54** As the world-order has its coming into being, so also it has its waning, its waning, and its destruction, according to some necessity the nature of which he does not make entirely clear.

We are not completely in the dark, however, about the nature of this necessity, for "necessity" is what Democritus called the vortex (**10.46**). The world-orders may indeed perish by collision, as Hippolytus says (**10.52**), but one may hazard a guess that they would perish in any case from mechanical failure. For the "resistance" of the middle exerts an effect upon the rotation of the whole which must in time dissipate its strength. At a certain moment the atoms, released from the hold of the vortex, must return into the disorderly motion which belongs to them by nature, and the world-order must perish, swallowed up in the eternal night of the infinite as though it had never been.

Only when we see them against the background of this fearful vision can we understand the shocked words with which Hippolytus, himself a Christian bishop, concludes his account of Democritus' philosophy:

> **10.55** This man ridiculed everything — as if all human concerns were absurd!

ELEVEN

Atomism: The Microcosm

The principles which are at work in the world-order at large are at work also in man; for "the living creature is a world-order in miniature" (**3.20**). Like the world-order man is composed of atoms and void, and like the world-order he comes into being not by design but by necessity, through the operation of the vortex.

The separation of the lighter from the heavier atoms does not happen all at once. It is a continuous process. In the words of a medical writer of the period:

11.1 When all things were being whirled about, the greatest part of the warmth was separated off into the proper regions; but much heat was retained in the earth — in some places more, in others less . . . .

This heat continues, even in our own day, to pass outwards toward the periphery, and the effects of its passage are visible:

11.2 Why is it that flat pieces of iron or lead float on water, whereas other things that are smaller and less heavy sink if they are round or elongated, like a needle? Also, why is it that certain bodies float on account of their smallness, such as motes and other earthy, dust-like particles in air? It cannot be right to suppose that the cause of all these is what Democritus says it is. For he says that heat particles, rising from the water, bear up those heavy bodies which are flat, whereas the narrower ones fall through because the particles opposing them are few in number.

But this ought to happen even more in air, as he himself points out, and the answer which he gives to his own objection is feeble. For he says that the "surge" — "surge" being the name he gives to the motion of the bodies which are borne upwards — does not move in a straight line.

That is to say, the heat particles do not always rise straight upwards through air as they do through water, but are deflected by the movements of the air itself. It is this "surge" which accounts for the ongoing process of evaporation which we see taking place from the surface of the sea:

> **11.3** We observe vapors and heat surging up from every river and even from the earth itself. They, like exhaled breath, have been squeezed out from here and are borne on high, and suffuse the sky with their own mist, and produce the high clouds by their gradual coming together.

We can see from this that even now much heat remains in the earth. But in the beginning there was very much more heat in it than there is now, and the surface of the earth was covered with warm mud. In this the first animals arose:

> **11.4** Democritus says that at first living creatures came into being without articulated forms, the moisture being productive of life.

Among these living creatures were men:

> **11.5** Democritus believed that at first men were begotten from water and slime.

> **11.6** He thought that they emerged from the ground like worms, without a maker and for no reason.

But the vortex not only brings man into being; it also threatens to destroy him. For the pressure of the surrounding air threatens, literally, to squeeze the life out of him:

> **11.7** Democritus says that breathing serves a certain purpose in animals that breathe. He says that it prevents the soul from being squeezed out. He does not say, however, that nature has brought

this about for that purpose; for in general, like the other philosophers of nature, he does not touch upon this sort of cause. He says that the soul and the hot are the same, these being the primary shapes among the spherical atoms. When these are packed together by the pressure of the surrounding air, then, he says, inhalation takes place to relieve them. For in air there are a large number of these bodies which he calls mind and soul. During inhalation, then, these enter with the air and check the pressure, thus preventing the soul in living creatures from passing out. Life and death, therefore, depend upon inhalation and exhalation. For when the surrounding pressure gets the upper hand, and the air outside is no longer able to enter and check it, then, since inhalation is impossible, death supervenes in living creatures. For death is the passing out of shapes of this sort from the body through the pressure of the surrounding air.

The weight of the atmosphere, pressing in upon the center, continually threatens to displace the lighter atoms which animate the body. Only by drawing breath can these be replenished in the body. Only, in short, by continual effort can man renew from moment to moment his precarious hold on life.

THE RISE OF CIVILIZATION

This struggle to keep body and soul together, to survive in the face of a hostile environment, is reflected in the whole history of man:

11.8   The first men to be born, they say, led an undisciplined and bestial life, setting out one by one to secure their sustenance and taking for their food both the tenderest herbs and the fruits of wild trees. Then, since they were attacked by the wild beasts, they came to each other's aid, being instructed by expediency, and when gathered together in this way by reason of their fear, they gradually came to recognize their mutual characteristics. And though the sounds which they made were at first unintelligible and indistinct, yet gradually they came to give articulation to their speech, and by agreeing with one another upon symbols for each thing which presented itself to them, made known among themselves the significance which was to be attached to each term. But since groups of this kind arose over every part of the inhabited world, not all men had the same language, inasmuch as every group organized the elements of its speech by mere chance. This is the explanation of the present existence of every conceivable kind of language, and, furthermore, out of these first groups to be formed came all the original nations of the world.

Now the first men, since none of the things useful for life had yet been discovered, led a wretched existence, having no clothing to cover them, knowing not the use of dwelling and fire, and also being totally ignorant of cultivated food. For since they were ignorant of the harvesting of the wild food, they laid by no store of its fruits against their needs; consequently large numbers of them perished in the winters because of the cold and the lack of food. Little by little, however, experience taught them both to take to the caves in winter and to store such fruits as could be preserved. And when they had become acquainted with fire and other useful things, the arts also and whatever else is capable of furthering man's social life were gradually discovered. Indeed, speaking generally, in all things it was necessity itself that became man's teacher, supplying in appropriate fashion instruction in every matter to a creature which was well endowed by nature and had, as its assistants for every purpose, hands and speech and sagacity of mind.

The lives of the first men were, in Hobbes's famous phrase, "solitary, poor, nasty, brutish, and short"; for they were the prey of animals swifter and stronger than themselves. It was fear of these that brought men together in the first instance. But having banded together, success taught them the value of cooperation. So it was with language: at first men made sounds at random; but as they came by degrees to realize the usefulness of such sounds in communicating with one another, the significance of words came to be fixed by agreement, and in this way the diversity of languages to be found among the different peoples of the earth arose.

Even so, men had as yet no settled mode of existence. They wandered from place to place, living off the land, and were at the mercy of cold and famine. Only gradually did they learn to use fire and to supplement their slender resources with means of their own contrivance. The mule, for example, was bred by men to plow the land:

11.9   For the mule is not a product of nature, but this craftily invented device is a figment of man's thought — a daring deed of adultery, as it were. It seems to me, Democritus says, that an ass forcibly impregnated a mare by chance, and when men found out about the offspring of this rape they made a practice of breeding such offspring.

11.10   In the most important things we are the pupils of the animals: of the spiders in spinning and mending, of the swallow in building houses, of the swan and the nightingale in singing, through imitation.

Sometimes men have hit upon the means of survival by chance. But chance cannot be relied upon:

> **11.11**   Luck is a giver of great gifts, but uncertain; nature is self-suffi-cient. Therefore by a lesser and certain means it overcomes the greater gift of hope.

> **11.12**   Men have made of luck a phantom — a pretext for their own folly. For rarely does luck conflict with intelligence, and most things in life can be set straight by a quick wit and sharp insight.

Man must rely upon what is given to him by nature, and in intelligence he possesses an instrument which enables him to impose upon his environment an order of his own making. The order which he creates does not infringe upon the order of nature; it supplements it. For man is himself a part of nature, and his capacity to create order is but a reflection of hers.

At the same time, the exercise of this capacity brings about changes in man himself. For as he learns, his capacity for thought is increased:

> **11.13**   Nature and teaching are very similar; for teaching transforms a man, and in transforming him makes his nature.

This transformation is not figurative but literal. Each discovery man makes changes his mode of life; but every change in his mode of life brings about a corresponding change in the configuration of the atoms of which he is constituted. Such changes, as we have already seen, affect the way he sees things and thinks about them (**10.9**), and so affect his power to act, to exercise the capabilities which are native to him. Thus, through the use of his capacity to impose order upon his environment, man makes himself. The gap between himself and the other animals, at first nonexistent, widens with every step he takes.

THE NATURE OF HAPPINESS

But the process is a slow one; it takes place "little by little," as **11.8** emphasizes again and again. For a long time men were wholly pre-occupied with the problem of survival. The securing of the necessities of life — food, shelter, protection against wild beasts — left him no time for the pursuits of leisure. Only when these basic wants were satisfied did music, the youngest of the arts, come into existence:

> **11.14**   For it did not separate off by necessity, but came into being from the existing abundance.

Abundance brought with it something else, too: a new conception of human existence — one which placed the goal of that existence not in survival as such but in the achievement of something to which survival is only a means, human happiness. Democritus has a fully worked out theory of the nature of human happiness. It is grounded firmly in his conception of human nature, and it is expressed in language which at every point makes the connection between the two clear:

> **11.15**   It is best for man to spend his life with as much equanimity and as little distress as possible. This would happen if a man did not base his pleasures on mortal things.

> **11.16**   Equanimity comes to men through proportionate pleasure and moderation in life. Excesses and defects are apt to change and cause great disturbances in the soul. Those souls which are moved over great distances have neither stability nor equanimity.

To be happy is to possess a soul unshaken by passion; for all violent emotions throw the soul into a state of turmoil in which equanimity is shattered. To speak of throwing the soul into turmoil is not to use metaphor but to describe quite literally what happens to the atoms which make up the soul. Their order and arrangement is so altered by violent movement that a man whose soul is in such a state is literally not himself.

The origins of this conception lie in Greek medicine. Health, as we have seen, depends upon a balance of contending forces. When excess or lack of moisture or dryness or heat or cold upsets this balance, the patient falls ill. But this disturbance is not limited to the body. Insofar as the condition of the body influences thought and feeling, the latter is equally affected. A medical writer of the period makes this point very well in a discussion of epilepsy:

> **11.17**   Men ought to know that pleasures, joys, laughter, and amusements, as well as pains, griefs, anxieties, and tears, arise from the brain and from nowhere else. It is by means of the brain specifically that we think, see, hear, and tell the difference between what is ugly and what is beautiful, what is evil and what is good, and what is pleasant and what is unpleasant — distinguishing them sometimes on the basis of convention, sometimes on that of expediency. It is the brain, again, that is the seat of madness and

delirium, that produces in us terrors and fears (not only by night but by day as well), brings insomnia, wandering of mind, thoughts that refuse to come, absent-mindedness, and eccentric behavior. All of these affections arise from the brain when it is in an unhealthy state — when it is abnormally hot or cold or wet or dry, or suffers from any other abnormal condition. Madness is caused by excess of moisture; for when the brain is abnormally moist it necessarily becomes agitated, and when it is agitated neither the sight nor the hearing is steady, but we see first one thing then another, and the tongue gives utterance to whatever is seen or heard at the moment. But so long as the brain is still, a man is of sound mind.

Democritus, who also wrote on medicine, shared these views:

11.18 Concerning thought he says simply that it arises "when the soul is mixed in due proportion." But if one becomes excessively hot or excessively cold, then thinking is changed, he says. It was for some such reason that the ancients, too, rightly regarded such a person as "out of his mind." So it is evident that he made thinking dependent upon the mixture of the body — which is perhaps reasonable enough in one who makes the soul a body.

The view expressed here is not at all original; we have met with it in earlier thinkers, and indeed it may go back, as Democritus suggested, to Homer. But in the hands of Democritus it is made to serve as a basis for a general theory of well-being:

11.19 Disease occurs in a household, or in a life, just as it does in a body.

In this sentence Democritus uses the ordinary word for disease, but it is clear that he is not using it in its ordinary sense. Normally it is used to refer to an unhealthy state of body or (less usually) to an unhealthy state of mind, such as madness. But here it can mean neither of these things; it can only refer to that form of distress in a household which results from conflict between its members, and to the still more important form of distress which a man suffers as a result of the same kind of conflict in himself.

Soul and Body

Such distress can be treated only by a science which deals with the soul as medicine deals with the body:

11.20 Medicine cures the diseases of the body; wisdom, on the other hand, relieves the soul of its sufferings.

As a means to happiness such wisdom is more valuable than the knowledge of the physician; for

11.21 Happiness and unhappiness belong to the soul.

11.22 It is more fitting that men should give an account of the soul than of the body. For the perfection of the soul corrects the imperfection of the body, while bodily strength without reasoning in no way improves the soul.

The basis for this last claim lies in the nature of man. For it is the soul that supplies movement and life to the body:

11.23 Some say that the soul moves the body housing it as it is moved itself. This is the view of Democritus, who talks as Philippus, the producer of comedies, does when he says that Daedalus made his wooden statue of Aphrodite move by pouring quicksilver into it! Democritus, too, speaks in the same way; for he says that spherical atoms move because it is their nature never to be still, and that as they move they draw the whole body along with them, and set it in motion.

These spherical atoms, as we have seen, constitute the soul (**11.7**). It is their "nature" to move simply because they are round; for, being round,

11.24 They are the most mobile, because they offer the fewest points of contact and are the least stable.

Hence they penetrate everywhere, setting the whole body in motion.

It follows that the soul is the agent in every bodily act, and is therefore responsible for that act:

11.25 If the body were to bring suit against the soul for all the pain and suffering it had endured during life, and were judge of its own case, it would condemn the soul with pleasure for destroying some parts of the body through neglect and debauching them through drunkenness, and for corrupting others and dissipating them in the pursuit of pleasure — just as it would blame the man who used without due care some tool or implement which was in poor condition.

11.26 What the body needs can be supplied generously without hardship or distress. The things which require hardship and distress and make life disagreeable are desired not by the body but by an illconstituted mind.

This appears very clearly when we compare the behavior of men with that of animals:

11.27 The needy animal knows how much it needs; but the needy man does not.

He does not know when to stop but always wants more, and so defeats his own purpose:

11.28 The desire for material possessions, if it is not limited by repletion, is far more unpleasant than extreme poverty. For the greater the desires, the greater the needs they create.

The moral is clear:

11.29 If one oversteps due measure, the most pleasant things become the most unpleasant.

Whereas

11.30 Moderation increases enjoyment, and makes pleasure even greater.

The injunction to observe moderation in all things is a familiar one; it is rooted, as we saw, in the traditional view of man's relation to the gods. To "lust after more" is to forget one's mortality, to bring down upon oneself the jealousy of the gods, which is death. Democritus enjoins moderation and the avoidance of excess for quite a different reason. It is not from fear of the gods that the wise man chooses moderation, but from fear of pain; so much is evident from **11.29**. To choose wisely is to look to the pleasureableness or painfulness of the consequences:

11.31 The landmark of what is beneficial and what is not beneficial is pleasure or displeasure.

A course of action is beneficial, then, if it produces pleasure. On the other hand, Democritus implies that not every pleasure is beneficial:

11.32 Accept no pleasure unless it be beneficial to you.

Do these two assertions not conflict? Not if we consider that for Democritus happiness lies in the maintenance of a certain condition in the soul. Whatever leads to the maintenance of this condition is beneficial. Pleasure is a *sign* to us that this condition exists in the soul; this is the meaning of **11.31**. In **11.32**, on the other hand, we are faced with a choice between actions which are *supposed* to be pleasurable but which may not be; for they may not promote that condition of the soul which we experience as pleasure.

The fact is that men's constitutions differ, and that what gives them pleasure varies with the individual:

11.33 For all men "good" and "true" are the same; but "pleasant" is different for different people.

What *is* the same for all men is that stable condition of the soul which is the source of happiness (**11.16**).

The wise man, then, will choose his pleasures with care; for equanimity comes to men through moderation in life:

11.34 Therefore one ought to pay attention to those things which are attainable, and be satisfied with what one has, paying little heed to objects of envy and wonder, and not letting one's thoughts dwell on them. One should consider rather the lives of those who suffer hardship, being mindful of what they suffer, in order that what one has may seem great and enviable, and the soul may not suffer some misfortune through over-covetousness.

To live otherwise is to court disaster:

11.35 It is not to live badly but to be a long time dying.

THE EDUCATION OF THE YOUNG

In fragment after fragment the importance of moderation is driven home:

11.36 Men pray to the gods for health; but they do not realize that they have this power in themselves. Through want of self-control they do the opposite, and betray their health to their desires.

11.37 It is hard to fight with desire; but to overcome it is the mark of a rational man.

11.38 It is childish, not manly, to have immoderate desires.

It is childish not merely in the sense that the child lacks self-control but in the sense that he does not know any better:

11.39 The cause of going wrong is ignorance of the better.

Hence the importance which Democritus attaches to education:

11.40 An imperturbable wisdom is worth everything.

But

11.41 Neither skill nor wisdom is attainable unless one learns.

11.42 Time does not teach us to be wise, but a proper upbringing and nature.

11.43 More men become good by training than by nature.

For teaching, Democritus is convinced, has the power to transform a man (**11.13**); how much more so a child:

11.44 It is possible without great expense to train children, and to place around their property and persons a wall of safety.

"Without great expense" because the required training may be given in the home by the parents. It is from them, in any case, that the child will learn:

11.45 The moderation of the father is the greatest example to his children.

11.46 The children of thrifty men, if they are left ignorant, are like sword dancers. If, when they come down, they miss the one spot where they must land, they are destroyed; and it is hard to hit the one spot, for in the space left there is only room for the feet. So it is with these children. If they fail to have impressed upon them their father's care and thrift, they are apt to be corrupted.

It is well, too, for the children to learn the importance of hard work. For education is not enough; if you would succeed, then, in Hesiod's words, you must "work unceasingly" (**1.20**):

11.47 The good things of life are produced by learning with hard work; the bad are reaped of their own accord, without hard work.

11.48 All toil is pleasanter than idleness when men succeed in acquiring the things for which they labor, or have some assurance of doing so. But in every failure to acquire one's object, the hard work is insufferable and wretched.

In any case it must be done, and the better the spirit in which it is done, the more easily it will go:

11.49 Hard work that is undertaken willingly is easier to bear than that which is done unwillingly.

There is consolation, too, in the fact that

11.50 Continual hard work becomes easier to bear through habituation.

It is important, therefore, to accustom children to work:

11.51 The worst thing of all is indulgence in the education of the young. For it is this which produces those pleasures from which evil arises.

11.52 Children who are relieved from hard work would not learn their letters, nor music, nor gymnastic, nor that sense of shame which is particularly productive of virtue. For it is from these especially that a sense of shame is wont to come.

DEMOCRITUS AND HESIOD

Not only in his attitude toward work but in other respects too, Democritus reminds us of Hesiod. His morality is prudential, marked by the sort of advice that we find in *Works and Days:*

11.53 Do not be suspicious of everybody; but be canny, and on the safe side.

11.54 Accept favors with the foreknowledge that you will have to give more in return for them.

11.55 When doing a favor, consider the recipient first, lest he prove false and repay good with evil.

11.56 Small favors, done at the right time, mean most to the recipients.

There is a certain coldness in this calculating shrewdness which comes out clearly in what Democritus has to say about children:

11.57 Men think that they must have children because it is natural to do so, and because it is an institution of long standing. This is quite clear with the other animals, too; for all have offspring according to nature, not because there is any profit in it. But once they are born they work hard and care for each of them as best they can, and fear for them while they are small; and if anything happens to them, they look after them. Such is the nature of everything that has a soul. But among men it has come to be felt that the parents should derive some benefit from their children.

Judged from this point of view, the game is not worth the candle:

11.58 I do not think that one ought to have children. For I can see that in having children there are many great dangers on the one hand, and many griefs, while on the other the advantages are few, and these are slight and weak.

11.59 A man who wants children would, I think, do better to get one from friends. The child will then be the sort he wants, for he can choose as he wishes. And the one that seems suitable will be most likely to realize his natural endowment. The great difference is that in this way it is possible to choose according to one's mind from many, whereas, if one begets his own children, there are many dangers involved; for he must live with whomever he begets.

There is little room for impulse in this morality. The prudent man counts the cost too closely. Nor, for that matter, is there much room for the older, warlike virtues which appear in the *Iliad*. Achilles is not a prudent man; on the contrary, he cares nothing for prudence and everything for honor, a thing which finds little place in Democritus' view of the good life. Even courage, the least expendable of the warlike virtues, is transformed into something quite different in Democritus' hands:

> 11.60 The brave man is he who overcomes not only his enemies but his pleasures. There are some men who are masters of cities but slaves to women.

> 11.61 To be ruled by a woman is the ultimate disgrace for a man.

The morality of Democritus is, in fact, the old peasant morality of Hesiod, raised to a new level by being grounded in a more general conception of human nature. In this respect it invites comparison with the less fully worked-out morality of Heraclitus. Both represent attempts to base a theory of the good life upon the nature of things, and so to provide it with an unshakable footing. In both, reason plays the central role. Yet there is no mistaking the difference between the two men, and this difference is not due merely to differences in their conception of the nature of things; in part it is due to the ambiguity of the word "reason." For Heraclitus reason is embedded in the very nature of things; it is only reflected in man because man is himself a part of nature. But Democritus does not view reason as embedded in nature; it is peculiar to man — a possession which at the same time sets him apart from nature and enables him to control it for his own ends.

Democritus and Pythagoras

There are, however, hints in Democritus of a larger conception of human life. The wisdom of the prudent man is of a practical nature; it is a wisdom of getting and spending. It does not look beyond "the good things of life," as that phrase is usually understood, but is directed toward the satisfaction which a moderate enjoyment of them brings.

But in **11.15** Democritus intimates that so long as a man bases his pleasures on "mortal things" equanimity is impossible in the long run. The reason for this will be clear from the following fragment:

11.62   Those who derive their pleasures from their bellies — overstepping due measure in eating or drinking or making love — find that they are brief and only last as long as they are eating and drinking, whereas the pains are many. They have a perpetual desire for the same things, and once men get what they desire the pleasure passes quickly, and there is nothing good in them but a brief enjoyment and then they want the same things again.

Now this remains true whether the element of excess is present or not. The transience of such pleasures lies in their very nature. To base one's life upon them is to build upon sand, for the pleasures of the body do not last. The wise man, seeing this, will seek his happiness in the pleasures of the soul:

11.63   The man who chooses the good of the soul makes a more divine choice; he who chooses the good of the body makes a mortal choice.

In such a man

11.64   Reason accustoms itself to derive pleasure from itself.

And of such pleasures the purest are those of inquiry:

11.65   I would rather discover a single cause than become king of the Persians.

For kingdoms perish, and the memory even of great deeds fades at last, but the laws of motion and impact remain, and to seek the truth about these things is to seek one's pleasure not in mortal things but in that which endures forever. The man who seeks his happiness in such things escapes the narrow confines of the here and now:

11.66   The whole world lies open to a wise man. For the native land of a good soul is the whole world-order.

It was, perhaps, this strain in his nature that drew Democritus to Pythagoras:

11.67 "He seems," says Thrasyllus, "to have been an admirer of the Pythagoreans. He even mentions Pythagoras himself, praising him in a work named after him. He seems to have gotten all his ideas from Pythagoras, and might be thought his pupil if chronology did not conflict with it." Glaucus of Rhegium, at any rate, says that he was a pupil of one of the Pythagoreans; and Glaucon was his contemporary. Apollodorus of Cyzicus says that he was an associate of Philolaus.

The stories may well be true. It is not difficult to see in the atoms of Democritus the units out of which the Pythagoreans attempted to construct the cosmos, endowed at last with those physical properties the want of which gave Aristotle such concern (**4.31**). But the similarities go deeper. Democritus repeatedly refers to the body as a "tent," a kind of temporary habitation for the soul. In **11.25** he likens it to a tool or implement which the soul uses for good or ill, and again and again the fragments suggest that he holds it of small account in itself:

11.68 In cattle excellence is displayed in strength of body; but in men it lies in strength of character.

11.69 Beauty of body is merely animal unless intelligence is present.

11.70 Men are not happy by virtue of their bodies or their possessions, but by virtue of right living and fullness of understanding.

"He who chooses the good of the soul makes a more divine choice" (**11.63**); yet the soul is not itself divine, and here the break with Pythagoreanism is clean. It cannot be divine, for it is not indestructible. When the living thing is no longer able to draw breath, the soul atoms are squeezed out and scattered abroad, and this is the end. The soul does not survive the body, and there is no life after death.

11.71 Some men, not understanding the dissolution of mortal nature, but conscious of the sufferings of life, are troubled while they live by anxieties and fears, inventing false stories of a time after death.

But this is absurd:

11.72 They are fools who hate life yet wish to go on living through fear of the unknown.

Their fears are in fact groundless, and the man who has once grasped this ceases to be oppressed by them. For as long as a man lives with anxiety and fears, he cannot achieve that equanimity of soul in which happiness lies, and reason alone is capable of exorcising them:

11.73   Cast out by reason ungoverned grief from your benumbed soul!

A clear view of the nature of things teaches us that atoms and the void alone exist, that the body feels only so long as it is animated by the soul, and that the soul is utterly dissolved at death. To achieve this understanding is to be released from fears and anxieties, and to possess a soul untroubled by phantoms.

THE CITY

We have been concerned, up to now, with the happiness of the individual. "To spend one's life with as much equanimity and as little distress as possible" is a goal suitable only for the individual. But man is a social animal, an animal to whom it has become second nature to live with his kind. A theory of the good life which took no cognizance of this fact would be unreal.

Moreover, the framework within which men live together and pursue their happiness is provided by the city. Upon the well-being of the city the well-being of all depends, and Democritus was very much aware of this:

11.74   One must consider above all else how the affairs of the city can best be managed, neither being desirous of honor beyond what is fitting nor setting up power for oneself against the best interests of the commonweal. For a well-run city provides the greatest guidance, and in it everything is contained. When it is secure, everything is secure; when it perishes, everything perishes.

11.75   Public distress is harder to bear than private distress; for there is no shred of hope of assistance.

In the city men find their security. When it breaks down, there is nowhere else to turn. There is nothing to do but revert to the anarchy in which the first men lived like animals. Hence Democritus' concern with *stasis* — that civil strife between rich and poor that increasingly threatened the security of the Greek city during the fifth century B.C.:

11.76 Civil strife is bad for both parties. For both the conquerors and the conquered alike the result is destruction.

11.77 It is only possible to produce great deeds, even wars among cities, through concord; otherwise it is impossible.

11.78 When the powerful have the courage to lend money to the have-nots, and assist them and do them favors, then compassion is present in their actions, and instead of being destitute they become their friends and help one another, and are in concord with their fellow citizens; and other good things happen which nobody could possibly catalogue.

Unless this happens, the have-nots may place themselves in the hands of a tyrant, hoping by this means to secure by force what those who have will not give willingly. This would be bad enough:

11.79 Poverty in a democracy is as preferable to what the ruling class calls happiness as freedom is to slavery.

But the collapse of the city would be worse still. For the alternative to it is savagery.

This explains the severity of Democritus' attitude towards those who by their actions threaten the security of the city:

11.80 Where animals are concerned, the rule for deciding whether to kill them or not is as follows: the man who kills those that do wrong, or intend to do so, is guiltless. And to do so is more conducive to well-being than not to.

11.81 As has been proposed regarding creatures and creeping things that are hostile, so I think we ought to act concerning men. To kill an enemy is in accord with ancestral custom in every society in which the law does not forbid it. But in every society there are native religious rites and treaties and oaths which prevent this.

Democritus is thinking of those who escape the consequences of their actions by taking sanctuary, as Orestes did after the murder of his mother. This is not right:

11.82 Those who do something which deserves exile or imprisonment or condemnation should *be* condemned, not acquitted. Whoever acquits against the law, deciding on the basis of gain or pleasure, acts unjustly; and this is bound to be on his conscience.

Membership in a city requires a man to live, not as he sees fit, but in obedience to the laws:

11.83 The laws would not prevent each man from living according to his own inclination if men did not injure one another. For envy provides the starting point for civil strife.

11.84 He who admires those who are well-off and are called happy by other men, and dwells upon them in his mind at all hours, is compelled continually to try something new and to attempt, through desire, to do something desperate which the laws prohibit.

It is impossible for such a man to be happy. For even if he succeeds temporarily, the possibility of being found out and punished by the magistrates hangs over his head like a sword:

11.85 The glory that results from justice is confidence of mind and imperturbability; but the fear that results from injustice is the limit of disaster.

11.86 The equable man, who is prone to do what is just and lawful, rejoices by day and night and is strong and carefree; but the man who cares nothing for justice and does not do as he ought to do — to him all such things are displeasing whenever he remembers one of them, and he is afraid and abuses himself.

The Just and the Unjust Man

The just man has nothing to fear; the unjust man has everything to fear. Yet as **11.84** shows, the fear of punishment alone is not sufficient to restrain the unjust man. For

11.87 Violent desires for one thing blind the soul to all others.

His greed makes him discount the risk involved, and leads him to hope that he will not be detected in wrongdoing. Some other way, then, must be found of dealing with such a man, and this is through the appeal to reason:

> **11.88** That man seems more effective in promoting virtue who employs exhortation and verbal persuasion than he who relies on law and compulsion. For it is likely that a man who is prevented from injustice by law will do wrong secretly; but it is not likely that a man who is led by persuasion to do what he ought will do anything disastrous, either secretly or openly. Wherefore, one who acts rightly through intelligence and understanding becomes courageous and at the same time upright.

If a man can be brought to see that it is to his own advantage to obey the laws, since by doing so he preserves the city and thereby the conditions under which alone happiness can be sought, then he will obey it freely. Such men alone are virtuous:

> **11.89** Good consists not in not doing wrong, but in not even wanting to do wrong.

The good man fears not so much the condemnation of his fellow men as the judgment of his own conscience:

> **11.90** One ought not to respect other men more than oneself, nor to harm them more than oneself, whether no one will know about it or everybody will. But one ought especially to respect oneself, and to set this up as a law in one's soul so as to do nothing which is unfitting.

To disobey this law is to invite a punishment more terrible than any that can be imposed by one's fellow men. For it is always possible to regard the judgment of others as unfair; but one's judgment upon oneself is inescapable. For when a man does something wrong "this is bound to be on his conscience" (**11.82**). Hence the wretchedness of the wrongdoer:

> **11.91** He who does wrong is more wretched than he who is wronged.

It is now clear why Democritus regards the sense of shame as "particularly productive of virtue" (**11.52**), and why he insists so strongly upon the importance of instilling it in the young. Other writers, too, stress the importance of a sense of shame; but they mean by it that respect for the opinion of others which prevents a man from doing what will appear base in their eyes. Democritus means by it the respect due to oneself. The sense of shame before others is less important than the sense of shame which a man feels at having done what he himself knows to be wrong. For what he has done "is bound to be on his conscience," and it can be wiped out only through repentance:

11.92   Repentance for wrongdoing is the saving grace of life.

The child who has learned self-respect will possess the key to happiness:

11.93   Those whose demeanor is well-ordered have a well-ordered life.

And this being so, he will freely obey the law; for

11.94   Respect for order yields to the ruler and the wiser man.

In this way Democritus appears to bridge the gap between the well-being of the individual and the well-being of the city. Far from finding that his happiness conflicts with the demands of justice, which require him to live in accordance with the laws, contrary to his inclinations (**11.83**), he finds that his happiness can only be found within the city. For the city equally restrains others from destroying him in the pursuit of their own well-being.

Conflicts of Interest

Yet there is a certain ambiguity in Democritus' system, and it is one of great significance for political theory. It concerns the nature of law itself.

To begin with, Democritus views all laws as man-made. Justice is not something which Zeus has given to men, as Hesiod teaches; it is something men have invented for themselves, and to that extent it is purely adventitious. When Democritus wishes to contrast those qualities of bodies which exist in nature with those which exist only for us, he does so by saying that the former are real whereas the latter exist only by convention. The distinction is clearly an invidious one; it implies that law is not grounded in the nature of things directly, but is made for a specific purpose, and is therefore justified only insofar as it fulfills this purpose:

11.95 The law wants to benefit the life of men; it achieves its end when men want to be benefited by it. When they obey it, it reveals its own virtue.

The individual who obeys the law does so because he is persuaded that it is to his benefit to do so. He sees clearly that if he disobeys the laws and preys on others, others in turn will prey upon him. The law that governs "fish, flesh, and fowl" will govern men, and the weak will go to the wall, to be devoured by the stronger.

How one looks upon this situation, however, is affected by whether one is strong or weak. The strong man might argue that it is only the weak who are benefited by the law. For in protecting the weak the city deprives the strong of their natural prey; consequently its legal provisions, far from benefiting the strong, hamper them at every turn. The strong man who realizes this has lost all reason for obeying the laws except fear of punishment, which, as we have seen, is admittedly inadequate (**11.84**). Indeed, such a man has good reason for *not* obeying the laws, namely, the same reason which makes the weak obey them: self-interest. For every individual pursues what is advantageous to himself.

Democritus acknowledges as much in **11.81**. In this fragment the city is caught between two conflicting claims. On the one hand there is the claim of self-interest, in accordance with which an enemy of the city (and all who break the laws are enemies of the city) must be exiled or put to death. On the other hand there are the "religious rites and treaties and oaths" which prevent this. Faced with this dilemma, what is the city to do? Democritus' own answer is clear: malefactors must be punished; the city's first duty is to itself. It must obey ancestral custom — not because it is ancient but because it is the means by which the city, originally as now, preserves itself in being.

It is obvious that the individual may at any time find himself confronted by the same dilemma. Self-interest may dictate a line of action directly contrary to what is permitted by usage or law; and where this is the the case it is difficult to see why, on Democritus' principles, the bypassing of the law, if it could be done with impunity, could not be justified. Democritus himself would have drawn back from this conclusion; so much is certain. But there were those among his contemporaries who were willing to follow the argument wherever it led, without regard to consequences, and to these we must now turn.

PART FOUR

THE UNSEATING

OF ZEUS

Protagoras, Antiphon, and Callicles

Reaction

TWELVE

Protagoras, Antiphon, and Callicles

During the course of the sixth and fifth centuries B.C. the life of the Greek city had been undergoing a profound transformation. A struggle for power had been going on which, in city after city, led to the emergence of new, democratic forms of government. Through revolution and constitutional reform "the many" had come to power, and this change brought others in its train. For the values in terms of which the old ruling class had justified their power did not justify the power of the new. Before they could do this, these values had to be reinterpreted.

We can see this process at work in the transformation of the word *aretē*. The word means "excellence"; the *aretē* of a man is that quality in him which makes him deserving of honor and respect. The *aretē* of a member of the old ruling class was associated with his wealth and family connections; these by themselves brought him influence in affairs of state. Under the democracy all this was changed; power was awarded not on the basis of birth but on the basis of a certain kind of ability. The *aretē* of the new democratic leader lay in the fact that he understood how to persuade the many that it was in their interests to pursue certain policies. This called for skill in speaking; indeed, the possession of this skill became the key to political success. Many sought it, and inevitably men appeared who professed to be able to teach it for a fee. These were the sophists.

239

The Sophists

In his *Protagoras*, Plato gives us a mocking portrait of three of the sophists gathered at the house of the wealthy Callias. When we were inside, says Socrates, recalling the scene,

12.1 We came upon Protagoras walking in the portico, with Callias the son of Hipponicus, his stepbrother Paralus the son of Pericles, and Charmides son of Glaucon on one side, and on the other Pericles' other son Xanthippus, Philippides the son of Philomelus, and Antimoerus of Mende, the most eminent of Protagoras' pupils, who is studying with him professionally with a view to becoming a sophist. Those who brought up the rear, listening to what was said, seemed to be foreigners for the most part whom Protagoras had picked up in various cities — he charming them with his voice, like Orpheus; they following, enchanted — but there were some Athenians dancing attendance as well. I was delighted to see how careful they were not to get in front of Protagoras; whenever he and those with him turned back, the group of listeners parted, some to one side, some to the other, in perfect order, and wheeling about came together again behind him. It was beautifully done.

"And after him I marked," as Homer says, Hippias of Elis, enthroned in the portico opposite; and sitting around him on benches Eryximachus, the son of Acumenus, Phaedrus of Myrrhinous, Andron the son of Androtion, some foreigners (fellow citizens of Hippias) and others. They appeared to be asking Hippias questions about nature and the heavenly bodies, while he, *ex cathedra*, replied to them and held forth on the subjects they inquired about.

"And there, too, did I descry Tantalus" — for as you know, Prodicus of Ceos is in town. He was in a room which Hipponicus used to use for storage, but which Callias had cleaned out to make room for all the people staying in the house and made into a bedroom. Well, Prodicus was still in bed, bundled up in blankets and rugs — of which there seemed to be a great heap — and near him, on the beds close by, lay Pausanias of the deme of Cerameis, and with Pausanias a boy still young — of good breeding I should say, and certainly very good-looking. I think I heard that his name is Agathon, and I should not be surprised to learn that he is Pausanias' favorite. Well, there were this boy and the two Adeimantuses — the son of Cepis and the son of Leucolophides — and others too. But what they were talking about I was unable to hear from outside, though I was longing to hear Prodicus, who seems to me a man of more than human sagacity. But his deep voice made a booming noise in the room which made his words inaudible.

Though it is scarcely daylight, the great men are already surrounded by an admiring crowd of young men. Prodicus of Ceos teaches rhetoric; he is an expert at drawing distinctions. Hippias is an expert on everything, from mathematics to mnemonics; for a fee he is willing to teach all of them, including rhetoric. Plato treats him here, as in the dialogues named after him, with scarcely veiled irony. But Protagoras is another matter. The oldest of the assembled sophists, he is accorded in this dialogue a respect which is surprising in Plato, who had no love for sophists.

Protagoras of Abdera

Protagoras, like Democritus, was a native of Abdera. Born early in the fifth century B.C., he spent more than forty years in the practice of his profession, travelling from city to city and offering instruction for a fee. It was rumored that he made more money by his teaching than the famous Phidias and ten other sculptors put together had made from their art, and his reputation was proportional to his success. He enjoyed the confidence of Pericles, for he was chosen to give laws to the colony which Athens founded at Thurii in Italy in 443 B.C. When he died, some seventy years of age, shortly after the beginning of the Peloponnesian War, he left behind him a reputation for wisdom such as few men can have enjoyed in their own time.

It is this reputation that has brought the young men of Athens flocking to see him on the occasion described by Plato in the *Protagoras*. The young Hippocrates, who has prevailed upon Socrates to introduce him to the great man, is typical of them. As Socrates explains, Hippocrates is eager to make a name for himself in the city, and he thinks that the best way to do this is to become a pupil of Protagoras. He wants to know just what effect it will have on him if he does.

12.2   Protagoras replied, "Young man, if you attend my classes your reward will be this: that on the very day on which you join them you will go home the better for it, and the same the day after that. Each day you will make some improvement."

Hearing this, I said, "Protagoras, what you say is not surprising; on the contrary it is reasonable, since even you, old and wise as you are, would become better if someone were to teach you something you happened not to know. But what I meant was this: suppose that Hippocrates here should suddenly change his mind and take a fancy to study with this young man who has just come to town, Zeuxippus of Heraclea. Suppose he approached him as he has you, and received from him the same answer that he has received from you — that each day he spent with him he would be better for it, and that he would make constant progress. And suppose Hippocrates were to ask him, 'In what way would I be better, as you say, and towards what would I make progress?' Zeuxippus would reply, 'In painting.' And if he went to the lessons of Orthagoras of Thebes, and, hearing from him the same as he has heard from you, asked him in what sense he would be better every day by attending his classes, Orthagoras would reply, 'In playing the flute.' Now then, tell this young man — and me, since I am asking for him — in what sense he will go away better on the day he joins your classes and toward what he will make progress each day thereafter."

Protagoras heard me out and said, "That is a good question, Socrates, and I enjoy answering good questions. Hippocrates, if he comes to me, will not have to put up with what he would have to put up with from any other sophist. For the others insult the intelligence of these young men who have just escaped from the arts and sciences by putting them to work again, against their wills, at arithmetic and astronomy and geometry and music (he glanced over at Hippias as he said this). If he comes to me he will learn nothing but what he came to learn, which is how to exercise good judgment in ordering both his own affairs and those of the city, and how to be a man of influence in public affairs, both in speech and in action."

"I wonder if I follow you," I said. "You seem to me to be speaking of the art of politics, and to be promising to make men good citizens."

"That," he said, "is exactly my profession."

Protagoras, then, pretends to make men better, and by this he means better able to manage the affairs of the city. But Socrates is not satisfied with this. When the Athenians have to solve a problem requiring special knowledge, they call in experts; but when matters of public policy are to be voted on, every man's opinion is considered to be of equal weight. This implies that the Athenians, at any rate, do not regard the management of public affairs as calling for any special knowledge. But if the management of public affairs is not a matter of knowledge, it is hard to see how it can be taught, since clearly only knowledge can be taught.

Protagoras' answer is simple: Socrates has the facts right, but he has drawn the wrong conclusions from them. The opinions of all are listened to precisely because all men *do* have a knowledge of what is right or wrong for the city. Unless this were true, no city would last. We tend to forget this when we see men doing what they know to be evil; but the point is that they *do* know that what they are doing is evil:

12.3 "The man who appears to you the most unjust of those who are brought up under the laws and among men is just — a practitioner of justice, even — in comparison with men knowing nothing of education or lawcourts or any form of compulsion which forced them constantly to be heedful of virtue — savages, in other words, like those which Pherecrates the poet brought on stage at the festival of Lenaea. If you found yourself among such people — people like the man-eaters in his chorus — you would be only too glad to meet up with Eurybatus and Phrynondas, bad as they are, and would long for the depravity of men in our own society."

THE TRANSMISSION OF *Arete*

How do men acquire this knowledge of right and wrong? You might as well ask, says Protagoras, how they learn Greek. They learn it when they are children — from their parents, from their teachers, from the magistrates, in short from everyone:

12.4   "As soon as a child can grasp what is said to him, his nurse, his mother, his tutor, and his father himself vie with each other to make him as good as possible; and they teach him with regard to every action he performs and every word he speaks that this is just and this unjust, this good and that bad, this holy and that unholy, and that he must do this and not do that. If he obeys willingly, well and good; if not, they straighten him out with threats and whippings like a warped and twisted plank.

"Afterwards they send him to school, charging his teachers to take more pains over the deportment of their children than their letters or music lessons. And the teachers do take pains over this, and when the children have learned their letters and are ready to understand the written word as formerly they learned the spoken, the teachers set the works of good poets before them and make them learn them by rote — poems in which they meet with many admonitions and many stories and praises and eulogies of good men of old, so that the child will be inspired to imitate them and long to become like them. And the music teachers, in the same way, stress self-control, so that their young charges will do no evil. And when they have learned to play the lyre they teach them the works of other good poets — lyric poets — which they accompany on the lyre, and they insist on familiarizing the souls of the children with rhythms and melodies, so that they become more civilized and more graceful and more in tune with themselves and more apt for speech and action. For rhythm and harmony are essential to the whole of human life.

"And in addition to all this, people send their children to a trainer, so that their bodies will be fit to meet the demands of their minds, lest they be compelled to play the coward because of the weakness of their bodies, both in war and in any other business.

"This is what people do who are able to do it, and the richest are the most able. It is their sons who begin their education earliest and are finished with it last. And when they have finished with teachers the city compels them to learn the laws and to live according to them, using them as a pattern, lest left to their own devices they do as they please. Just as the teachers of those who are not yet able to write well draw the letters in lightly before giving them their slates, and make them follow the outlines as a guide, so the city sketches in the laws which have been discovered by good lawgivers of old, and compels men to rule and be ruled in accordance with these. And she punishes anyone who steps outside the lines, and the name given to this punishment, both here and in many other cities, is 'correction,' since the penalty serves a corrective purpose."

In all these ways society takes care to see that its values are perpetuated.

But are we not all sophists in that case? Why should Protagoras receive money for doing what the rest of us do every day without pay? The answer, Protagoras replies, is simple. Though all are teachers of virtue, some are better at it than others:

> **12.5** "Such a one I claim to be — better than others at helping men to become noble and good, and worth all that I charge and more, as my pupils themselves agree."

The sophist, then, has a place in the educational system; for he possesses a skill not possessed by ordinary men. He understands the art of persuasion, and can fix the images of virtue and vice in the souls of young men more firmly than any ordinary man can. When they leave his hands they will possess those virtues which society has all along sought to implant in them. It would be surprising indeed if young men such as these did not exercise a power in public affairs consonant with their aretē.

One difficulty, however, remains. Protagoras seems to assume that the ideas of right and wrong which society implants in us by these methods are correct. No doubt they *seem* correct in the eyes of the society which inculcates them. But the question before us is not whether they *seem* right, but whether they *are* right. This question is not raised in the *Protagoras* itself; in that dialogue Plato is after other game. But we know from other considerations what answer Protagoras would make to it: if the values of a society *seem* right to it, they *are* right.

"MAN IS THE MEASURE"

The argument leading to this conclusion was set forth by Protagoras in a book entitled *On Truth*, of which the opening sentence has been preserved:

> **12.6** Of all things the measure is man: of existing things, that they exist; of nonexistent things, that they do not exist.

There is a passage in Plato's *Cratylus* which provides a clue to the meaning of this enigmatic statement:

> **12.7** *Socrates:* Does it seem to you, Hermogenes, that this is true of existing things: that what a thing is differs with the individual, as Protagoras maintains when he says that "of all things the measure is man" — so that as things *appear* to me, so they *are* for me, and as they *appear* to you so they *are* for you? Or does it seem to you that they have some fixed nature of their own?

It is clear from this question that by "man" Protagoras means the individual, and that by "measure" he means judge; the individual is the sole judge of whether a thing has or has not a certain nature. If it *seems* to him that it has such-and-such a nature, then for him it *has* such-and-such a nature.

An example will help that may have been Protagoras' own. It comes from Plato's *Theaetetus*, a dialogue in which the view we are considering is examined at some length:

> **12.8** *Socrates:* Isn't it true that sometimes, when the same wind is blowing, one of us feels cold and the other not? Or that one feels only slightly cold while the other feels very cold?
>
> *Theaetetus:* Certainly.
>
> *Socrates:* Shall we say, in such a case, that the wind is, in itself, either cold or not cold? Or shall we agree with Protagoras that it is cold to him who feels cold but not to him who doesn't?
>
> *Theaetetus:* Evidently the latter.

On Protagoras' view, then, it makes no sense to ask whether the wind *in itself* is cold or not. For to ask this question is to assume that the wind has a nature of its own, which is exactly what Protagoras denies. The wind which *is* for me is *cold* for me; the wind which *is* for you is *not cold* for you.

A curious consequence of this is that all beliefs are true:

12.9   *Socrates:* He says, doesn't he, that what is *believed* by each person *is so* for him who believes it?

Theodorus: Yes, that is what he says.

Now if this is to be universally true it must apply to statements of value also. If certain modes of behavior *seem* right to a given society, such behavior will *be* right for that society. There is no point in asking, as we did earlier, whether they are right *apart* from this seeming. They are what they seem to be, no more and no less.

But at this point a difficulty arises:

12.10   *Socrates:* Do you know, Theodorus, what amazes me about your friend Protagoras?

Theodorus: What?

Socrates: Well, gratifying as it is to be told that what each of us believes is true, I am surprised that he does not begin his *Truth* by saying that of all things the measure is the pig, or the dog-faced baboon, or some sentient creature still more uncouth. He would then have addressed us in a manner befitting a great man, disdainfully, showing us that while we were admiring him as if he were a god, for his wisdom, he was no wiser than a tadpole, to say nothing of any other man.

For what else are we to say, Theodorus? If what each man believes to be true through sensation is true for him — and no man can judge of another's experience better than the man himself, and no man is in a better position to consider whether another's opinion is true or false than the man himself, but (as we have said more than once) each man is to have his own opinions for himself alone, and all of them are to be right and true — then *how*, my friend, was Protagoras so wise that he should consider himself worthy to teach others and for huge fees? And how are we so ignorant that we should go to school to him, if each of us is the measure of his own wisdom?

How, in short, can Protagoras pretend to be wiser than the young Hippocrates, who wishes to be his pupil, if the beliefs he has are no truer than those Hippocrates already has?

THE SOPHIST AS EDUCATOR

To this question Protagoras replies with a distinction:

12.11   When you talk this way of pigs and dog-faced baboons, you not only play the pig yourself, but encourage your hearers to treat my writings in the same way; and that is not right. For I maintain that the truth is as I have written; each of us is the measure of what is and what is not, but people differ from one another in this: that different things appear and are to different people. And I am very far from denying that wisdom and the wise man exist, but on the contrary I say that that man is wise who, when bad things appear and are to any of us, brings about a change in us so that good things appear and are.

Don't quibble with my use of language, but try to understand what I mean. Remember what was said earlier: to the man who is sick his food seems bitter and is bitter; to the man who is well it is and seems just the opposite. Now neither of these men is to be made wiser, for that is impossible; nor should it be claimed that the sick man is ignorant because he believes what he does, or the well man wise because he believes otherwise. But a change must be brought about from the one condition to the other, because the other is better. So it is with education: a change must be brought about from a worse condition to a better; but whereas the physician produces this change by drugs, the sophist does it by words. No one has ever yet made anyone who previously had false beliefs have true ones; for it is impossible to believe what is not, nor anything but what one experiences, and this is always true. But I believe that one can make a man who is in a depraved condition of soul and has beliefs of a like nature good, so that he has different beliefs. These appearances some, through inexperience, call "true"; but I say that some are "better" than others, but not "truer." And the wise, friend Socrates, I am very far from calling frogs, but when they have to do with the body I call them physicians, and when they have to do with plants, farmers. For I maintain that the latter induce in sickly plants good and healthy and true sensations instead of bad, and that wise and good orators make good things instead of wicked things appear just to their cities. For I believe that whatever *seems* right or wrong to each city *is* right or wrong for it, so long as it continues to think so. But the wise man causes the good things instead of the bad to appear and to be for them in each case.

Protagoras is arguing here, as Plato himself so often does, from the analogy of the physician. The latter sets himself to bring about a change in the patient so that wine will seem to him to be sweet instead of bitter. There is no point in asking whether the wine is *really* bitter; if it *seems* bitter to the patient, then for him it *is* bitter. But patient and physician are agreed that it is better for the wine to appear sweet to the patient than it is for it to taste bitter to him, and the usefulness of the doctor to the patient lies in the fact that the doctor knows how to change the patient by means of drugs so that the wine no longer tastes bitter to him.

Now Protagoras would have us believe that the sophist stands in the same relation to his pupil as the physician does to his patient. The pupil's state of mind is an unhealthy one, for to act in accordance with the laws instead of following his impulses seems bad to him instead of good. The sophist must, by his arts, bring about a change in the pupil so that to act in accordance with the laws appears good to him. In this case, too, it is useless to ask whether the pupil's present belief is false; if to act in accordance with the laws *seems* bad to him, it *is* bad for him. The pupil is not being asked to exchange a false belief for a true one; for all beliefs are true for those who hold them. But all agree that it is *better* for justice to seem good to a man than for injustice to seem good to him.

But at this point we run into difficulties. Is it really true that "all agree" that justice is better than injustice? Suppose someone refuses to accept this; what right have we to say that he is "depraved"? For to say this is to suggest that it is somehow *wrong* to think that injustice is good. But on Protagoras' view this is impossible; all beliefs are right for those who hold them, including the belief that it is right to act unjustly. If, then, we call a pupil who persists in this belief "depraved," we are merely using the word as a stick to beat him with, and education becomes a process by means of which the older members of a society coerce the young into agreeing with them — except that this is done not by forcing a certain type of behavior on the young but by persuading them to abandon their views in favor of ours. At this the sophist is a past master, and his superior wisdom really consists in nothing but this: that he is more efficient at changing men's minds than most of us.

But the statesman stands in the same relation to the city as the sophist does to his charges. He does not merit power because his views are any sounder than those of the ordinary man. He merits it by virtue of the fact that he has learned the art of persuasion — perhaps from Protagoras himself — and learned it so well that he is able to make the views of the ordinary man conform to his own. He will, of course, *call* these views of his "sounder," because the ordinary man, in his innocence, supposes that there *are* right and wrong views of what is good for the city, and the statesman will naturally use language which accords with the understanding of the ordinary man if he wishes to persuade him to his own way of thinking. But the statesman, at any rate if he knows what he is doing, will understand that no policy is right or wrong in itself, but that "whatever *seems* right or wrong to each city *is* right or wrong for it."

PROTAGORAS AND DEMOCRITUS

It is certain that Protagoras would have shrunk from the implications of this view. Everything that we know of him testifies to his political conservatism. Nor is this particularly surprising; for "moral relativism" can have the effect of enhancing in men's eyes the social value of those very virtues which thought has undermined, and these are the virtues which Protagoras himself extols in the great myth with which he entertains his hearers in the house of Callias.

There was a time, he says, when men lived dispersed, and there were no cities:

> **12.12** "As a result, they were destroyed by wild beasts, since they were in every way weaker, and their craftsmanship, while adequate for supplying them with food, was inadequate for waging war on the wild beasts; for as yet they had no knowledge of statecraft, of which the science of war is a part. They kept trying to form a community, and to provide security for themselves by founding cities. But whenever they formed a community they injured one another for want of statecraft, and so they began to be scattered again and to perish.
>
> "Then Zeus, fearing that the race of man would be destroyed altogether, sent Hermes to bring to men respect and justice, so that there might be orderly cities and friendly ties to bring men together. Hermes asked Zeus how he should give justice and respect to men. 'Shall I distribute them as the arts were distributed — on the principle that one man skilled in medicine suffices to treat many laymen, and so with the other craftsmen? Shall I distribute justice and respect to men in this way, or to all alike?' 'To all alike,' said Zeus; 'let all have their share. There could never be cities if only a few had a share in these virtues, as they do in the other crafts. Moreover, you must lay it down as my law that if anyone is incapable of acquiring a share of respect and justice, he shall be put to death as a public pest.' "

It is only a myth; Protagoras knows that justice is a man-made thing. But he also recognizes that the virtues he extols — respect and justice — are what bring order into human life and create bonds of friendship between men. And so these are the virtues he would inculcate in the young Hippocrates.

So much is clear. But suppose that the young Hippocrates were to say to him, "Protagoras, according to you it is 'better' for men to respect one another and obey the law. Well and good. But on your principles, what can this possibly mean? So far as I can see, it can only mean that it appears so to you, and in consequence *is* so — for you. But it does not, I confess, appear so to me, and I see no reason why I should allow your views to take the place of mine. If that is to happen, you must first convince me that mine are 'worse,' and I do not see, frankly, how you can hope to do that without, at some point, appealing to a criterion of 'better' and 'worse' that does not depend upon what you think or I think or anybody else thinks. For otherwise the whole business will start again." On Protagoras' principles it is difficult to see what answer he could possibly make to this.

The weakness in Protagoras' position was immediately perceived by Democritus. Democritus saw that a criterion of "better" and "worse" was needed which would not vary with men's opinions, and he thought that he could supply such a criterion. It is to every man's advantage to be just, whether he realizes it or not; for unless he is just, the city cannot survive. As Protagoras himself admitted, there could never be cities unless all had a share in the civic virtues (**12.12**). But the importance of the city's survival derives from the fact that without it happiness is impossible. Happiness can be achieved only within a city; indeed, it is a reflex in the individual soul of that external stability which the city provides. But happiness has a physical aspect, and it was here that Democritus thought a criterion might be found. The happiness of the happy man is but the outward and visible sign of the arrangement of atoms in his soul; and the presence or absence of such an arrangement is not a matter of opinion but of truth. There is no room here for "moral relativism"; the man who thinks that injustice is good is simply wrong, and what is more he can be shown to be wrong, for injustice can be shown to lead to unhappiness (**11.86**). Morality has been grounded in the nature of things — the arrangement of atoms in the void.

Unfortunately, this view also has its difficulties. For it is not certain that the man who seeks his own advantage is more likely to secure it through obedience to the laws in every case. On the contrary, he may find that his interests are harmed by obedience to the laws; for though law exists for the good of all, there is no guarantee that the interests of any particular individual will be served by them. This point was instantly taken up and exploited by the sophist Antiphon.

ANTIPHON

We know little of Antiphon beyond the fact that he was an Athenian and a contemporary of Socrates, which would make him a little younger than Protagoras. His chief work was entitled *On Truth*, from which several lengthy excerpts have come down to us. These excerpts, incomplete as they are, give us a remarkable insight into the degree of sophistication (in both senses of the term) which political thinking had reached by the last half of the fifth century B.C.

The longest and most valuable of these excerpts states in the clearest possible manner the distinction between man-made and natural law:

12.13 Justice [on the ordinary reckoning] consists in not breaking the rules of the city of which one is a citizen. A man will be just, then, in a way most advantageous to himself if, in the presence of witnesses, he holds the laws of the city in high esteem, and in the absence of witnesses, when he is alone, those of nature. For the laws of men are adventitious, but those of nature are necessary; and the laws of men are fixed by agreement, not by nature, whereas the laws of nature are natural and not fixed by agreement. He who breaks the rules, therefore, and escapes detection by those who have agreed to them, incurs no shame or penalty; if detected, he does. But if a man attempts what is impossible according to the laws of nature, the evil that befalls him is no less if no one observes him, and no greater if everyone does. For he is not hurt because of opinion, but because of truth.

There are, Antiphon holds, certain laws which nature herself imposes upon us. The most obvious of these is the law of self-preservation. This law was not passed by an assembly; it is a law of nature, and applies to every living thing. The penalty for not obeying it is death. In addition to these laws men have made others, affecting their relations with one another in the city. These laws come into being by agreement and are conventions. The penalty for not obeying them does not follow automatically, as in the case of transgressions against the laws of nature, but is contingent upon being found out, and is not certain even then.

These two sorts of law, then, are to be sharply distinguished. But they are not merely different; they are, Antiphon argues, usually opposed:

12.14   The point of the inquiry is this: that most of the things which are just by law are hostile to nature. For a law has even been passed stating what the eyes should and should not see, what the ears should and should not hear, what the tongue should and should not speak, what the hands should and should not do, where the feet should and should not go, and what the mind should and should not desire. And those acts which the laws prohibit are no more agreeable or more akin to nature than those which they enjoin. But life and death are the concern of nature, and living creatures live by what is advantageous to them and die from what is not advantageous; and the advantages which accrue from law are chains upon nature, whereas those which accrue from nature are free.

The law of preservation bids men live. But men "live by what is advantageous to them." By implication, therefore, the law of nature requires a man to pursue whatever is advantageous to him. Now the test of whether a thing is advantageous to us is whether it is "agreeable" to us; but the laws of the city demand of us conduct which brings pain to the individual who obeys them. Hence obedience to the laws is not advantageous, and is not to be chosen.

The argument proceeds on lines that are familiar to us from Democritus, to whom Antiphon was plainly indebted. But it is Antiphon who adds the premise that obedience to the laws brings pain to those who obey them. This premise, which is crucial, he drives home by examples:

> **12.15** Take the case of those who defend themselves only after suffering injury and are not themselves the instigators of it; or of those who do good to their parents, though they are bad; or of those who allow others to swear out a complaint while not doing so themselves. One might find many of these cases that are hostile to nature. In each case there is more suffering when less is possible, and less pleasure when more is possible, and suffering when it is possible not to suffer.

Suppose, to take Antiphon's first example, that a man seeks my life. Other things being equal, it is to my advantage to strike first, for attack is the best defense in such cases; and in doing so I would be obeying the law of my nature. But man-made law asserts that I have no right to strike except in self-defense. That is to say, I must wait for my enemy to attack me at a time and place of *his* choosing instead of at a time and place of *my* choosing; and to do this is plainly to my disadvantage, for it increases my chances of being killed at the first onslaught.

The usual reply to this is that if I am killed, the man who kills me will be brought to trial and severely punished. But, as Antiphon goes on to point out, this does not bring *me* back to life, and it by no means follows that my slayer, even if he is brought to trial, will be punished:

> **12.16** If some benefit accrued to those who subscribed to the laws, while loss accrued to those who did not subscribe to them but opposed them, then obedience to the laws would not be without profit. But as things stand, it seems that legal justice is not strong enough to benefit those who subscribe to laws of this sort. For in the first place it permits the injured party to suffer injury and the man who inflicts it to inflict injury, and it does not prevent the injured party from suffering injury nor the man who does the injury from doing it. And if the case comes to trial, the injured party has no more of an advantage than the one who has done the injury; for he must convince his judges that he has been injured, and must be able, by his plea, to exact justice. And it is open to the one who has done the injury to deny it; for he can defend himself against the accusation,

and he has the same opportunity to persuade his judges that his
accuser has. For the victory goes to the best speaker.

Thus, even if my slayer is apprehended and brought to trial, Antiphon
argues, it is by no means certain that he will be convicted. For the person
who brings suit must (under Athenian law) himself persuade the jury
of the defendant's guilt, while the defendant, on his side, will try to
persuade the jury that he is innocent. And since persuasion is a matter
of technique, victory will go to the one who is most skilled in the art
of speaking, or who has enough money to hire a professional speech
writer to write his speech for him.

In the light of all this we can see why, in Antiphon's view, a man will
conduct himself "in a way most advantageous to himself if, in the presence of witnesses, he holds the laws of the city in high esteem, and in
the absence of witnesses, when he is alone, those of nature" (12.13).
And since, by definition, the just man is he who does not transgress the
laws of his city, it follows that it is better to act unjustly than justly. It
is better because it is more advantageous; and by this Antiphon means
more advantageous to the individual.

CALLICLES

The full implications of this position become clear, however, only
when we turn to the more outspoken Callicles. We know nothing of
Callicles except what Plato tells us in his *Gorgias*. He was not a sophist;
indeed, he expresses his contempt for sophists as worthless persons. But
his contempt for them is the contempt of the man of action and practicing politician for the mere theorist. He is able to speak of them as he
does because he has squeezed them dry. But he has learned his lesson
well, and it is for this reason that he is included here. He gives classical
expression to the philosophy of politics implicit in the line of argument
we have been following.

In the *Gorgias* he listens in disgusted silence while Socrates compels
Gorgias the rhetorician to admit that the teacher of rhetoric has a moral
responsibility to his pupils to impart a knowledge of justice to them. But
when Gorgias' young pupil Polus is forced to admit to the paradox that
the unjust man, *i.e.*, the man who breaks the laws for his own advantage,
is worse off than the just man, Callicles can contain himself no longer:

> 12.17 Socrates, you throw your weight around like a regular mob-
> orator. You are haranguing us in this fashion now simply be-
> cause Polus has got himself into the same position that he ac-
> cused Gorgias of being led into by you. For you asked Gorgias

whether he would teach a man who came to him knowing nothing of the nature of justice but wishing to learn rhetoric. And Gorgias was ashamed and said that he would, because convention demanded it and men would be vexed with him if he refused. It was because of this admission that he was forced to contradict himself, which delighted you. Polus mocked you then, and rightly in my opinion; but now he has got himself in the same fix. For my part, I reject precisely the admission that Polus made to you — that to act unjustly is more shameful than to suffer injustice; for it is from this admission that he in turn has been tripped up by you and had his mouth stopped by your arguments, being ashamed to say what he thought.

You say that you are seeking the truth, Socrates; but in fact this is merely the claptrap of the mob-orators — notions that are not admirable by nature but only by convention. For the most part, nature and convention are opposed to one another, so that when a man is ashamed and doesn't dare to say what he thinks, he is easily driven into saying the opposite of what he thinks. Knowing this trick, you make dishonest use of it in argument. When your opponent speaks on the basis of convention, you question him on the basis of nature; when he talks about nature, you talk about convention. Thus, in the present case, when we were talking about doing injustice and suffering it, and Polus was speaking of what is shameful by convention, you followed it up by speaking of what is shameful by nature.

By nature everything is shameful that is evil, such as suffering injustice; *doing* injustice is shameful only by convention. To suffer injustice is not the part of a man; it is the part of a slave — one for whom it is better to be dead than alive, and who, when he is insulted and injured, is unable to help himself or anyone else he cares for. But as far as I am concerned those who make the laws are weak men — the "many." So they make the laws for themselves and for their own advantage, and dispense praise and blame accordingly. And to frighten those who are stronger and able to get the upper hand of them they say that getting the upper hand is shameful and unjust, and that this is in fact what injustice is: to seek to get the upper hand of others. Being inferior themselves, they are content to be considered the equals of their betters.

This, then, is why it is said to be unjust and shameful to seek to get the upper hand of the many, and why men call it "wrong." But in my opinion nature herself makes it plain that it is right for the better to have the upper hand of the worse, and the more powerful of the less. It is evident in many fields, not only among animals but also among the cities and races of men, that right has always been considered to be that the stronger rule the weaker and have the upper hand of them. With what right did Xerxes invade Greece, or his father Scythia? And one might give a thousand instances of the same kind. It is my opinion that these men act in accordance with nature — yes, by Heaven, and in accordance with nature's own law — though not perhaps in accordance with the laws which *we* make. *We* mold the best and the strongest among us from the time they are infants, catching them young, like lions, and by spells and charms we enthrall them, telling them that all are to have equal rights, and that this is admirable and as it should be. But as for me, I fancy that when some man arises with sufficient strength he will shake off all this, burst his bonds and break loose. He will trample underfoot our scraps of paper and tricks, our charms and our "laws," all of which are against nature. The "slave" will rise in revolt and show himself our master, and there will shine forth the true light of natural justice . . . .

That is the truth of the matter, and you will come to see it if you put aside philosophy and turn to more important things.

Callicles is not an "immoralist"; on the contrary, he asserts that the strong *ought* to rule. It is *right* that they should, for this is according to nature. As proof of this he appeals to the behavior of animals and to the relations between cities. In nature the stronger animals eat the weaker; but man, too, is an animal, and therefore the same law applies to him. That it does so is plain enough from the relations which hold between one city and another; it is precisely the same as that in which men stand to one another in a state of nature — so much so that warfare between them is taken for granted by Democritus, and passed over without comment (**11.77**).

It is, moreover, Democritus who provides the principle upon which the whole argument turns, namely, the principle that what is natural is somehow better than what is artificial. The law of self-preservation is "higher" than man-made law, because it is grounded in man's nature, and hence is closer to what is most fundamental in his being. In the hands of Callicles the law of nature becomes what it had threatened to become all along; the highest principle of morality — not relative but absolute because grounded in the very nature of things. The effects of these teachings need not be guessed at, for they are writ large in the events of the times, and the reaction to them was swift.

THIRTEEN

Reaction

In 399 B.C. Socrates, the teacher of Plato, was brought to trial before an Athenian jury. The indictment was as follows:

13.1   Meletus, son of Meletus, of the deme of Pitthus, indicts Socrates, son of Sophroniscus, of the deme of Alopece, on his oath, as follows. Socrates is guilty of not recognizing the gods which the city recognizes, and of introducing new and different deities. He is also guilty of corrupting the young. The penalty demanded is death.

The connection between the different parts of the indictment is brought into sharper focus by the cross-examination to which Meletus is subjected by Socrates in Plato's account of the trial:

13.2   Tell me, Meletus; in what way do I corrupt the young? I take it from the terms of the indictment you have brought that I do so by teaching them not to recognize the gods which the city recognizes, but new and strange divinities. Isn't this what you maintain — that I corrupt them by teaching them this?

   That is precisely what I maintain.

   Then Meletus, in the name of the gods of whom we are even now speaking, explain yourself a little more clearly, both to me and to these gentlemen here. I cannot make out whether you are saying that I teach men to believe that there are gods (and I believe that there are gods, and I am not completely godless, nor am I at fault on this score) but that they are not gods which the city recognizes but others, or are you saying that I do not believe

257

in the existence of any gods at all, and that this is what I teach to others?

That is exactly what I maintain: that you do not believe in the existence of any gods at all.

You amaze me, Meletus. Why do you say this? Do I not recognize the sun and moon to be gods, just as other men do?

No, he does not, gentlemen of the jury! He says that the sun is a stone, and that the moon is made of earth.

Do you imagine, friend Meletus, that you are accusing Anaxagoras? And have you so low an opinion of these gentlemen as to suppose them illiterate, so that they do not know that the writings of Anaxagoras of Clazomenae are full of such doctrines? Fancy your supposing that the young men learn these from me, when they can buy them for a drachma at most in the public market place and laugh at Socrates if he pretends that they are his — especially when they are so very singular! Do you really think that I have no belief in the existence of *any* god at all?

None whatever.

The exchange shows that Meletus' evidence for supposing that Socrates does not believe in the gods is simply that, like Anaxagoras, Socrates allegedly teaches that the sun is a stone and the moon a mass of earth. He is, in short, a natural philosopher.

That Socrates is fully aware of the real nature of the charge against him is evident from the opening words of his defense:

13.3   The proper course for me to take, men of Athens, is to begin by defending myself against the first of the false accusations brought against me, and my first accusers, and afterwards to defend myself against the later ones. For many have accused me in your presence, and for a great many years, though nothing of what they have said is true. And I fear these people more than I do Anytus and his friends. They are dangerous enough; but the others are still more dangerous, gentlemen of the jury — I mean those who got hold of you when most of you were still children, and accused me falsely, saying that there is a certain "wise man," one Socrates, a "contemplator of the heavens," who has investigated all things below the earth and "makes the weaker argument the stronger." It is the men who have spread this report of me, gentlemen, who are my really dangerous accusers. For those who hear them are convinced that men who investigate these things do not believe in gods.

Those who inquire into such things are atheists; Socrates inquires into such things; therefore, Socrates is an atheist. Such is the reasoning which Socrates must combat. And as he intimates, the argument goes back almost twenty-five years to the production of Aristophanes' *Clouds*.

Aristophanes' *Clouds*

The *Clouds* illustrates very clearly indeed the reaction of a highly intelligent man to the teachings of the natural philosophers. In it an old man named Strepsiades, who is burdened with the debts of a worthless son, decides to send him to study under Socrates, in hopes that he will learn enough to enable him to outwit his creditors. Since the son will have none of it, the old man is obliged to go himself. He finds Socrates suspended in a basket, contemplating the sun. The latter explains to Strepsiades condescendingly that he has to mingle the subtle essence of his mind with the air, which is of like nature, in order to penetrate the things of heaven. After a good deal more of this nonsense the Chorus enters, done up as clouds. These, Socrates explains, "are the only true goddesses; all the rest are pure myth":

13.4
STREPSIADES

But by the Earth! is our father, Zeus, the Olympian, not a god?

SOCRATES

Zeus! what Zeus! Are you mad? There is no Zeus.

STREPSIADES

What are you saying now? Who causes the rain to fall? Answer me that!

SOCRATES

Why, these, and I will prove it. Have you ever seen it raining without clouds? Let Zeus then cause rain with a clear sky and without their presence!

STREPSIADES

By Apollo! that is powerfully argued! For my own part, I always thought it was Zeus pissing into a sieve. But tell me, who is it makes the thunder, which I so much dread?

SOCRATES

These, when they roll one over the other.

STREPSIADES

But how can that be? you most daring among men!

SOCRATES

Being full of water, and forced to move along, they are of necessity precipitated in rain, being fully distended with moisture from the regions where they have been floating; hence they bump each other heavily and burst with great noise.

STREPSIADES

But is it not Zeus who forces them to move?

SOCRATES

Not at all; it's the aerial Whirlwind.

STREPSIADES

The Whirlwind! ah! I did not know that. So Zeus, it seems, has no existence, and it's the Whirlwind that reigns in his stead? But you have not yet told me what makes the roll of the thunder?

SOCRATES

Have you not understood me then? I tell you, that the Clouds, when full of rain, bump against one another, and that, being inordinately swollen out, they burst with a great noise.

STREPSIADES

How can you make me credit that?

SOCRATES

Take yourself as an example. When you have heartily gorged on stew at the Panathenaea, you get throes of stomach-ache and then suddenly your belly resounds with prolonged rumbling.

STREPSIADES

Yes, yes, by Apollo! I suffer, I get colic, then the stew sets to rumbling like thunder and finally bursts forth with a terrific noise. At first, it's but a little gurgling *pappax, pappax!* then it increases, *papapappax!* and when I take my crap, why, it's thunder indeed, *papapappax! pappax!! papapappax!!!* just like the clouds.

SOCRATES

Well then, reflect what a noise is produced by your belly, which is but small. Shall not the air, which is boundless, produce these mighty claps of thunder?

STREPSIADES

And this is why the names are so much alike: crap and clap. But tell me this. Whence comes the lightning, the dazzling flame, which at times consumes the man it strikes, at others hardly singes him. Is it not plain, that Zeus is hurling it at the perjurers?

SOCRATES

Out upon the fool! the driveller! he still savours of the golden

age! If Zeus strikes at the perjurers, why has he not blasted
Simon, Cleonymus and Theorus? Of a surety, greater perjurers
cannot exist. No, he strikes his own temple, and Sunium, the
promontory of Athens, and the towering oaks. Now, why should
he do that? An oak is no perjurer.

STREPSIADES

I cannot tell, but it seems to me well argued. What is the
lightning then?

SOCRATES

When a dry wind ascends to the Clouds and gets shut into
them, it blows them out like a bladder; finally, being too confined, it bursts them, escapes with fierce violence and a roar to
flash into flame by reason of its own impetuosity.

STREPSIADES

Ah, that's just what happened to me one day. It was at the
feast of Zeus! I was cooking a sow's belly for my family and I
had forgotten to slit it open. It swelled out and, suddenly bursting,
discharged itself right into my eyes and burnt my face.

The views parodied here are probably those of Diogenes of Apollonia,
but they differ little, if at all, from those of Anaximenes. In fact, they
go back to the origins of Greek philosophical thought, and are typical
expressions of the attempt which characterizes that tradition from the
first to explain thunder, lightning, earthquakes, and similar phenomena
in terms of the action of impersonal forces. So far as that attempt succeeded, it struck at the roots of the popular conception of the gods. The
impersonal agencies of the natural philosophers simply took over the
functions of the gods, and "natural" explanations took the place of
religious.

In his life of Pericles, Plutarch relates a story which illustrates this
process in a striking way:

13.5   It is said that once the head of a one-horned ram was sent to
Pericles from his country place, and that Lampon the prophet,
seeing that the horn grew strong and solid from the middle of
the forehead, said that though there were in the city two powerful parties (those of Pericles and Thucydides the son of Melesias)
the mastery would devolve upon one of them, namely, the one to
whom this sign had appeared. Anaxagoras, however, cutting
through the skull, showed that the brain had not filled out its
cavity, but had drawn together to a point like an egg at that spot
where the root of the horn had its origin.

Here the new and the old appear side by side. Lampon the prophet sees the ram's horn as a disruption of nature, brought about by the gods as a sign to men; Anaxagoras sees it as due simply to natural causes, and as without any significance at all.

It was the attitude of Anaxagoras which triumphed. We can see it at work in the author of a work on epilepsy, written at about the same time:

> **13.6**   In my opinion the so-called "sacred disease" is no more sacred than any other. On the contrary, it occurs naturally and for a reason. Men suppose it to be sacred through ignorance, and through wonder at the fact that it resembles no other disease. But the theory of divine origin, while it gains some support from men's ignorance, is undermined by the facile method of healing applied to it, which consists of ritual purifications and incantations. If a disease is to be considered sacred merely because it excites astonishment, there will be many sacred diseases, not just one. For I will show that there are many diseases no less wonderful and portentous, which no one would think to call "sacred."

That this same attitude was found outside medical circles is evident from Herodotus' account of the madness of Cambyses. The first sign of this madness occurred during Cambyses' invasion of Egypt. Finding Memphis in the midst of a religious celebration in honor of the sacred calf called Apis, Cambyses, in a fit of rage, struck the calf with his own dagger, so that it died. The Egyptians, of course, believed that his subsequent madness was the direct result of this crime, and that it was inflicted on him by the gods; but Herodotus says:

> **13.7**   . . . it may, however, have arisen from some one of the many diseases that afflict mankind. For Cambyses is said to have suffered from birth from some great disease which men call the "sacred disease"; and it would not be strange if, his body being afflicted with a great illness, his mind was diseased.

Aristophanes, who saw clearly what all this was leading up to, summed it up in the figure of Strepsiades, fresh from his first lesson in natural philosophy:

> **13.8**   PHIDIPPIDES
>
> Oh! My poor father! what has happened to you? By the Olympian Zeus! you are no longer in your senses!
>
>   STREPSIADES
>
> Look! "the Olympian Zeus." Oh! you fool! to believe in Zeus at your age!

PHIDIPPIDES

What is there in that to make you laugh?

STREPSIADES

You are then a tiny little child, if you credit such antiquated rubbish! But come here, that I may teach you; I will tell you something very necessary to know to be a man; but do not repeat it to anybody.

PHIDIPPIDES

Tell me, what is it?

STREPSIADES

Just now you swore by Zeus.

PHIDIPPIDES

Sure I did.

STREPSIADES

Do you see how good it is to learn? Phidippides, there is no Zeus.

PHIDIPPIDES

What is there then?

STREPSIADES

The Whirlwind has driven out Zeus and is King now.

PHIDIPPIDES

What drivel!

STREPSIADES

You must realize that it is true.

In this passage the *Theogony* of Hesiod has been brought up to date. As the Fourth Age culminated in the overthrow of Cronus by his own son Zeus, so the Fifth Age, the age of iron, has culminated in the overthrow of Zeus by the vortex, the "aerial Whirlwind." But this great feat has been accomplished not by gods but by men, and by a particular class of men, namely, all those who have investigated the "things in the heavens and below the earth."

THE JUST AND THE UNJUST DISCOURSES

That this was not simply the opinion of Aristophanes but of others, too, is clear from the words of Socrates himself:

13.9   Another reason for my unpopularity is that young men with plenty of leisure time, the sons of the rich, follow me about of their own accord; for they enjoy hearing people cross-examined. And they frequently imitate me, and take it upon themselves to cross-examine others; and I suppose that they find great plenty of men who think that they know something but in fact know little or nothing. And the result is that those who are cross-examined by them are angry with *me* instead of with themselves, and they say that Socrates is an abomination and corrupts the young. And when someone asks them "By doing what?" or "By teaching what?" they have nothing to say, but are at a loss; but in order not to appear so, they fall back on the stock charges that are levelled at all philosophers, *i.e.*, that they investigate things in the heavens and below the earth, and do not believe in gods, and make the weaker argument appear stronger.

The charge of impiety is simply a stock charge, directed automatically at anyone who inquires into natural philosophy. The charge of making the weaker argument appear stronger, *i.e.*, of subverting justice, calls for further notice. For Strepsiades goes to Socrates, after all, not in order to learn what causes it to rain but in order to learn "how to win lawsuits, whether they be just or not." And when at last the old man prevails on his shiftless son Phidippides to take his place as Socrates' pupil, it is to this theme that Aristophanes returns.

Socrates, wearied of the whole affair, hands over the instruction of Phidippides to the Just and the Unjust Discourses themselves, who agree to state their cases in turn:

13.10   JUST DISCOURSE

Very well, I will tell you what was the old education, when I used to teach justice with so much success and when modesty was held in veneration. Firstly, it was required of a child, that it should not utter a word. In the street, when they went to the music-school, all the youths of the same district marched lightly clad and ranged in good order, even when the snow was falling in great flakes. At the master's house they had to stand with their legs apart and they were taught to sing either, "Pallas, the Terrible, who overturneth cities," or "A noise resounded from afar" in the solemn tones of the ancient harmony. If anyone indulged in buffoonery or lent his voice any of the soft inflexions, like those which to-day the disciples of Phrynis take so much pains to form, he was treated as an enemy of the Muses and belaboured with blows. In the wrestling school they would sit with outstretched legs and without display of any indecency to the curious. When they rose, they would smooth over the sand, so as to leave no trace to excite obscene thoughts. Never was a child rubbed with oil below the belt; the rest of their bodies thus retained its fresh bloom and down, like a velvety peach. They were not to be seen approaching a lover and themselves rousing his passion by soft modulation of the voice and lustful gaze. At table, they would not have dared, before those older than themselves, to have taken a radish, an aniseed, or a leaf of parsley, and much less eat fish or thrushes or cross their legs.

Unjust Discourse

What antiquated rubbish! Have we got back to the days of the festivals of Zeus Polieus, to the Buphonia, to the time of the poet Cecides and the golden cicadas?

Just Discourse

Nevertheless by suchlike teaching I built up the men of Marathon. But you, you teach the children of to-day to bundle themselves quickly into their clothes, and I am enraged when I see them at the Panathenaea forgetting Athené while they dance, and covering their tools with their bucklers. Hence, young man, dare to range yourself beside me, who follow justice and truth; you will then be able to shun the public place, to refrain from the baths, to blush at all that is shameful, to fire up if your virtue is mocked at, to give place to your elders, to honour your parents, in short, to avoid all that is evil. Be modesty itself, and do not run to applaud the dancing girls; if you delight in such scenes, some courtesan will cast you her apple and your reputation will be done for. Do not bandy words with your father, nor treat him as a dotard, nor reproach the old man, who has cherished you, with his age.

Unjust Discourse

If you listen to him, by Bacchus! you will be the image of the sons of Hippocrates and will be called *mother's big ninny*.

Just Discourse

No, but you will pass your days at the gymnasia, glowing with strength and health; you will not go to the public place to cackle and wrangle as is done nowadays; you will not live in fear that you may be dragged before the courts for some trifle exaggerated by quibbling. But you will go down to the Academy to run beneath the sacred olives with some virtuous friend of your own age, your head encircled with the white reed, enjoying your ease and breathing the perfume of the yew and of the fresh sprouts of the poplar, rejoicing in the return of springtide and gladly listening to the gentle rustle of the plane tree and the elm. (*With greater warmth from here on*) If you devote yourself to practising my precepts, your chest will be stout, your colour glowing, your shoulders broad, your tongue short, your hips muscular, but your tool small. But if you follow the fashions of the day, you will be pallid in hue, have narrow shoulders, a narrow chest, a long tongue, small hips, and a big thing; you will know how to spin forth long-winded arguments on law. You will be persuaded also to regard as splendid everything that is shameful and as shameful everything that is honourable; in a word, you will wallow in degeneracy like Antimachus.

But in the cross-examination which follows, it is the Unjust Discourse that triumphs:

UNJUST DISCOURSE

13.11 . . . Have you ever seen chastity of any use to anyone? Answer and try to confute me.

JUST DISCOURSE

To many; for instance, Peleus won a sword thereby.

UNJUST DISCOURSE

A sword! Ah! what a fine present to make him! Poor wretch! Hyperbolus, the lamp-seller, thanks to his villainy, has gained more than . . . I do not know how many talents, but certainly no sword.

JUST DISCOURSE

Peleus owed it to his chastity that he became the husband of Thetis.

UNJUST DISCOURSE

. . . who left him in the lurch, for he was not the most ardent; in those nocturnal sports between the sheets, which so please women, he possessed but little merit. Get you gone, you are but an old fool. But you, young man, just consider a little what this temperance means and the delights of which it deprives you — young fellows, women, play, dainty dishes, wine, boisterous laughter. And what is life worth without these? Then, if you happen to commit one of these faults inherent in human weakness, some seduction or adultery, and you are caught in the act, you are lost, if you cannot speak. But follow my teaching and you will be able to satisfy your passions, to dance, to laugh, to blush at nothing. Suppose you are caught in the act of adultery. Then up and tell the husband you are not guilty, and recall to him the example of Zeus, who allowed himself to be conquered by love and by women. Being but a mortal, can you be stronger than a god?

GORGIAS OF LEONTINI

This mode of reasoning may bear little resemblance to that of the historical Socrates, but it bears a striking resemblance to that of the great sophist Gorgias, who arrived in Athens in 427 B.C. with an embassy from Leontini, a city in Sicily, and created a sensation with his oratory. A lengthy specimen of this oratory has come down to us. It is in the form of a speech in defense of Helen, wife of Menelaus, who (according to legend) precipitated the Trojan War by eloping with Paris. The version which follows is much shortened, but it preserves something of the pompous and long-winded style which was Gorgias' trademark:

13.12   Either it was through the caprice of Fate, the counsel of the gods, and the casting vote of Necessity that Helen acted as she did, or because she was violently abducted, or seduced, or a prisoner of love.

If she acted as she did for the first reason, those who censure her should themselves be censured; for human thought cannot impede divine will. It is natural, not that the stronger be impeded by the weaker, but that the weaker be ruled and led by the stronger, and that the stronger lead and the weaker follow. God is stronger than man in might and wisdom and every other respect. If, then, we are to posit Fate or God as the reason, we must absolve Helen of her ill-repute.

If she was forcibly captured, and lawlessly raped and unjustly assaulted, it is clear that the captor committed a crime by violating her, and the captive suffered by being violated. In this case, the barbarian agent of the barbarous act, as far as the story, the law, and the deed are concerned, deserves blame in the story, loss of rights in the law, and punishment for the deed. Helen was assaulted, deprived of her country, obscured from her friends; how could we possibly blame her and not pity her? He committed a dreadful crime, but she suffered; therefore we should pity her and despise him.

If the story is that he seduced her and beguiled her soul, it is not hard to defend her and absolve her of the blame; the defense would run like this. Words are tremendously powerful and produce the most godlike effects in the smallest, most obscure bodies; for words can put an end to fear, assuage grief, effect joy, and increase pity . . . . The same argument applies to the power of words with respect to the soul's disposition as to the disposition of drugs with respect to the body's nature. Just as different drugs draw off different humors from the body and some put an end to illness, others to life, so it is with words — some cause pain, some pleasure, some fear, some courage, and some drug and enchant the soul with evil persuasion. What is there to prevent our thinking that Helen, too, went to Troy influenced by words, but none the less unwillingly, as one captured by violent captors? For it is possible to see that the power of persuasion, though it lacks the appearance of compulsion, has the same strength.

The fact that, if my account is persuasive, she did no wrong but rather suffered one, has been expounded. I shall now examine the fourth reason, in the fourth part of my account. If love was the cause of all these things it will not be difficult for her to escape blame for her alleged crime. The objects of our sight do not have the nature we would like them to have, but that which each has chanced upon; and the soul is fashioned in its ways, too, through sight. For the sight of hostile forces, equipped in warlike array of bronze and iron, so disturbs the soul that men are frequently thrown into confusion by it and flee in panic from the impending danger as if it were actual. For the force of habit born of law is expelled through fear at the sight which comes upon them and causes them to neglect both the noble which is adjudged through the law, and the good which results from victory. And conversely, whenever artists compose one perfect figure or body from many colors and bodies, they give pleasure to the sight. The sculpting of statues and production of images affords the eyes divine delight; thus, some things naturally please or pain the sight, and many things produce in many men love and desire for many actions or bodies. If, therefore, Helen's eye was entranced by Alexander's body, and she delivered up her soul to an eager contest of love, what is so strange in that? If love, being divine, has divine power from the gods, how could the weaker reject or fight against it? If love is some human illness and a fault of ignorance in the soul, it should not be blamed as a sin but deemed a misfortune.

Since, then, Helen escapes all blame, being either enraptured by love or seduced by words or compelled by divine necessity to do as she did, how justified should we consider the man who censures her?

I have removed from the story a woman's ill-repute; I have abided by the law which I propounded at the beginning of my account; I tried to remove the injustice of blame, the ignorance of beliefs. I wanted to write this to praise Helen and to please myself.

That this is a display piece is obvious. Gorgias does not care in the least whether Helen is innocent or guilty. His sole purpose is to show that he can make what appears to all men to be wrong appear to them to be right, and by this means demonstrate in the clearest possible way "the power of persuasion, when added to speech, to make any impression it wishes on the soul," as he says elsewhere. To impart this power to others, for a fee, is what Gorgias professes. The purposes to which it is put is not his concern; or, as Aristophanes put it, "if well-paid, these men also teach one how to win lawsuits, whether they be just or not."

THE SOPHISTS AS SKEPTICS

"These men" are clearly the sophists; yet in the *Clouds* Aristophanes makes no distinction between the sophists and those who investigate things in the heavens and below the earth, and to us it would appear that he confused the two. But the fact that so many of his fellow citizens shared his confusion suggests that there may have been some basis for it.

To begin with, many of the sophists did in fact concern themselves with philosophical questions. When we meet Hippias in **12.1**, he is surrounded by a crowd of young men who are asking questions about natural science. Gorgias himself composed a work on nature, in which he argued that nothing exists, that if anything did exist we could have no knowledge of it, and that even if we had knowledge of it our knowledge would not be communicable (see Appendix B). Protagoras wrote a work on the gods which began with the ominous words:

> **13.13** Concerning the gods, I do not know whether they exist or not. For many are the obstacles to knowledge: the obscurity of the subject and the brevity of human life.

There is nothing impious in this statement. Protagoras may, for all we know, have argued that since we can know nothing certain concerning the gods the best course is to observe the religious conventions of the city to which one belongs. That would be quite in keeping with the conservatism of his political views. But it is dangerous to arouse doubts where there were none before, and it is not surprising that at a later date the story grew up that Protagoras was tried for impiety on account of his book, and his writings burnt.

If there is doubt about the views of Protagoras, there is none whatever about those of his younger contemporary the sophist Prodicus, whom we also met in **12.1**:

> **13.14** Prodicus says that the ancients worshipped as gods the sun, the moon, rivers, springs, and all things useful to human life, simply because of their usefulness — just as the Egyptians deify the Nile. For this reason bread is worshipped as Demeter, wine as Dionysus, water as Poseidon, fire as Hephaestus, and so on for each of the things that are useful to men.

The gods, in short, are merely personifications of natural phenomena; apart from these they have no existence.

From here it was but a step to the view of Critias, another of those present at the famous gathering at the house of Callias, and a writer of sorts who expressed what (in intellectual circles) must have been a widely held view of the origin of religion:

> **13.15** There was a time when the life of man was disorderly and bestial and subject to brute force; when there was no reward for the good and no punishment for the bad. At that time, I think, men enacted laws in order that justice might be absolute ruler and have arrogance as its slave; and if anyone did wrong he was punished. Then, when the laws prohibited them from doing deeds of violence, they began to do them secretly. Then, I think, some shrewd and wise man invented fear of the gods for mortals, so that there might be some deterrent to the wicked even if they did or said or thought something in secret. Therefore he introduced the divine, saying that there is a god, flourishing with immortal life, hearing and seeing with his mind, thinking of all things and watching over them and having a divine nature; who will hear everything that is said among mortals and will be able to see all that is done. And if you plan any evil in secret it will not escape the notice of the gods, for they are of surpassing intelligence. In speaking thus he introduced the prettiest of teachings, concealing the truth under a false account. And in order that he might better strike fear into the hearts of men he told them that the gods dwell in that place which he knew to be a source of fears to mortals — and of benefits too — namely, the upper periphery where they saw lightnings and heard the dreaded rumblings of thunder and saw the starry body of the heaven, the beauteous embroidery of that wise craftsman Time, where the bright glowing mass of the sun moves and whence dark rains descend to earth. With such fears did he surround men, and by means of them he established the deity securely in a place befitting his dignity, and quenched lawlessness. Thus, I think, did some man first persuade mortals to believe in a race of gods.

In holding and teaching such views the sophists struck at the heart of the old morality. For in the last analysis that morality was grounded in the will of Zeus. "For Cronus' son set up this law for men. Fish, flesh, and fowl each other may devour, for right is not in them. But right he gave to men, and this is best by far" (1.16). With the disappearance of Zeus the basis of the old morality crumbled away.

Aristophanes is quite clear about this. The net result of the education of Phidippides in the new learning is that he can now prove by logic that it is right for sons to beat their own fathers:

13.16   PHIDIPPIDES

... Answer me, did you beat me in my childhood?

STREPSIADES

Why, assuredly, for your good and in your own best interest.

PHIDIPPIDES

Tell me, is it not right, that in turn I should beat you for your good, since it is for a man's own best interest to be beaten? What! must your body be free of blows, and not mine? am I not free-born too? the children are to weep and the fathers go free? You will tell me, that according to the law, it is the lot of children to be beaten. But I reply that the old men are children twice over and that it is far more fitting to chastise them than the young, for there is less excuse for their faults.

STREPSIADES

But the law nowhere admits that fathers should be treated thus.

PHIDIPPIDES

Was not the legislator who carried this law a man like you and me? In those days he got men to believe him; then why should not I too have the right to establish for the future a new law, allowing children to beat fathers in their turn? We make you a present of all the blows which were received before this law, and admit that you thrashed us with impunity. But look how the cocks and other animals fight with their fathers; and yet what difference is there betwixt them and ourselves, unless it be that they do not propose decrees?

STREPSIADES

But if you imitate the cocks in all things, why don't you scratch up the dunghill, why don't you sleep on a perch?

PHIDIPPIDES

That has no bearing on the case, good sir; Socrates would find no connection, I assure you.

THE REACTION OF ANYTUS

For the passing of the old morality Aristophanes held the natural philosophers and the sophists jointly responsible, and in the *Clouds* he stated the case against them so powerfully that more than twenty years later the backwash from it could sweep Socrates to his death. That Aristophanes' contemporaries shared his views is evident not merely from the well-known prosecutions of Anaxagoras and Socrates but from the care which even a conservative like Protagoras is obliged to take to avoid bringing their wrath upon himself. As he confesses to Socrates:

> **13.17** A man has to be careful when he goes as a stranger into great cities and persuades the best of the young men to abandon the company of others, friends and foreigners alike, both young and old, and to associate with himself on the ground that they will become better through association with him. For such conduct arouses no small amount of jealousy and ill will and intrigue.

There is a striking example of this kind of ill will in Plato's *Meno*. Meno, Socrates explains to the democratic leader Anytus, longs to acquire "the kind of wisdom and virtue which fits men to manage an estate or govern a city." To whom should he be sent?

> **13.18** Or is it clear from what we have just said that he should go to those who profess to be teachers of virtue, and who advertise themselves as the common property of any of the Greeks who want to learn from them for a flat rate?
>
> *Anytus:* Who do you mean, Socrates?
>
> *Socrates:* Why surely you know as well as anyone that they are the people called "sophists."
>
> *Anytus:* By Heracles, say no more, Socrates! Let none of my kinsmen nor friends, neither Athenian nor foreign, be seized by such madness that he allows himself to be corrupted by association with those men! For they are the manifest ruin and corruption of all who come in contact with them.
>
> *Socrates:* How so, Anytus? Can they be so different from others who claim to know how to perform some useful service that they alone not only do no good to what is placed in their hands, as others do, but actually do the opposite and ruin it — and openly demand a fee for doing so? I can hardly believe you. I know of one man, Protagoras, who has made more money from his wisdom than Pheidias, who was so famous for the beautiful works which he produced, and ten other sculptors put together. It would be strange indeed if those who repair old shoes and mend clothing were unable, even for thirty days, to get away with returning the clothes or shoes in worse condition than they received them (for they would starve to death in no time if they did) while for more than forty years Protagoras has taken in all of Greece while corrupting those who associated with him and sending them away worse than they came. For I believe that he

was close to seventy when he died, and had practiced his trade for forty years. And during all that time — indeed to this day — he has not ceased to be well thought of; and not Protagoras only, but a great many others as well, some of whom lived before his time and some of whom are living still. Now are we to suppose, as you seem to think, that these men deliberately deceived and ruined the young men; or are we to suppose that they were themselves unaware of doing so? And if the latter, are we to suppose that these, whom some consider the wisest of all men, were as mad as all that?

Anytus: Far from it, Socrates; it is the young men who give them money who are mad, and those who are responsible for them and entrust them to the care of such men are madder still. But maddest of all are the cities that allow them to enter, and do not drive them out, whether it is a stranger who tries this sort of thing or a citizen.

Socrates: Has one of the sophists done you an injury, Anytus, that you are so hard on them?

Anytus: Not at all; I have never in my life had anything to do with any of them, nor would I allow any of my people to do so either.

Socrates: Then you really have had no experience of them at all?

Anytus: No, and never hope to.

Socrates: Amazing. How do you know, then, whether a thing has any good in it, or evil, when you have had no experience of it whatever?

Anytus: Easily. I know what they are, these people, experience or no experience.

The hostility of Anytus was shared by many honest men, and it was to result in the death of Socrates himself. But the passage just quoted raises a new question: was this hostility justified? Socrates does not, in anything he says, deny the *fact* of corruption; but he raises in **13.17** the question whether it is really likely that the sophists alone are responsible for it.

His own view of the matter, or Plato's rather, is stated clearly in the *Republic* where he addresses the young Adeimantus:

13.19 Do you believe, as the many do, that there are young men who are corrupted by the sophists, and that individual sophists are really able to corrupt anyone to any extent worth mentioning? Is it not those who say this who are the greatest sophists, and who educate in the most effective way young and old alike, both men and women, making them into just the sort of people they want them to be?

When do they do this? he asked.

Why, when the many are crowded together in assemblies or courtrooms or theaters or camps, I said, or in any other public place where a gathering of many people with a great uproar censure something that has been said or done, or praises others — always immoderately, with loud shouts and much clapping of hands, until "the rocks and region round reecho," redoubling the noise of their pleasure and their praise. Don't you suppose that when this happens the heart of a young man is, as the saying goes, moved within him? What private instruction can stand up against it? Will it not be swept clear away by the flood of censure and approval and carried headlong downstream with it, until he too will affirm the same things to be honorable or base that they do, and will do as they do, and become like them?

Indeed, Socrates, it is inevitable.

Moreover, I said, we have not yet mentioned the most powerful force of all.

What is that? he asked.

Why, the actual penalties imposed by these "educators" and "sophists" upon those who are not convinced by words. You know, don't you, that they punish the man who is not persuaded by them with loss of civic rights and fines and death.

They certainly do, he said.

Well, what other sophist, do you think, or private teaching opposed to these, will be able to hold out against them?

None, I imagine, he said.

No, I replied; even to attempt it is the sheerest folly. For humanly speaking there is not, never was, nor ever will be any different standard of virtue than that which is inculcated by them . . . . Each of these private individuals who teach for pay, and whom these people call "sophists," supposing them to be rivals, teach nothing but the opinions of the many, which they form when they are gathered together; and each calls this "wisdom." It is as though a man who had a large and powerful beast in his keeping were to make a study of its moods and desires — how it should be approached and handled, when it is most savage or most gentle and from what causes, what sounds it makes on each of these occasions, and again what sounds, when made by another, serve to placate it or anger it, and then after studying all these things by living with it after a long time were to call this "wisdom" and, having reduced it to a science, turn to teaching it — not really knowing whether these opinions and desires were honorable or base, good or bad, just or unjust, but simply applying these names to the same things to which the great beast applied them, calling the things that pleased it "good" and those that annoyed it "bad." For he would not be able to give any other account of them except that what was "necessary" was "just" and "honorable," not being aware how great a difference there is between what is necessary and what is good, or being able to show it to another. Doesn't it seem to you that such a one would be a queer sort of educator?

It does indeed, he said.

It will be apparent that Aristophanes and Plato took very different views of the role played by the sophists in the breakdown of the traditional morality. Aristophanes looked upon that morality and found it good; its breakdown he saw as the work of the sophists and natural philosophers who had undermined its religious foundations. But Plato saw further. He saw that in an important sense the teaching of the sophists was merely an expression of conventional morality itself — but an expression that revealed more clearly the weaknesses inherent in it.

We can see what those weaknesses were, for they are already implicit in Hesiod. Hesiod tells us that we must "listen . . . to justice, and forget, completely, violence" (**1.16**). Why? Because "justice conquers violence and triumphs in the end" (**1.18**). "Otherwise," he tells us with startling candor, "I'd not myself be righteous, nor have my son be so; for it is bad to be a man of justice if the less just's to have the greater right" (**1.19**). In short, it is *expedient* to follow justice, for justice is the will of Zeus.

What happens when we take away Zeus — when Zeus has been driven out and the Vortex rules in his stead? Will it still be expedient to follow justice? Yes, insofar as those who make the laws have the power to enforce them. But the eyes of those who make the laws, unlike those of Zeus, cannot be everywhere at once, and it is not, therefore, in every case expedient to obey the law. On the contrary, when the law sleeps it will almost certainly prove expedient to take advantage of the fact. How does this differ from the philosophy, say, of Antiphon, who says that when a man is under observation it will pay him to act justly, but that when he is unobserved it will pay him to act otherwise? There is no difference at all: in the teaching of the sophist the prudential morality of Hesiod has come home to roost.

THE MELIAN DEBATE

If this is true, we should expect to find evidence of it in the behavior of the "great beast" itself; and indeed nothing is simpler. Two passages will suffice; they are drawn from Thucydides' great history of the Peloponnesian War. The first describes an event which occurred in the sixteenth year of the war. In this year the Athenians, Thucydides tells us, made an expedition against Melos, a small island in the Cyclades. Upon arrival they sent representatives to negotiate, and the following exchange took place:

13.20   *Athenians.* — 'For ourselves, we shall not trouble you with specious pretences — either of how we have a right to our empire because we overthrew the Mede, or are now attacking you because of wrong that you have done us — and make a long speech which would not be believed; and in return we hope that you, instead of thinking to influence us by saying that you did not join the Lacedaemonians, although their colonists, or that you have done us no wrong, will aim at what is feasible, holding in view the real sentiments of us both; since you know as well as we do that right, as the world goes, is only in question between equals in power, while the strong do what they can and the weak suffer what they must.'

Melians. — 'As we think, at any rate, it is expedient — we speak as we are obliged, since you enjoin us to let right alone and talk only of interest — that you should not destroy what is our common protection, the privilege of being allowed in danger to invoke what is fair and right, and even to profit by arguments not strictly valid if they can be got to pass current. And you are as much interested in this as any, as your fall would be a signal for the heaviest vengeance and an example for the world to meditate upon.'

Athenians. — 'The end of our empire, if end it should, does not frighten us: a rival empire like Lacedaemon, even if Lacedaemon was our real antagonist, is not so terrible to the vanquished as subjects who by themselves attack and overpower their rulers. This, however, is a risk that we are content to take. We will now proceed to show you that we are come here in the interest of our empire, and that we shall say what we are now going to say, for the preservation of your country; as we would fain exercise that empire over you without trouble, and see you preserved for the good of us both.'

Melians. — 'And how, pray, could it turn out as good for us to serve as for you to rule?'

Athenians. — 'Because you would have the advantage of submitting before suffering the worst, and we should gain by not destroying you.'

Melians. — 'So that you would not consent to our being neutral, friends instead of enemies, but allies of neither side.'

Athenians. — 'No; for your hostility cannot so much hurt us as your friendship will be an argument to our subjects of our weakness, and your enmity of our power.'

Melians. — 'Is that your subjects' idea of equity, to put those who have nothing to do with you in the same category with

peoples that are most of them your own colonists, and some conquered rebels?'

Athenians. — 'As far as right goes they think one has as much
of it as the other, and that if any maintain their independence it
is because they are strong, and that if we do not molest them it is
because we are afraid; so that besides extending our empire we
should gain in security by your subjection; the fact that you are
islanders and weaker than others rendering it all the more important that you should not succeed in baffling the masters of
the sea.'

Melians. — 'But do you consider that there is no security in the
policy which we indicate? For here again if you debar us from
talking about justice and invite us to obey your interest, we also
must explain ours, and try to persuade you, if the two happen to
coincide. How can you avoid making enemies of all existing
neutrals who shall look at our case and conclude from it that one
day or another you will attack them? And what is this but to
make greater the enemies that you have already, and to force
others to become so who would otherwise have never thought
of it?'

Athenians. — 'Why, the fact is that continentals generally give
us but little alarm; the liberty which they enjoy will long prevent
their taking precautions against us; it is rather islanders like yourselves, outside our empire, and subjects smarting under the yoke,
who would be the most likely to take a rash step and lead themselves and us into obvious danger.'

Melians. — 'Well then, if you risk so much to retain your empire, and your subjects to get rid of it, it were surely great base-
ness and cowardice in us who are still free not to try everything
that can be tried, before submitting to your yoke.'

Athenians. — 'Not if you are well advised, the contest not
being an equal one, with honour as the prize and shame as the
penalty, but a question of self-preservation and of not resisting
those who are far stronger than you are.'

Melians. — 'But we know that the fortune of war is sometimes
more impartial than the disproportion of numbers might lead one
to suppose; to submit is to give ourselves over to despair, while
action still preserves for us a hope that we may stand erect.'

Athenians. — 'Hope, danger's comforter, may be indulged in by
those who have abundant resources, if not without loss at all
events without ruin; but its nature is to be extravagant, and those
who go so far as to put their all upon the venture see it in its
true colours only when they are ruined; but so long as the discovery would enable them to guard against it, it is never found
wanting. Let not this be the case with you, who are weak and
hang on a single turn of the scale; nor be like the vulgar, who,
abandoning such security as human means may still afford, when

visible hopes fail them in extremity, turn to invisible, to prophecies and oracles, and other such inventions that delude men
with hopes to their destruction.'

Melians. — 'You may be sure that we are as well aware as you
of the difficulty of contending against your power and fortune,
unless the terms be equal. But we trust that the gods may grant
us fortune as good as yours, since we are just men fighting against
unjust, and that what we want in power will be made up by the
alliance of the Lacedaemonians, who are bound, if only for very
shame, to come to the aid of their kindred. Our confidence, therefore, after all is not so utterly irrational.'

Athenians. — 'When you speak of the favour of the gods, we
may as fairly hope for that as yourselves; neither our pretensions
nor our conduct being in any way contrary to what men believe
of the gods, or practise among themselves. Of the gods we believe,
and of men we know, that by a necessary law of their nature they
rule wherever they can. And it is not as if we were the first to
make this law, or to act upon it when made: we found it existing
before us, and shall leave it to exist for ever after us; all we do
is to make use of it, knowing that you and everybody else, having the same power as we have, would do the same as we do.
Thus, as far as the gods are concerned, we have no fear and no
reason to fear that we shall be at a disadvantage. But when we
come to your notion about the Lacedaemonians, which leads you
to believe that shame will make them help you, here we bless
your simplicity but do not envy your folly. The Lacedaemonians,
when their own interests or their country's laws are in question,
are the worthiest men alive; of their conduct towards others much
might be said, but no clearer idea of it could be given than by
shortly saying that of all the men we know they are most conspicuous in considering what is agreeable honourable, and what
is expedient just. Such a way of thinking does not promise much
for the safety which you now unreasonably count upon.'

Melians. — 'But it is for this very reason that we now trust to
their respect for expediency to prevent them from betraying the
Melians, their colonists, and thereby losing the confidence of their
friends in Hellas and helping their enemies.'

Athenians. — 'Then you do not adopt the view that expediency
goes with security, while justice and honour cannot be followed
without danger; and danger the Lacedaemonians generally court
as little as possible.'

Melians. — 'But we believe that they would be more likely to
face even danger for our sake, and with more confidence than
for others, as our nearness to Peloponnese makes it easier for
them to act, and our common blood insures our fidelity.'

Athenians. — 'Yes, but what an intending ally trusts to, is not
the goodwill of those who ask his aid, but a decided superiority
of power for action; and the Lacedaemonians look to this even

more than others. At least, such is their distrust of their home resources that it is only with numerous allies that they attack a neighbour; now is it likely that while we are masters of the sea they will cross over to an island?'

Melians. — 'But they would have others to send. The Cretan sea is a wide one, and it is more difficult for those who command it to intercept others, than for those who wish to elude them to do so safely. And should the Lacedaemonians miscarry in this, they would fall upon your land, and upon those left of your allies whom Brasidas did not reach; and instead of places which are not yours, you will have to fight for your own country and your own confederacy.'

Athenians. — 'Some diversion of the kind you speak of you may one day experience, only to learn, as others have done, that the Athenians never once yet withdrew from a siege for fear of any. But we are struck by the fact, that after saying you would consult for the safety of your country, in all this discussion you have mentioned nothing which men might trust in and think to be saved by. Your strongest arguments depend upon hope and the future, and your actual resources are too scanty, as compared with those arrayed against you, for you to come out victorious. You will therefore show great blindness of judgment, unless, after allowing us to retire, you can find some counsel more prudent than this. You will surely not be caught by that idea of disgrace, which in dangers that are disgraceful, and at the same time too plain to be mistaken, proves so fatal to mankind; since in too many cases the very men that have their eyes perfectly open to what they are rushing into, let the thing called disgrace, by the mere influence of a seductive name, lead them on to a point at which they become so enslaved by the phrase as in fact to fall wilfully into hopeless disaster, and incur disgrace more disgraceful as the companion of error, than when it comes as the result of misfortune. This, if you are well advised, you will guard against; and you will not think it dishonourable to submit to the greatest city in Hellas, when it makes you the moderate offer of becoming its tributary ally, without ceasing to enjoy the country that belongs to you; nor when you have the choice given you between war and security, will you be so blinded as to choose the worse. And it is certain that those who do not yield to their equals, who keep terms with their superiors, and are moderate towards their inferiors, on the whole succeed best. Think over the matter, therefore, after our withdrawal, and reflect once and again that it is for your country that you are consulting, that you have not more than one, and that upon this one deliberation depends its prosperity or ruin.'

Melos decided to fight; the Athenians laid siege to the city. After a time Melos surrendered unconditionally. "The Athenians," says Thucydides, "put to death all the men of military age whom they took and sold the women and children as slaves."

THE MYTILENEAN DEBATE

The morality of expediency has nowhere been more brilliantly, or more brutally, stated than in Thucydides' account of the debate at Melos. Yet precisely because of that brilliance and brutality a certain suspicion has always attached to it. It seems highly unlikely that Thucydides is reporting actual speeches here; there is something artificial, something stagy, about them which fits better with their representing an attempt on Thucydides' part to set forth what he himself felt to be the principles underlying Athenian policy. The speeches are such as would have been made by men fully conscious of the principles upon which they act; but for that reason they raise the question whether Thucydides has correctly analyzed these acts.

For this reason it is well to supplement Thucydides' account of the debate at Melos with an account of another debate, which certainly took place and which Thucydides was not likely to have seriously misrepresented — a debate which was conducted before the Athenian assembly itself on the fate of Mytilene. Mytilene, the chief city of Lesbos, an island off the Ionian coast, revolted against Athenian rule in the fourth year of the war. The Athenians reduced the island city by blockade and decided to put to death the entire male population. The next day, however, they began to have second thoughts; there was a change of feeling, and the authorities were prevailed upon to reopen the debate. Of the various speeches Thucydides has given us two: one by Cleon, a demagogue described as "the most violent of the citizens," urging the carrying out of the original decree; the other by an otherwise unknown citizen named Diodotus, urging that the decree be rescinded.

Cleon's summing up shows clearly the grounds for his position:

13.21 To sum up shortly, I say that if you follow my advice you will do what is just towards the Mitylenians, and at the same time expedient; while by a different decision you will not oblige them so much as pass sentence upon yourselves. For if they were right in rebelling, you must be wrong in ruling. However, if, right or wrong, you determine to rule, you must carry out your principle and punish the Mitylenians as your interest requires; or else you must give up your empire and cultivate honesty without danger. Make up your minds, therefore, to give them like for like; and do not let the victims who escaped the plot be more insensible than the conspirators who hatched it; but reflect what they would have done if victorious over you, especially as they were the aggressors.

It is they who wrong their neighbour without a cause, that pursue their victim to the death, on account of the danger which they foresee in letting their enemy survive; since the object of a wanton wrong is more dangerous, if he escape, than an enemy who has not this to complain of. Do not, therefore, be traitors to yourselves, but recall as nearly as possible the moment of suffering and the supreme importance which you then attached to their reduction; and now pay them back in their turn, without yielding to present weakness or forgetting the peril that once hung over you. Punish them as they deserve, and teach your other allies by a striking example that the penalty of rebellion is death. Let them once understand this and you will not have so often to neglect your enemies while you are fighting with your own confederates.

In part Cleon is urging this course of action on grounds of self-interest. Athens is an imperial power, and to feel pity, to listen to the claims of decency, is entirely against the interests of an imperial power. Revolt must be punished severely and promptly; hesitation in this matter will merely invite further revolt. But Cleon also urges the *justice* of this course of action. In revenging yourselves on the Mytileneans you will, he says, be doing the right thing as well as acting in your own interest. For the Mytileneans attacked you without provocation; punish them as they deserve, then, and do not let your anger cool.

Diodotus, too, argues on grounds of self-interest; but he will make no concessions to "justice":

13.22 'I have not come forward either to oppose or to accuse in the matter of Mitylene; indeed, the question before us as sensible men is not their guilt, but our interests. Though I prove them ever so guilty, I shall not, therefore, advise their death, unless it be expedient; nor though they should have claims to indulgence, shall I recommend it, unless it be clearly for the good of the country. I consider that we are deliberating for the future more than for the present; and where Cleon is so positive as to the useful deterrent effects that will follow from making rebellion capital, I who consider the interests of the future quite as much as he, as positively maintain the contrary. And I require you not to reject my useful considerations for his specious ones: his speech may have the attraction of seeming the more just in your present temper against Mitylene; but we are not in a court of justice, but in a political assembly; and the question is not justice, but how to make the Mitylenians useful to Athens.

'Now of course communities have enacted the penalty of death for many offences far lighter than this: still hope leads men to venture, and no one ever yet put himself in peril without the inward conviction that he would succeed in his design. Again, was there ever city rebelling that did not believe that it possessed either in itself or in its alliances resources adequate to the enterprise? All, states and individuals, are alike prone to err, and there is no law that will prevent them; or why should men have exhausted the list of punishments in search of enactments to protect them from evil-doers? It is probable that in early times the penalties for the greatest offences were less severe, and that, as these were disregarded, the penalty of death has been by degrees in most cases arrived at, which is itself disregarded in like manner. Either then some means of terror more terrible than this must be discovered, or it must be owned that this restraint is useless; and that as long as poverty gives men the courage of necessity, or plenty fills them with the ambition which belongs to insolence and pride, and the other conditions of life remain each under the thraldom of some fatal and master passion, so long will the impulse never be wanting to drive men into danger. Hope also and cupidity, the one leading and the other following, the one conceiving the attempt, the other suggesting the facility of succeeding, cause the widest ruin, and, although invisible agents, are far stronger than the dangers that are seen. Fortune, too, powerfully helps the delusion, and by the unexpected aid that she sometimes lends, tempts men to venture with inferior means; and this is especially the case with communities, because the stakes played for are the highest, freedom or empire, and, when all are acting together, each man irrationally magnifies his own capacity. In fine, it is impossible to prevent, and only great simplicity can hope to prevent, human nature doing what it has once set its mind upon, by force of law or by any other deterrent force whatsoever.

'We must not, therefore, commit ourselves to a false policy through a belief in the efficacy of the punishment of death, or exclude rebels from the hope of repentance and an early atonement of their error. Consider a moment! At present, if a city that has already revolted perceive that it cannot succeed, it will come to terms while it is still able to refund expenses, and pay tribute afterwards. In the other case, what city think you would not prepare better than is now done, and hold out to the last against its besiegers, if it is all one whether it surrender late or soon? And how can it be otherwise than hurtful to us to be put to the expense of a siege, because surrender is out of the question; and if we take the city, to receive a ruined town from which we can no longer draw the revenue which forms our real strength against the enemy? We must not, therefore, sit as strict judges of the offenders to our own prejudice, but rather see how by moderate chastisements we may be enabled to benefit in future by the revenue-producing powers of our dependencies; and we must make up our minds to look for our protection not to legal terrors but to careful administration. At present we do exactly the opposite. When a free community, held in subjection by force, rises, as is only natural, and asserts its independence, it is no sooner reduced than we fancy ourselves obliged to punish it severely; although the right course with freemen is not to chastise them rigorously when they do rise, but rigorously to watch them before they rise, and to prevent their ever entertaining the idea, and, the insurrection suppressed, to make as few responsible for it as possible.

'Only consider what a blunder you would commit in doing as Cleon recommends. As things are at present, in all the cities the people is your friend, and either does not revolt with the oligarchy, or, if forced to do so, becomes at once the enemy of the insurgents; so that in the war with the hostile city you have the masses on your side. But if you butcher the people of Mitylene, who had nothing to do with the revolt, and who, as soon as they got arms, of their own motion surrendered the town, first you will commit the crime of killing your benefactors; and next you will play directly into the hands of the higher classes, who when they induce their cities to rise, will immediately have the people on their side, through your having announced in advance the same punishment for those who are guilty and for those who are not. On the contrary, even if they were guilty, you ought to seem not to notice it, in order to avoid alienating the only class still friendly to us. In short, I consider it far more useful for the preservation of our empire voluntarily to put up with injustice, than to put to death, however justly, those whom it is our interest to keep alive. As for Cleon's idea that in punishment the claims of justice and expediency can both be satisfied, facts do not confirm the possibility of such a combination.

'Confess, therefore, that this is the wisest course, and without conceding too much either to pity or to indulgence, by neither of which motives do I any more than Cleon wish you to be influenced, upon the plain merits of the case before you, be persuaded by me to try calmly those of the Mitylenians whom Paches sent off as guilty, and to leave the rest undisturbed. This is at once best for the future, and most terrible to your enemies at the present moment; inasmuch as good policy against an adversary is superior to the blind attacks of brute force.'

The contrast between the two speeches is very marked. The head-strong violence of Cleon is set against the dispassionate calm of Diodotus in the most striking way. Nor is there any doubt as to where our sympathies lie. Diodotus speaks with the voice of reason; he is cool and collected. Moreover he comes to what seem (to our modern tastes) to be the correct conclusions. He has little faith in the value of punishment; he feels that an ounce of prevention is worth a pound of cure; that severity with wrongdoers merely plays into the hands of the "reactionaries," and so on. And listening, we are apt to be deceived into thinking that he is guided by the same humanitarian motives that move modern men to say these same things. But it is not so; we are expressly warned against being swayed too much by pity or by ordinary decent feelings. We are to make our decisions simply on "the plain merits of the case" before us, and the argument, throughout, turns on the appeal to self-interest: "The question is not justice, but how to make the Mytileneans useful to Athens." The same cold-blooded calculation that marks Democritus' discussion of the question whether a man ought to have children (**11.58**) marks that of Diodotus. It is a more disturbing speech than that of Cleon precisely because it rules out humanitarian considerations on principle. But it is the logical fruit of the morality of self-interest, and that morality was embedded in the very fibre of a people who, no more than a generation since, had been peasants very much like old Strepsiades, and whose education reflected still the mentality of *Works and Days*.

Epilogue

If the full weight of Plato's attack on the morality of self-interest fell mainly on the sophists, it was because he recognized in their theory of man and society the reflex of that morality. And no one understood that theory as well as he, or expressed it as well. It is stated in the *Republic* by the young Glaucon:

1   Men say that by nature it is good to do wrong, but bad to be wronged; but that the bad involved in being wronged far exceeds the good in doing wrong. So whenever men wrong one another and are wronged, and have a taste of both, then those who find that they cannot have the one without the other decide that it is to their advantage to make an agreement with one another neither to do wrong nor to be wronged. And this, they say, was the beginning of making laws and covenants, and of giving the names "lawful" and "just" to the command of law; and this is the origin and essential nature of justice: a compromise between what is best of all — doing wrong and getting away with it — and what is worst — being wronged and not being able to get revenge. Justice, being midway between the two, is cherished not as a good but as something to be honored where the ability to do wrong is lacking. For a man who had the power to do it, and was really a man, would never covenant with anybody *neither* to do wrong *nor* be wronged. He would be mad to do so. This, then, Socrates, is the true nature of justice, and these are the circumstances out of which it arises, according to the theory.

We have heard all this before. It is the sophistic theory of justice, in the extreme form in which we find it stated by Callicles. The laws of the city are the invention of the weak, who are cunning enough to see that it is to their mutual interest to restrain the stronger. But the theory does not rest upon any investigation into the way in which human societies have actually arisen in the past. It derives its whole force from a certain theory as to the nature of man, as Glaucon goes on to point out:

2   That those who do right do so unwillingly, because they are unable to do wrong, will be evident if we imagine a just man and an unjust man to each of whom we give license to do whatever he wishes, and then follow them in thought to see where the desire of each will lead him. We shall, in such a case, catch the just man red-handed doing the same as the unjust man, because of the self-interest which every creature pursues by its very nature as a good, though in law it is diverted by force into paying deference to "equality."

The license I mean would be of the same sort as the power which men say the ancestor of Gyges the Lydian had. This man was a shepherd in the service of the ruler of Lydia. A heavy rain and earthquake opened the ground, and a chasm appeared at the place where he was. Seeing it, and wondering at it, he went down into it and saw (so the story goes), among other marvelous things, a bronze horse, hollow, with a door leading into it. And peering through it he saw a corpse larger than that of a man, wearing only a gold ring on its finger, which he removed before leaving. And when the shepherds next met to make up their customary monthly report to the king on the condition of the flocks, he also attended, wearing the ring.

Now as he sat there among the rest he happened to turn the collet of the ring towards himself, so that it was in his palm; and when this happened he became invisible to those sitting around him, and they spoke of him as if he were absent. He was amazed, and feeling about for it he turned the ring back again so that the collet was outside and he became visible. Seeing this, he made trial of the ring to see if it really had this power, and found that whenever he turned the collet inwards he became invisible and that whenever he turned it outwards he became visible. Perceiving this, he straightway arranged matters so that he was one of the messengers sent to the king. When he arrived he seduced the queen and with her help set upon the king, killed him and seized the throne.

Suppose, now, that there were two such rings, and the just man were to wear one and the unjust man the other. There would be, I think, no one so adamantine as to continue in justice and to have the strength of mind to refrain from touching the property of others, when it was perfectly possible for him to take whatever he wished with impunity, even from the open market place, and to enter people's houses and make love to anyone he wished, and to kill or free from prison anyone he wished, and in every other respect to behave among men as though he were a god. And in doing this his conduct would be no different from the other man's, but they would both follow the same path.

This, one might argue, is strong evidence that no one is just of his own accord, but only under compulsion, and that no one regards justice as benefitting him personally, since each, when he thinks it possible to commit an injustice, does so. For every man believes that injustice is far more profitable to himself than justice, and according to the author of this theory he is quite right. For if a man who obtained such license neither committed injustice nor touched the property of another he would be regarded as a miserable idiot by those who knew of it — though they would praise him to each other's faces, deceiving each other through fear of suffering injustice.

This is the theory which lies behind that of the "conventional" nature of law. Though men behave themselves in the city, so that it is difficult to see their real nature under these artificial conditions, it may be seen quickly enough when the law sleeps or has no force behind it. Then it is revealed, and we see men for what they are: ruthless, grasping, self-centered animals to whom nothing is sacred, and to whom the law of self-preservation and the unlimited satisfaction of one's desires is the highest court of appeal.

But behind this theory lay another still. Dim, shadowy, it was the root from which, it seemed to Plato, all the rest sprang. And this was the theory of the nature of nature itself which had slowly emerged from the investigations of the natural philosophers. In the *Laws* Plato looks back on this process of development, as we have followed it, and tries to appraise its significance.

Where I come from, says the principal speaker in that dialogue, we have books that treat of the gods, some in verse, some in prose:

3 The oldest of these tell how, in the beginning, the heaven and the rest came into being, and after a while they proceed to give a theogony and to tell of the birth of the gods and their society. Whether these accounts are good or bad for their hearers in other respects, it is not easy to blame them for being old. But as regards the careful respect due to parents, I would not recommend them as being salutory, nor as being wholly true. But let's set aside and forget about these ancient accounts; let them be told in whatever way is pleasing to the gods. The blame for our troubles should be laid at the door of the new "intellectuals." For the result of the arguments of such men is this. When you and I say that the gods exist, and produce as evidence things like the sun, moon, stars, and earth as being gods and divine,

then the converts of these "intellectuals" retort that these are only earth and stones, and are incapable of being concerned in human affairs, and that our beliefs are merely embroidered with arguments to make them more credible.

If we are to come to grips with these people, the speaker continues, we must get at the assumptions which underlie what they say:

4   *Athenian:* It is clear, these people hold, that the greatest and most beautiful things are the products of nature and chance, while the lesser are the products of art. Art, receiving from nature the birth of the great and primary things, molds and forms the lesser ones which we call "artificial."

Clinias: What do you mean?

Athenian: I will put it more clearly. They maintain that fire and water and earth and air all exist "naturally" and "by chance"; they are not the product of art. And these, which are completely inanimate, go to make up the bodies which come next in order — the earth, sun, moon, and stars. Moving at random, each according to its own power, they come together in certain "fitting" ways — hot things with cold, dry with wet, soft with hard, and so on with all the other combinations which necessarily result from the chance mingling of opposites; and in this way they give birth to the whole heaven and all that is in it — and all animals and plants, too, once the seasons have come into being from the same causes. And none of this, they maintain, involved any intelligence or any god or the exercise of any art, but as I said a moment ago it all just happened "naturally" and "by chance." Art, they say, came later — a product of these same causes, and as perishable as mortals themselves. And she has begotten certain trifles having little to do with "truth" — images such as those produced by painting or music and the arts which accompany these. The arts which produce anything of real value, such as medicine or agriculture or gymnastic, have more in common with nature. Politics, they admit, has some small basis in nature; but mostly it is a product of art. Thus all legislation is not "natural" but "man-made," for law is nothing "true."

Clinias: What do you mean?

Athenian: First of all, my friend, these men say that the gods exist by art — not by nature but by certain conventions which differ from place to place just as each community agreed in drawing up its own constitution. Some things are beautiful "by nature," others "by convention." Just things do not exist at all by nature; but men are forever disputing about them and constantly change them around. And whenever they change them each change becomes authoritative for the moment, though it is made by art and convention and not in any way by nature.

All these, my friends, are the views of the "intellectuals" — both poets and private citizens who affirm that the height of justice is to succeed by force. An outbreak of irreligion attacks the young men who hear this, as though the gods were different from the concepts of them which the law requires us to have. Hence factions arise when their instructors draw them towards the "real life" which is "according to nature," and which "in truth" consists in living so as to be "master" of others rather than a "slave," according to "legal convention."

Everything, then — the sophistic theory of society, of man, of the gods — turns upon certain assumptions about nature itself, assumptions derived in the last analysis from the philosophers of nature. It is the assumption that nature is devoid of mind or purpose, and that the world-order is the product not of design but of chance, *i.e.*, of atoms in motion, subject only to those laws of impact and recoil of which the symbol is the vortex itself, maker of heaven and earth. From this the rest follows. As nature is driven by the laws of impact, so men are driven by the laws of nature, subject only to those appetites which drive other animals, restrained only by those fears which restrain them. And the city? The city can only be what Callicles took it to be: an artificial thing, cemented together by the basest of human emotions — fear — and shored up by mutual deception.

If these conclusions were insupportable, the assumptions from which they sprang must be subjected to a new appraisal. This was the work which Plato set himself, and which was to be continued in his pupil Aristotle. A phase of thought was over, and a new one was beginning. The battle with the natural philosophers had been joined.

APPENDIX A

THALES OF MILETUS

Our earliest source of information about Thales is Herodotus, who says that he predicted the eclipse of the sun which took place on May 28, 585 B.C., during a battle between the Medes and the Lydians:

1   In the sixth year of the war (which they had been fighting with equal fortune) an engagement took place during which, in the midst of the battle, day suddenly became night. This event had been foretold to the Ionians by Thales of Miletus, and it actually occurred in the year in which he said it would.

There is no reason to doubt Thales' interest in such matters; it is attested by the anecdotes related by Plato and Aristotle (**9.50–51**). What is uncertain is the extent of his interest in the wider problems dealt with by his successors.

The first to speak of Thales as a natural philosopher in the full sense of the word is Aristotle:

2   Some men say that the earth rests on water. This is the most ancient account we have received. And this, men say, is the account of Thales of Miletus: that it stays where it is because it floats like a log or something of the sort.

3   Most of the early philosophers thought that the first principles in the form of matter were the only principles of everything. The source of all existing things — that from which first of all they come into being and into which they finally perish, the substance remaining but changing in its qualities — this, they say, is the element and first principle of existing things. Therefore they think that nothing comes into being or passes away, because a certain sort of nature is always preserved . . . . For there must be some nature (either one or more than one) from which other things come into being while this is preserved.

However, they do not all give the same account of the number and form of such a first principle. Thales, the originator of this sort of philosophy, says that it is water (for which reason he declared that the earth rests on water). Possibly he based this assumption on the observation that the nourishment of all things is moist, and that heat itself comes into being from this and lives by it (that from which they come to be being the first principle of all things). He bases his assumption, then, on this and on the fact that the seeds of all things have a moist nature, water being the natural first principle of moist things.

There are some who think that the very ancient first theologians made this sort of assumption about nature; for they made Ocean and Tethys the ancestors of coming into being, and the oath of the gods water, which they called Styx (for the most ancient is the most honored, and an oath is the most honored thing). Whether there was any such ancient and venerable belief concerning nature is unclear. At any rate, Thales is said to have made this declaration about the first cause.

Virtually all that we know about Thales as a natural philosopher is contained in these two passages.

Aristotle tells us that Thales made the earth rest on water, and that he made water the "element" and "first principle" of existing things. There is no reason to doubt the first of these statements. It is repeated, with the addition of circumstantial detail, by Seneca:

4   For Thales says that the earth is supported by water and sails like a ship; and when it is said to quake it is pitching because of the movement of the water.

It is clear, then, that Thales was concerned with the problem of the earth's support and the causes of earthquakes — problems subsequently dealt with by his successors (**2.19–21**; **3.13**, with note). But Anaximander and Anaximenes were not primarily concerned with the explanation of particular phenomena; they were concerned with the origin and nature of the world-order as a whole. Did Thales, too, address himself to this problem?

The evidence is doubtful. To begin with, it is not at all clear how much weight we should attach to Aristotle's assertion that Thales made water the "element" and "first principle" of existing things (the technical terms are Aristotle's own). He makes it with an assurance which is belied by his subsequent statement that at any rate Thales is *said* to have held this view. Second, assuming that Thales *did* assign some sort of primacy to water, it is impossible to tell, from what Aristotle says, precisely what sort of primacy it had — whether Thales was thinking of it from a physiological point of view as something found in all living things (as Aristotle himself suggests), or whether he actually conceived of it as a "first principle" in the sense in which air was a "first principle" for Anaximenes. This last is unlikely; the evidence suggests that Thales was interested less in the origin of the world-order than in the nature of living things.

This impression is borne out by the only other passages in which Aristotle reports his views:

5   It seems, from the anecdotes that are told about him, that Thales supposed the soul to be a source of motion — if, indeed, he said that the lodestone has a soul because it moves iron.

6   Some people say that the soul is mingled in the whole; for which reason, perhaps, Thales thought that everything was full of gods.

The reasoning here is clear enough: the soul is a source of motion; the lodestone has the power to move iron; therefore the lodestone, too, has soul. But again it is difficult to know how much confidence to place in Aristotle's report, for he himself seems to have very little. The remainder of what we are told of Thales comes from later authors and is of little value.

It is clearly impossible to form an impression of Thales' views from Aristotle's account of them; nor does Aristotle's account, such as it is, indicate that the scope of Thales' thought invites comparison with that of Anaximander. It is only with the latter that we first meet with problems which transcend the explanation of particular phenomena, and it is precisely his concern with these larger problems that entitles Anaximander to be considered the first of the natural philosophers.

APPENDIX B

GORGIAS, *On Nature*

Sextus Empiricus gives an epitome of a work by Gorgias entitled *On Not-Being* or *On Nature*. This work appears to be directed against the Eleatics. Parmenides had maintained that being is, and that it alone can be thought or spoken of. Gorgias, on the contrary, maintains that being is not, that if it did exist it would be unknowable, and that even if it were knowable it could not be spoken of. He sought to prove these theses by arguments which travesty those of the Eleatics.

Whether this *tour de force* was intended seriously is difficult to determine. Aristotle apparently took it seriously enough to write a monograph (now lost) criticizing it; but Plato nowhere suggests that Gorgias was anything more, or pretended to be anything more, than a rhetorician. The epitome of Sextus is offered here without any attempt to answer the problems it raises.

1 In his book *On Not-Being* or *On Nature* Gorgias sets out to prove three successive points: first, that nothing exists; second, that even if it does it is incomprehensible by men; and third, that even if it is comprehensible it is certainly not expressible and cannot be communicated to another.

That nothing exists he proves in the following way. If anything exists, it must be either what is or what is not or what is *and* what is not. But, as he proceeds to show, what is does not exist, nor does what is not exist, nor does what is *and* what is not exist. Therefore nothing exists.

Now what is not does not exist. For if what is not exists it will at one and the same time be and not be. For insofar as it is conceived as what is not it will not exist; while on the other hand, insofar as it *is* what is not it *will* exist. But it is completely absurd that something should exist and not exist at one and the same time. Therefore what is not does not exist. (Moreover, if what is not *does* exist, what is will not exist; for these are contrary to one another. Thus, if existence were to characterize what is not, nonexistence will characterize what is. But it is not the case that what is does not exist; neither, therefore, will what is not exist.)

Furthermore, what is does not exist either. For if what is exists, either it is eternal or created or both eternal *and* created at the same time. But, as we shall prove, it is neither eternal nor created nor both eternal *and* created. Therefore what is does not exist.

For if what is is eternal (this is the first possibility to be considered), it has no beginning. For everything that is created has some beginning; but the eternal, being uncreated, had no beginning. And having no beginning it is infinite. But if it is infinite it is nowhere. For if it is somewhere, that in which it is is different from it, and thus what is, since it is encompassed by something, will no longer be infinite. For what encompasses is greater than that which is encompassed, but nothing is greater than the infinite. So, then, the infinite is not anywhere. (Nor is it encompassed by itself. For in that case that in which it is will be the same as that which is in it, and what is will become two different things: place and body. For that in which it is is place, while that which is in it is body. But this is absurd; therefore what is does not exist in itself.) Hence, if what is is eternal it is infinite; but if it is infinite it is nowhere; and if it does not exist anywhere it does not exist. Therefore, if what is is eternal it does not exist in respect to having a beginning.

Furthermore, it is impossible for what is to be created. For if it has been created, it has been created either out of what is or out of what is not. But it has not been created out of what is. For if it *is* it has not been created but exists already. Nor has it been created out of what is not; for what is not cannot create anything, since that which is creative of anything must of necessity have a share of existence. What is, then, is not created either.

For the same reasons it is not both together, *i.e.*, eternal *and* created; for these are destructive of one another. If what is is eternal it has not been created, and if it has been created it is not eternal. Therefore, if what is is neither eternal nor created, nor both together, it will not exist.

(Moreover, if it exists it is either one or many. But, as will be shown, it is neither one nor many; therefore, what is does not exist. For if it is one, either it is a quantity or it is continuous or it is a magnitude or it is a body; but whichever of these it is it is not one. For if it is a quantity it will be divided [*i.e.*, into the units which make up that quantity]; if it is continuous it will be cut up; similarly, if it be conceived as a magnitude it will not be indivisible; and if it is a body it will be threefold, for it will have length, breadth, and depth. But it is absurd to say that what is is none of these; therefore, what is is not one. Nor is it many. For if it is not one it is not many either; for the many is made up of ones, so that if the one is destroyed the many are destroyed too.)

From the foregoing it will be evident that neither what is nor what is not exists. That they do not both exist together — both what is and what is not — is easy to prove. For if both what is not *and* what is exist, what is not will be the same as what is so far as existence is concerned. And for this reason neither of them exists. For it is admitted that what is not does not exist; and it has been shown that what is is the same as what is not. Therefore it too will not exist. Not only that, but if what is is the same as what is not, both of them cannot exist. For if both exist they are *not* the same; and if they *are* the same, both cannot exist. For if what is does not exist and what is not does not exist, and both together do not exist, and if besides these possibilities no other is conceived, then nothing exists.

The next thing to be proved is that even if anything exists it is unknowable and inconceivable by man. For (says Gorgias) if the objects of thought are not things that exist, then what is is not thought . . . . But the objects of thought (to take them first) are not existing things, as we shall show, and therefore what is is not thought.

Now it is clear that the objects of thought are not existing things. For if the objects of thought are existing things, *all* objects of thought exist, and in whatever way anyone thinks them — which is ridiculous. For if someone thinks of a man flying, or of a chariot running along on the sea, it does not follow straightway that a man *is* flying or that a chariot *is* running along on the sea. So the objects of thought are not existing things.

Furthermore, if the objects of thought are existing things, non-existent things will not be thought. For opposites characterize opposites, and what is not is opposite to what is. Hence if "being thought" characterizes what is, then "not being thought" characterizes what is not. But this is absurd; for Scylla and Chimera and many things that do not exist are thought. Therefore what is is not thought.

And just as things are called visible things because they are seen, and things heard audible because they are heard, and we do not reject visible things because they are not heard or dismiss audible things because they are not seen (for each ought to be judged by the sense peculiar to it and not by another), so also objects of thought will exist even though they are not visible to sight or audible to hearing, because they are apprehended by the test proper to them [merely by being thought]. So that if someone *thinks* that a chariot is running along on the sea, then he ought to believe that there *is* a chariot running along on the sea, even though he does not see it — which is absurd. Therefore what is is not thought or comprehended.

But even if it be comprehended it cannot be communicated to another person. For if existing things are *objects* seen and heard and, in general, perceived by the senses, and exist outside us; and if those that are visible are comprehended through vision while those that are audible are comprehended through hearing, and not the other way around; how, then, *can* they be conveyed to another person? For it is by means of *words* that we communicate, and words are not real, existent things. We do not, therefore, indicate existing things to our fellow men but words, which are different from real things. Thus, just as what is visible cannot become audible, and *vice versa*, so too, since what is is outside of us, it could not become our words. And not being words, it cannot be made apparent to another person.

(Indeed, words arise, he says, from the impression which external objects, *i.e.*, the objects of sensation, make on us. For when we meet with a taste the word which expresses that quality is produced in us, and when we meet with a color the word which expresses the color. But if so, words are not suited to the explanation of what lies outside us, but on the contrary what lies outside us is that which indicates our words. Moreover, it is not possible to object that words exist in the same sense that the objects of vision and hearing exist, and can therefore indicate real, existent things, being real and existent themselves. For even if words are real, he says, they differ from the rest of the things that are real, and visible bodies differ very greatly from words. For what is visible is apprehended by one sense organ, words by another. Words, therefore, do not manifest most real things, just as they do not make clear another's nature.)

BIBLIOGRAPHICAL ESSAY

In the visual art of a people we are often able to grasp intuitively the peculiar quality of their way of seeing things, and an evening spent in poring over the plates in a book such as E. Ayerton and S. Moulinier's *The Doric Temple* (London, 1961) may yield a deeper insight into the Greek mind than many learned works. Yet the literary remains, because their appeal is more complex, tend to leave a deeper and more lasting impression on us, and to bring us closer still to the thought of a people.

The books which above all dominated the Greek mind were the poems of Homer and Hesiod. These are available in excellent translations. For Homer there is Richmond Lattimore's translation of the *Iliad* (*The Iliad of Homer*, Chicago, 1951) and Robert Fitzgerald's translation of the *Odyssey* (*The Odyssey of Homer*, New York, 1961); for Hesiod, H. G. Evelyn-White's translation of the *Theogony* and *Works and Days* in the Loeb Classical Library (*Hesiod, the Homeric Hymns and Homerica*, London, 1914). In his exploration of these works the reader will find M. I. Finley's *The World of Odysseus* (New York, 1954) a useful companion.

The poems of Homer and Hesiod were written in the eighth century B.C.; the poetry of the succeeding period, during which the foundations of Greek philosophy were laid, is of a quite different character. A good selection of it will be found translated by Richmond Lattimore in *Greek Lyrics* (Chicago, 1960) and *The Odes of Pindar* (Chicago, 1947).

The great tragedies of the fifth century B.C., by Aeschylus, Sophocles, and Euripides, have been translated by many hands for the modern reader. Perhaps the best collection is that edited by David Grene and Richmond Lattimore in four volumes for the University of Chicago Press (Chicago, 1959). A good translation (anonymous) of the comedies of Aristophanes will be found in the second volume of *The Complete Greek Drama*, edited by Whitney J. Oates and Eugene O'Neill, Jr. (New York, 1938).

Finally, there are the *Histories* of Herodotus, translated by Aubrey de Selincourt in the Penguin series, and Thucydides' magnificent *History of the Peloponnesian War*, translated by Rex Warner for the same series.

Of these books all but one (*The Doric Temple*) are available in paperbound editions at modest prices.

EARLY GREEK PHILOSOPHY

The indispensable work for any detailed study of the early Greek philosophers is H. Diels's *Die Fragmente der Vorsokratiker*, first published in 1903 and edited since Diels's death by W. Kranz. This great collection of materials has never been translated into English, but K. Freeman's *Companion to the Pre-Socratic Philosophers: A Companion to Diels'* FRAGMENTE DER VORSOKRATIKER (Oxford, 1946) gives a useful summary of its contents. The same author's *Ancilla to the Pre-Socratic Philosophers: A Complete Translation of the Fragments in Diels'* FRAGMENTE DER VORSOKRATIKER (Oxford, 1948) includes most of the primary materials.

Most books on early Greek philosophy contain a generous amount of material in translation. The best of these is W. K. C. Guthrie's *History of Greek Philosophy* (Cambridge, England, 1962—), of which the first two volumes, carrying the history of Greek philosophy down to Democritus, have already appeared. *The Presocratic Philosophers: A Critical History with a Selection of Texts* (Cambridge, England, 1957), by G. S. Kirk and J. E. Raven, is a useful one-volume work. Two older books worth mentioning are John Burnet's *Early Greek Philosophy* (London, 1930) and F. M. Cornford's *From Religion to Philosophy* (London, 1912). Burnet, whose book held the field for a generation and is a classic, was inclined to stress the rational elements in early Greek philosophy, and to emphasize the radical nature of the break between myth and reason. Cornford, who combined the gifts of a poet with those of a classical scholar, took a very different view of Greek philosophy, insisting on its continuity with religion and on the mythical elements to be found in it even in its full development. Both books are available in paperbound editions, and taken together provide an instructive lesson in the kinds of approach to Greek philosophy which are possible.

HESIOD

A growing body of evidence suggests that many elements in Hesiod's account of creation derive from much older, Near Eastern accounts. The evidence is clearly presented in F. M. Cornford's *Principium Sapientiae: The Origins of Greek Philosophical Thought* (Cambridge, England, 1952). Part Two of this book, "Philosophical Cosmogony and its Origins in Myth and Ritual," begins with Anaximander and moves backward in time to Hesiod and to parallels in Babylonian sources.

The Intellectual Adventure of Ancient Man (Chicago, 1946) by H. and H. A. Frankfort, J. A. Wilson, and T. Jacobsen is a useful introduction to ancient Near Eastern ideas of man and the cosmos; it has been published in paperbound form as *Before Philosophy* (Harmondsworth, England, 1949). The relevant Near Eastern texts will be found in translation in

J. B. Pritchard's *Ancient Near Eastern Texts Relating to the Old Testament*, 2nd ed. (Princeton, 1955).

ANAXIMANDER

The best account of Anaximander's thought as a whole is Charles H. Kahn's *Anaximander and the Origins of Greek Cosmology* (New York, 1960). This is a scholarly work and uses Greek terms freely; but a great deal may be gained from it, even by the student without a knowledge of Greek — above all from the concluding chapter, "Milesian Speculation and the Greek Philosophy of Nature," which offers a bird's-eye view of the whole Ionian tradition.

A valuable feature of Kahn's book is that it uses early Greek medical writings to throw light on some of the chief theoretical conceptions of Ionian physics. One of the first to realize the value of these writings for our knowledge of early physical ideas was W. A. Heidel, whose *Heroic Age of Science: The Conception, Ideals and Methods of Science among the Ancient Greeks* (Baltimore, 1933) is based largely on his study of these works. This book was followed some years later by a smaller one entitled *Hippocratic Medicine: Its Spirit and Method* (New York, 1941). The most important of the early Greek medical writings are available in W. H. S. Jones's *Hippocrates* in the Loeb Classical Library (4 vols.), John Chadwick and W. N. Mann's *The Medical Works of Hippocrates* (Oxford, 1950) and Tage U. H. Ellinger's *Hippocrates on Intercourse and Pregnancy* (New York, 1952).

There is a good discussion of early Greek geographical knowledge in J. L. Myres's "An Attempt to Reconstruct the Maps Used by Herodotus," *Geographical Journal* (1896), 605-629. The history of the development of this knowledge is sketched in W. A. Heidel's little book *The Frame of the Ancient Greek Maps: With a Discussion of the Sphericity of the Earth* (New York, 1937).

Interest in Anaximander naturally tends to center on the single fragment which has come down to us. This is discussed in a masterly way by Gregory Vlastos in an article entitled "Equality and Justice in the Early Greek Cosmologies," *Classical Philology* (1947), 156-178, which shows in detail the centrality of the notion of cosmic justice in Anaximander and his successors. The same author's "Isonomia," *American Journal of Philology* (1953), 337-366, develops this idea in connection with Alcmaeon's theory of health as a balance of powers.

ANAXIMENES AND XENOPHANES

In Anaximenes the conception of soul first comes into prominence. Aristotle's review of the opinions of his predecessors regarding the soul is well worth reading. It will be found in Book One, Chapter Two of his treatise *On the Soul*. (The best collection of Aristotle's writings is *The Basic Works of Aristotle*, edited by Richard McKeon, New York, 1941.) Among modern studies E. Rohde's *Psyche: The Cult of Souls and Belief in Immortality among the Greeks* (London, 1925) is a classic.

With Xenophanes the development of philosophical theology begins. This development is traced in W. Jaeger's *The Theology of the Early Greek Philosophers* (London, 1947). The reader will do well to consult, in addition, the lengthy review of this book by Gregory Vlastos entitled "Theology and Philosophy in Early Greek Thought," *Philosophical Quarterly* (1952), 97-123.

PYTHAGOREANISM

The treatment of the Pythagoreans in W. K. C. Guthrie's *History of Greek Philosophy*, Volume One, is so full (it is as long as many books) that it deserves special mention here. F. M. Cornford wrote a number of short pieces dealing with different aspects of Pythagoreanism. His *Plato and Parmenides* (London, 1939) opens with an excellent chapter on "The Earliest Pythagorean Cosmogony." Another essay, "The Invention of Space," in *Essays in Honor of Gilbert Murray* (London, 1936), throws an interesting sidelight on this chapter. There is a charming piece by Cornford entitled "The Harmony of the Spheres" in *The Unwritten Philosophy and Other Essays* (Cambridge, England, 1950), and a lengthy essay in two parts dealing with the central paradox in Pythagoreanism, "Mysticism and Science in the Pythagorean Tradition," *Classical Quarterly* (1922), 137-150; (1923), 1-12.

The question of the genuineness of the fragments attributed to the fifth century Pythagorean Philolaus will probably never be settled to everyone's satisfaction. Among recent writers J. E. Raven, in *The Presocratic Philosophers* (308-311), rejects them altogether as post-Aristotelian forgeries; G. de Santillana and W. Pitts defend them vigorously in an article entitled "Philolaus in Limbo: or, What Happened to the Pythagoreans?" *Isis* (1951), 112-120.

The literature dealing with Pythagorean mathematics is fascinating. The "standard" view is that of T. L. Heath (*A History of Greek Mathematics*, 2 vols., Oxford, 1921), who considers much of the work incorporated in Euclid's *Elements* to have originated with the Pythagoreans. W. A. Heidel, in "The Pythagoreans and Greek Mathematics," *American Journal of Philology* (1940), 1-33, contends that no special mathematical discoveries can be attributed to Pythagoras himself, and that the role of the Pythagoreans in the history of Greek mathematics has been greatly exaggerated. The relevant materials are collected in *Greek Mathematical*

Works (Volume One: From Thales to Euclid) with an English translation by Ivor Thomas (Cambridge, Massachusetts, 1951). T. L. Heath's *Thirteen Books of Euclid's Elements* (3 vols., New York, 1956) contains much useful material on Pythagorean geometry. The reader interested in mathematical curiosities will enjoy Martin Gardner's "Simple Proofs of the Pythagorean Theorem," *Scientific American* (1964), 118-125.

For a brief but excellent account of Pythagorean political activities in southern Italy the reader is referred to J. S. Morrison's "Pythagoras of Samos," *Classical Quarterly* (1956), 135-156.

HERACLITUS

G. S. Kirk's *Heraclitus: The Cosmic Fragments* (Cambridge, England, 1954) is excellent but demands a knowledge of Greek. Two shorter pieces which do not are Gregory Vlastos' "On Heraclitus," *American Journal of Philology* (1955), 337-368, and Charles H. Kahn's "A New Look at Heraclitus," *American Philosophical Quarterly* (1964), 189-203. Philip Wheelwright's *Heraclitus* (Princeton, 1959) is also stimulating.

PARMENIDES

There is a full discussion of the fragments in Leonardo Tarán's *Parmenides: A Text with Translation, Commentary and Critical Essays* (Princeton, 1965); but this work is comparable in difficulty to Kirk's *Heraclitus*. The student without Greek would do better to begin with the chapter in F. M. Cornford's *Plato and Parmenides* (London, 1939) entitled "Parmenides' *Way of Truth*."

Parmenides is all argument, and the assessment of these arguments is no easy matter, though it would be difficult to guess this from the tone of some of the literature dealing with them. The modern student could do worse than turn to Plato's discussion of Parmenides in his dialogue *The Sophist*, translated with a running commentary by F. M. Cornford in *Plato's Theory of Knowledge* (London, 1935). Aristotle, too, discusses the Eleatics in the first book of his *Physics* (Chapters Two and Three). The reader who finds the argument hard to follow may find it useful to consult W. D. Ross's *Aristotle's Physics: A Revised Text with Introduction and Commentary* (Oxford, 1936), 337-341.

ZENO AND MELISSUS

The materials for a study of Zeno's paradoxes are collected in H. P. D. Lee's *Zeno of Elea: A Text with Translation and Notes* (Cambridge, England, 1936). The simplest and clearest exposition of them is Gregory

Vlastos' "Zeno" in W. Kaufman's *Philosophical Classics* (Englewood Cliffs, New Jersey, 1951), I, 27-45. However, the discussion of the Dichotomy in this essay has been superseded by Vlastos' article "Zeno's Race Course," *Journal of the History of Philosophy* (1966), 95-108; his discussion of the Arrow by "A Note on Zeno's Arrow," *Phronesis* (1966), 3-18.

Criticism of the arguments, especially the arguments against motion, begins with Aristotle in his *Physics* (Book Six, Chapter Nine) and extends down to the present. Some idea of the extent of the literature on the subject can be gained from F. Cajori's "The History of Zeno's Arguments on Motion," *American Mathematical Monthly* (1915), 1 ff., 39 ff., 77 ff., 109 ff., 143 ff., 253 ff., 292 ff. Much of this literature is of a technical nature, and much of it credits Zeno with a mathematical subtlety for which there is no evidence in the texts themselves.

For a time Cantor's discoveries in mathematics were thought to supply an answer to the paradoxes. This view was maintained, for example, by Bertrand Russell in his *Principles of Mathematics* (London, 1903). William James, on the other hand, maintained in *Some Problems of Philosophy* (New York, 1911) that Russell had entirely missed the point of the paradoxes. More recently Max Black's "Achilles and the Tortoise," *Analysis* (1951), 91-101 has elicited a number of articles on Zeno. Many of them are listed on page 109 n. of Black's *Problems of Analysis* (Ithaca, New York, 1954), which reprints the original article together with three further essays on the paradoxes. Other recent discussions are A. Grünbaum's "Modern Science and Refutation of the Paradoxes of Zeno," *Scientific Monthly* (1955), 234-239, and G. Whitrow's *The Natural Philosophy of Time* (New York, 1963), 135-157.

The influence of Zeno's dialectic on the Socrates of Plato's early dialogues, together with Plato's attempt to reshape the method into an instrument capable of advancing knowledge, may be studied in Richard Robinson's *Plato's Earlier Dialectic*, 2nd ed. (Oxford, 1953). Aristotle's treatment of dialectic, and the extent to which the practice of dialectic affected the form of Aristotle's logic, is discussed in E. Kapp's *The Greek Foundations of Traditional Logic* (New York, 1942). The influence of the competitive spirit on Greek and later Scholastic thought is traced by J. Huizinga's fascinating book *Homo Ludens: A Study of the Play Element in Culture* (London, 1949).

EMPEDOCLES

A critical problem for the understanding of Empedocles is the relation between his work on nature and the *Purifications*; for in the former Empedocles seems to leave no room for the immortal soul which is presupposed in the latter. The question is discussed in an excellent article by Charles Kahn entitled "Religion and Natural Philosophy in Empedocles' Doctrine of the Soul," *Archiv für Geschichte der Philosophie* (1960), 3-35.

Empedocles appears to have carried the investigation of the origins of life much further than his predecessors. The whole subject is treated in W. K. C. Guthrie's little book *In the Beginning: Some Greek Views on the Origins of Life and the Early State of Man* (London, 1957). The work of Empedocles seems to have had a decisive effect on the development of Greek biology, and a great deal of it was taken up into Atomism. This is particularly true of his theory of sensation, which Theophrastus treats at some length in his work *On the Senses*, translated by G. M. Stratton in *Theophrastus and the Greek Physiological Psychology before Aristotle* (New York, 1917).

ANAXAGORAS

The fragments of Anaxagoras raise a number of difficulties. These have been stated clearly by Gregory Vlastos in "The Physical Theory of Anaxagoras," *Philosophical Review* (1950), 31-57. Vlastos not only offers an ingenious solution of the difficulties but takes into account earlier work on the subject.

Anaxagoras' contributions to astronomy are dealt with in T. L. Heath's *Aristarchus of Samos, the Ancient Copernicus: A History of Greek Astronomy to Aristarchus, Together with Aristarchus' Treatise on the Sizes and Distances of the Sun and Moon* (Oxford, 1913). As the title indicates, this book covers the whole range of early Greek astronomical thought.

The question of the origin of the ideal of the philosophic life is discussed by W. Jaeger in an essay "On the Original Cycle of the Philosophic Ideal of Life," printed as an appendix to his *Aristotle: Fundamentals of the History of His Development*, 2nd ed. (Oxford, 1948). Jaeger holds that the ideal of the contemplative life derives from Plato or from the Platonic school, a view which is disputed by A. Cameron in *The Pythagorean Background to the Theory of Recollection* (Menasha, Wisconsin, 1938).

THE ATOMISTS

There is a very full treatment of the atomists, together with translations of most of the materials, in Cyril Bailey's *The Greek Atomists and Epicurus* (Oxford, 1928). Atomism was taken up into the philosophy of Epicurus, whose ideas may be studied in *Epicurus: Letters, Principal*

Doctrines and Vatican Sayings (New York, 1964). In this form they reached Lucretius, the Roman poet whose work on *The Nature of the Universe* has been translated by R. E. Latham for the Penguin series.

The connection between Democritus' physical theories and his ethical views is developed in an interesting way by Gregory Vlastos in "Ethics and Physics in Democritus," *Philosophical Review* (1945), 578–592; (1946), 53–64.

THE SOPHISTS

W. Jaeger discusses the place of the sophists in Greek life in the first volume of his *Paideia: The Ideals of Greek Culture,* 2nd ed. (New York, 1945). Their teachings are set forth clearly and simply in John Burnet's *Greek Philosophy: Thales to Plato* (London, 1932), 105–125.

The best introduction to the thought of Protagoras is that contributed by Gregory Vlastos to *Plato's Protagoras* (Indianapolis, 1956). In this dialogue Plato was concerned with Protagoras as a political thinker, and this is the role in which he appears also in T. A. Sinclair's *History of Greek Political Thought* (London, 1951), Chapter Four: "Protagoras, the First Great Political Thinker." In the *Theaetetus* Plato is concerned with him as an epistemologist. The reader will find a useful commentary on this dialogue in F. M. Cornford's *Plato's Theory of Knowledge: The Theaetetus and the Sophist of Plato Translated with a Running Commentary* (London, 1935).

Antiphon, too, is dealt with in Sinclair's *History of Greek Political Thought.* Callicles is known to us only from Plato's *Gorgias.* His resemblance to Nietzsche is brought out by E. R. Dodds in the appendix to his *Plato's Gorgias: A Revised Text with Introduction and Commentary* (Oxford, 1959). Dodds's comments on the exchange between Socrates and Callicles *(Gorgias* 481 B – 522 E) are equally fascinating, though they present difficulties for the Greekless reader.

Plato deals with individual sophists in a number of dialogues. Hippias appears in no less than two of them, the *Hippias Major* and the *Hippias Minor.* Another debate with a sophist will be found in Book One of the *Republic,* where the thesis that justice is the interest of the stronger is defended by Thrasymachus. The argument is sometimes hard to follow, but the student will find help in R. C. Cross and A. D. Woozley's *Plato's Republic: A Philosophical Commentary* (London, 1964), Chapter Two: "The Argument with Thrasymachus."

REACTION

The speech of Gorgias should be compared with Helen's defense of her conduct in Euripides' *The Trojan Women* (lines 914–1059), translated by Richmond Lattimore in *The Complete Greek Tragedies.*

The influence of philosophical ideas on Thucydides is very marked. For quite different appraisals of him the reader should look at F. M. Cornford's *Thucydides Mythistoricus* (London, 1907) and C. N. Cochrane's *Thucydides and the Science of History* (London, 1929). Another curious document bearing the marks of the "new thought" is the essay on the political situation in Athens falsely attributed to Xenophon. The reader will find a translation of it, with full analyses and commentary, in Hartvig Frisch's *The Constitution of the Athenians* (Copenhagen, 1942).

The whole subject of Greek values is discussed at length in Arthur W. H. Adkins' *Merit and Responsibility: A Study in Greek Values* (Oxford, 1960). It is, of course, the constant preoccupation of Plato in his early and middle dialogues — above all in his *Republic*. His analysis of the situation cuts deeper, I think, than most modern ones, including E. R. Dodds's fascinating book *The Greeks and the Irrational* (Berkeley, 1951), the sixth chapter of which ("Rationalism and Reaction in the Classical Age") treats the subject from a psychological point of view.

EPILOGUE

There are excellent translations of Plato's *Republic* and *Laws* in Edith Hamilton and Huntington Cairns's *Plato: The Collected Dialogues* (New York, 1961), which contains all of Plato's dialogues in a variety of good modern translations, as well as a full and useful index.

NOTE ON THE SOURCES

The writings of the early Greek philosophers are now lost to us. Our knowledge of them is derived entirely from later authors, who occasionally quote from them but more often merely report (sometimes at second or third hand) what was said in them. The testimony of these writers is of very unequal value, and there is no simple rule for determining the reliability of a given account. It is not merely a question of the author's distance in time from the early philosophers, but of the kind of evidence available to him, his ability to assess it, and the nature of his interest in it. It is impossible to go into these questions in a brief Note; it must suffice to indicate who the main authorities are whose names appear in the list of references.

THE FRAGMENTS

The fragments of early Greek philosophy which we possess in the form of quotations constitute by far the most valuable source of information. These come from a variety of sources. Plato, who is the earliest, rarely quotes his predecessors and is not concerned about literal accuracy. To some extent this is true of Aristotle as well. We owe most of the fragments to writers of a later age, of whom the following are outstanding.

Plutarch lived during the last half of the first century A.D. and into the second. He studied at the Academy which Plato founded at Athens, lived long in Rome, and wrote voluminously. In the collection of his ethical, religious, physical, literary, and political essays entitled *Moralia*, or *Moral Essays*, he quotes frequently from the early Greek philosophers. There is an English translation of these essays by a variety of hands in the Loeb Classical Library, where the quotations may be studied in context.

Sextus Empiricus, who lived during the late second century A.D., was a physician of the empirical school (whence the name "Empiricus") and an admirer of the skeptic Aenesidemus. He produced an exposition of the skeptical philosophy entitled *Outlines of Pyrrhonism*, followed by two works of criticism entitled *Against the Dogmatists* and *Against the*

309

Schoolmasters, in which he quotes the opinions of earlier philosophers on cognition and the reliability of the senses. These works are translated by R. B. Bury in four volumes in the Loeb Classical Library.

Clement of Alexandria, who lived during the last half of the second century A.D. and into the third, was a convert to Christianity and wrote his *Protrepticus,* or *Exhortation to the Greeks,* as well as his *Stromateis,* or *Miscellanies,* in an effort to demonstrate the superiority of Christian to Greek philosophy. The *Protrepticus* is translated by G. W. Butterworth in the Loeb Classical Library.

Hippolytus, bishop of Rome in the third century A.D., wrote a *Refutation of All Heresies* in nine books, in which he maintained that the heresies in question were simply revivals of views first put forward by the ancient philosophers. This involved frequent quotation from the philosophers themselves.

Diogenes Laertius lived about the first half of the third century A.D. His book *The Lives and Opinions of the Philosophers* is a ragbag of odds and ends of material of very unequal value. Among the things of value are a number of brief quotations from the early philosophers. The book is translated by R. D. Hicks in two volumes in the Loeb Classical Library.

Stobaeus, or John of Stobi, probably lived in the late fifth century A.D. He made a collection of extracts from Greek thought which has come down to us in two parts: the *Eclogae Physicae Dialecticae et Ethicae,* or *Physical, Logical and Ethical Extracts,* and the *Florilegium,* or *Anthology.* Stobaeus was particularly interested in ethical questions and is a chief source for the ethical fragments of Democritus.

Simplicius, who lived in the sixth century A.D., is the most valuable of our sources. He wrote extensive commentaries on the *Categories,* the *De Caelo,* the *Physics,* and the *De Anima* of Aristotle, and in expounding Aristotle's criticisms of the early Greek philosophers thought it useful to state the views criticized in the words of the philosophers themselves. He did this at great length because, as he says, some of the older writings had become quite rare.

The Testimony

Where the fragments fail we have to fall back upon the reports of a variety of authors. Plato's accounts of earlier views are apt to be careless, and it is not always easy to be sure when he is serious. The first to show an interest in the development of earlier thought is Aristotle, who regularly begins his discussions of philosophical problems by reviewing the opinions of his predecessors (Book One of his *Metaphysics* is an excellent example of the method).

Since the publication of Harold Cherniss' *Aristotle's Criticism of Presocratic Philosophy* (Baltimore, 1935), there has been a tendency to distrust Aristotle as a source of information concerning early Greek philosophy. The charge of untrustworthiness is serious, for Theophrastus, the source of much of our knowledge for the early period, was the pupil of Aristotle, and as J. B. McDiarmid has shown in his "Theophrastus on the Presocratic Causes," *Harvard Studies in Classical Philology* (1953), 1–156, his history of earlier thought was greatly influenced by Aristotle's account of it. If the tradition stemming from Theophrastus is poisoned at the source, it is clear that we know a good deal less about early Greek philosophy than we once thought we did. The question is too complex for summary treatment, but Aristotle receives perhaps more justice as a historian in W. K. C. Guthrie's "Aristotle as a Historian of Philosophy," *Journal of Hellenic Studies* (1957), 34–41. The reader will find a similar defense of Theophrastus in C. H. Kahn's *Anaximander and the Origins of Greek Cosmology* (New York, 1960), 17–24.

Theophrastus' history was entitled *Opinions of the Physicists*. It was in sixteen (or eighteen) books, of which the last, *On Sensation*, has come down to us almost in its entirety. (It is translated in G. M. Stratton's *Greek Physiological Psychology before Aristotle*, London, 1917). In addition, a number of extracts from the first book, *On Material Principles*, were copied by Simplicius into his commentary on Aristotle's *Physics*. This work of Theophrastus is the source of what is called the "doxographical tradition," of which a somewhat oversimplified account follows.

Of the various summaries of early Greek philosophy which later writers compiled from Theophrastus' history, two have come down to us: the *Epitome* falsely attributed to Plutarch, and the *Physical Extracts* of Stobaeus, mentioned earlier. According to Diels, both depend on an earlier summary made by an otherwise unknown compiler named Aetius, probably in the second century A.D. Aetius, whose name occurs frequently in the References, derived his information from Theophrastus by way of a lost work which Diels calls the *Vetusta Placita*.

The summary of earlier thought which appears in Book One of Hippolytus' *Refutation of All Heresies* also derives ultimately from Theophrastus, though it is independent of Aetius. The material dealing with Anaximander, Xenophanes, and Anaxagoras is of greater value than that dealing with Pythagoras, Heraclitus, the Eleatics, Empedocles, and the Atomists. The *Stromateis*, or *Miscellanies*, falsely ascribed to Plutarch, from which Eusebius copied extracts into his *Preparation of the Gospel* in the fourth century A.D., also derive ultimately from Theophrastus, as does the work of Diogenes Laertius, written two centuries earlier.

REFERENCES TO DIELS-KRANZ

The names of Simplicius, Hippolytus, Aetius, and the rest occur most frequently in the References which follow. There are, of course, other sources; the list given at the back of K. Freeman's *Companion to the Pre-Socratic Philosophers* (Oxford, 1946) runs to more than thirty pages. There the reader will find notes giving the place of origin, approximate date, and principal works of each.

The works of most of these authors are difficult of access; but most of the materials relevant to early Greek philosophy have been collected in H. Diels's great work *Die Fragmente der Vorsokratiker* (Berlin, 1903), now in its eleventh edition, and edited since Diels's death by W. Kranz. This is the work referred to in the References as "DK." Diels assigned a number to each of the early philosophers, and divided the materials relating to each into "B-materials" (the fragments) and "A-materials" (the ancient testimony). Thus "DK 28 B 8" means that the passage in question will be found in Diels-Kranz under "Parmenides" as fragment 8. So far as possible each reference to the sources has been followed by an indication of its location in Diels.

REFERENCES

The student will find that a reading of the brief Note on the Sources which precedes will facilitate his understanding of the references.

CHAPTER ONE · HESIOD

1.1 Hesiod *Theogony* 116–134
1.2 Hesiod *Theogony* 695–703
1.3 Euripides frag. 484
1.4 Hesiod *Theogony* 156–186
1.5 Aeschylus frag. 44
1.6 Herodotus *Histories* iv. 8
1.7 Hesiod *Theogony* 720–745
1.8 Hesiod *Theogony* 881–885
1.9 Homer *Iliad* xv. 185–199
1.10 Hesiod *Works and Days* 109–126
1.11 Hesiod *Works and Days* 127–139
1.12 Hesiod *Works and Days* 140–155
1.13 Hesiod *Works and Days* 156–169b
1.14 Hesiod *Works and Days* 169c–201
1.15 Hesiod *Works and Days* 202–212
1.16 Hesiod *Works and Days* 275–280
1.17 Hesiod *Works and Days* 225–247
1.18 Hesiod *Works and Days* 216–218
1.19 Hesiod *Works and Days* 267–273
1.20 Hesiod *Works and Days* 381–383
1.21 Hesiod *Works and Days* 410–413
1.22 Hesiod *Works and Days* 361–362
1.23 Hesiod *Works and Days* 349–351

CHAPTER TWO · ANAXIMANDER

2.1 Diogenes Laertius ii. 2 (DK 12 A 1)
2.2 Simplicius *Phys.* 24, 13 (DK 12 A 9)
2.3 Hippolytus *Ref.* i. 6. 1 (DK 12 A 11)
2.4 Aristotle *Physics* iii. 4. 203 b 6 (DK 12 A 15)
2.5 Aristotle *Physics* i. 4. 187 a 20 (DK 12 A 9)
2.6 Simplicius *Phys.* 150, 24 (DK 12 A 9)
2.7 [Plutarch] *Strom.* 2 (DK 12 A 10)
2.8 Aristotle *De caelo* ii. 13. 295 a 10 (DK 59 A 88)

2.9   [Hippocrates] *Nat. puer.* 17 (VII, 498 Littré)

2.10   Hippolytus *Ref.* i. 6. 4 (DK 12 A 11)

2.11   Aetius ii. 13. 7 (DK 12 A 18)

2.12   Aetius ii. 20. 1 (DK 12 A 21)

2.13   Simplicius *De caelo* 471, 4 (DK 12 A 19)

2.14   Aetius ii. 15. 6 (DK 12 A 18)

2.15   Aetius ii. 21. 1 (DK 12 A 21)

2.16   Aetius ii. 25. 1 (DK 12 A 22). Aetius actually says that the diameter of the ring bearing the moon is nineteen times as large as the earth. This is generally agreed to be a mistake for eighteen, and I have translated accordingly. For a similar mistake see Aetius ii. 20. 1 (DK 12 A 21), corrected by Aetius himself at ii. 21. 1 (DK 12 A 21) with the concurrence of Hippolytus *Ref.* i. 6. 5 (DK 12 A 11).

2.17   [Plutarch] *Strom.* 2 (DK 12 A 10)

2.18   Hippolytus *Ref.* i. 6. 3 (DK 12 A 11), reading γυρών with Diels.

2.19   Theo of Smyrna, p. 198, 18 Hill (DK 12 A 26)

2.20   Aristotle *De caelo* ii. 13. 295 b 10 (DK 12 A 26)

2.21   Simplicius *De caelo* 532, 14

2.22   Aristotle *Meterologica* ii. 1. 353 b 6 (DK 12 A 27)

2.23   Alexander *Meteor.* 67, 11 (DK 12 A 27)

2.24   Agathermus i. 1 (DK 12 A 6)

2.25   Herodotus *Histories* iv. 36

2.26   Herodotus *Histories* iv. 42

2.27   Herodotus *Histories* iv. 45

2.28   Herodotus *Histories* ii. 17

2.29   Herodotus *Histories* ii. 23

2.30   Aetius v. 19. 4 (DK 12 A 30)

2.31   [Plutarch] *Strom.* 2 (DK 12 A 10)

2.32   Censorinus *De die nat.* iv. 7 (DK 12 A 30)

2.33   Plutarch *Symp.* viii. 8, p. 730 E (DK 12 A 30)

2.34   Simplicius *Phys.* 24, 18 (DK 12 B 1)

2.35   Aetius v. 30. 1 (DK 24 B 4)

2.36   [Hippocrates] *Nat. hom.* 7. Cf. Aristotle *Physics* iii. 5. 204 b 22 where, according to Simplicius, Anaximander is meant.

2.37   Herodotus *Histories* iii. 40

2.38   Herodotus *Histories* vii. 10

2.39   Sophocles *Antigone* 1347–1352

2.40   Aetius iii. 3. 1 (DK 12 A 23). Seneca *Quaest. nat.* ii. 18 (DK 12 A 23) supplies further details.

2.41   Aetius i. 3. 3 (DK 12 A 14)

2.42   Augustine *C. D.* viii. 2 (DK 12 A 17)

2.43   Aristotle *Physics* viii 1. 250 b 11

2.44   Hippolytus *Ref.* i. 6. 2 (DK 12 A 11)

CHAPTER THREE · ANAXIMENES AND XENOPHANES

3.1   Simplicius *Phys.* 24, 26 (DK 13 A 5)

3.2   Hippolytus *Ref.* i. 7. 2–3 (DK 13 A 7)

3.3   Plutarch *De prim. frig.* 7, p. 947 F (DK 13 B 1). Diels prints this as a fragment, but the actual wording is Plutarch's.

3.4   [Plutarch] *Strom.* 3 (DK 13 A 6)

3.5   Hippolytus *Ref.* i. 7. 5–6 (DK 13 A 7)

3.6 Aetius ii. 22. 1 (DK 13 A 15)

3.7 Hippolytus *Ref.* i. 7. 4 (DK 13 A 7)

3.8 Hippolytus *Ref.* i. 7. 6 (DK 13 A 7)

3.9 Aristotle *Meteorologica* ii. 1. 354 a 28 (DK 13 A 14)

3.10 Aetius ii. 14. 13 (DK 13 A 14)

3.11 Aetius ii. 10. 3 (DK 13 A 20)

3.12 Aristotle *De caelo* ii. 13. 294 b 13 (DK 13 A 20). It is possible that this theory, too, originated with Anaximander; cf. Ammianus Marcellinus xviii. 7. 12 (DK 12 A 48) and Cicero *De div.* i. 50. 112 (DK 12 A 5a).

3.13 Aristotle *Meteor.* ii. 7. 365 b 6 (DK 13 A 21)

3.14 *Schol. Arat.* p. 515, 27 M (DK 13 A 18)

3.15 Aetius i. 7. 13 (DK 13 A 10). But the tradition is confused; see Cicero *De nat. div.* i. 10. 26 (DK 13 A 10) and Augustine *C. D.* viii. 2 (DK 13 A 10).

3.16 Aetius i. 3. 4 (DK 13 B 2)

3.17 Homer *Iliad* v. 696–698

3.18 Aristotle *De anima* i. 2. 403 b 26

3.19 Aristotle *De anima* i. 2. 404 b 2 (DK 59 A 100)

3.20 Galen *De usu partt.* iii. 10 (DK 68 B 34). David *Prol.* 38, 14 Busse (DK 68 B 34) attributes the saying to Democritus.

3.21 Theophrastus *Phys. op.* fr. 2 *ap.* Simplicius *Phys.* 25, 1 (DK 64 A 5)

3.22 Simplicius *Phys.* 153, 20 (DK 68 B 8)

3.23 Simplicius *Phys.* 152, 22 (DK 68 B 5)

3.24 Simplicius *Phys.* 152, 13 (DK 64 B 3)

3.25 Simplicius *Phys.* 152, 18 (DK 64 B 4), omitting the first sentence.

3.26 Aetius iii. 4. 4 (DK 21 A 46)

3.27 Aetius iii. 4. 4 (DK 21 B 30)

3.28 [Plutarch] *Strom.* 4 (DK 21 A 32)

3.29 Hippolytus *Ref.* i. 14. 5–6 (DK 21 A 33)

3.30 Sextus Empiricus *Adv. math.* x. 314 (DK 21 B 33)

3.31 *Schol. BLT* Eust. *ad Hom.* c. 44 (DK 21 B 32)

3.32 Clement *Strom.* v. 109 (DK 21 B 14)

3.33 Clement *Strom.* vii. 22 (DK 21 B 16)

3.34 Clement *Strom.* v. 110 (DK 21 B 15)

3.35 Clement *Strom.* v. 109 (DK 21 B 23)

3.36 Sextus Empiricus *Adv. math.* ix. 144 (DK 21 B 24)

3.37 Simplicius *Phys.* 23, 10 (DK 21 B 26)

3.38 Simplicius *Phys.* 23, 19 (DK 21 B 25)

3.39 Aristotle *Metaphys.* i. 5. 986 b 24 (DK 21 A 30)

3.40 Diogenes Laertius ix. 19 (DK 21 A 1)

3.41 Diogenes Laertius ix. 19 (DK 21 A 1)

3.42 Sextus Empiricus *Adv. math.* ix. 193 (DK 21 B 11)

3.43 Athenaeus xi. 462 C (DK 21 B 1), lines 13–24

3.44 Hesiod *Theogony* 108–115

3.45 Stobaeus *Ecl. phys.* i. 8. 2 (DK 21 B 18)

3.46 Sextus Empiricus *Adv. math.* vii. 110 (DK 21 B 34)

3.47 Herodianus *On Anomalous Words*, p. 41, 5 (DK 21 B 38)

3.48 Plutarch *Symp.* ix. 7, p. 746 B (DK 21 B 35)

CHAPTER FOUR · PYTHAGOREANISM

4.1 Diogenes Laertius viii. 15

4.2 Porphyrius *Vita Pythagorae* 19 (DK 14 A 8a)

4.3 Clement *Strom.* iii. 17 (DK 44 B 14). I am inclined to accept the fragments of Philolaus as genuine, though in deference to dissenters I have made use of them only when it seemed clear on independent grounds that the teaching in question was genuinely Pythagorean.

4.4 Diogenes Laertius viii. 26–28 (DK 58 B 1a). This account comes from Alexander Polyhistor, who claimed to have found it in certain "Pythagorean notebooks." Its reliability has been questioned, though it seems to contain elements of genuine Pythagorean doctrine of an early period (cf. Guthrie, *A History of Greek Philosophy*, I, 201, n. 3).

4.5 Pindar *Nemea* 6. 1–4

4.6 Pindar *Nemea* 7. 55–58

4.7 Pindar *Pythia* 8, 92–97

4.8 Pindar *Nemea* 11, 13–16

4.9 Pindar *Isthmia* 5, 16

4.10 Aristotle *Nicomachean eth.* x. 7. 1177 b 32

4.11 Diogenes Laertius viii. 36 (DK 21 B 7)

4.12 Herodotus *Histories* ii. 123 (DK 14, 1)

4.13 Diogenes Laertius viii. 13

4.14 Diogenes Laertius viii. 19

4.15 Diogenes Laertius viii. 9

4.16 Diogenes Laertius i. 12

4.17 Diogenes Laertius viii. 6 (DK 22 B 129)

4.18 Iamblichus *Vita Pythag.* 18, 89

4.19 Diogenes Laertius viii. 11–12

4.20 Proclus *in Euclid I*, 32, p. 379, 2 (DK 58 B 21)

4.21 Plutarch *Quaest. conv.* viii. 2. 4, 720 A

4.22 Proclus *in Euclid I*, p. 328, 7

4.23 Proclus *in Euclid I*, p. 64, 16. The five regular solids were called "cosmic" because of Plato's use of them in his *Timaeus* in the construction of the world-order.

4.24 Proclus *in Euclid I*, p. 84, 13

4.25 Aristotle *Metaphys.* i. 5. 985 b 23 (DK 58 B 4)

4.26 Galileo *Opere Complete di Galileo Galilei* (Firenze, 1842) IV, 171. Quoted in E. A. Burtt, *Metaphysical Foundations of Modern Science*, Anchor Books edition (New York, 1954), 75.

4.27 Aristotle *De caelo* ii. 9. 290 b 12 (DK 58 B 35). The persons referred to are identified as Pythagoreans in *De caelo* ii. 9. 291 a 8. There is a full discussion of the "harmony of the spheres" in T. L. Heath's *Aristarchus of Samos* (Oxford, 1913), 105–115.

4.28 Porphyry *in Ptolem. Harm.* p. 56 Düring (DK 47 B 1)

4.29 Shakespeare *Merchant of Venice*, Act 5, Scene 1

4.30 Plutarch *Quaest. conv.* ix. 5. 745 E

4.31 Aristotle *Metaphys.* i. viii. 989 b 29 (DK 58 B 22). Cf. Aristotle *De caelo* iii. 1. 300 a 17.

4.32 Aristotle *Metaphys.* xiii. 6. 1080 b 18 (DK 58 B 9)

4.33 Aristotle *Metaphys.* xiv. 2. 1091 a 15 (DK 58 B 26)

4.34 Aristotle *Metaphys.* i. 5. 987 a 15 (DK 58 B 8)

4.35 Aristotle *Phys.* iv. 6. 213 b 22 (DK 58 B 30). That the void is really air is clear from Aristotle *Phys.* iii. 4. 203 a 10 (DK 58 B 28), where the "unlimited" is identified with "the even," and *Phys.* iii. 4. 204 a 31 (DK 58 B 29), where "the even" is identified with air.

4.36 [Hippocrates] *De carn.* 6 (VIII, 592 Littré). Cf. [Hippocrates] *Nat. puer.* 12, where the principle is illustrated in a striking way.

4.37 Meno *ap.* Anonymous Londinensis xviii. 8 (DK 44 A 27)
4.38 Stobaeus *Ecl. phys.* i. 15. 7 (DK 44 B 17)
4.39 Aristotle *De caelo* ii. 13. 293 a 20 (DK 58 B 37)
4.40 Simplicius *De caelo* 511, 26 (DK 58 B 37), commenting on **4.39.**
4.41 Diogenes Laertius viii. 25 (DK 58 B 1a). See note on **4.3.**
4.42 Aetius ii. 1. 1 (DK 14, 21)
4.43 Diogenes Laertius viii. 26 (DK 58 B 1a)
4.44 Plato *Phaedo* 86 B
4.45 Diogenes Laertius vii. 32
4.46 Diogenes Laertius viii. 20 (DK 14, 9)
4.47 Diogenes Laertius viii. 3
4.48 Diodorus Siculus xii. 9. 2 ff. (DK 14, 14)
4.49 Plato *Gorgias* 507 E
4.50 Stobaeus *Ecl. phys.* i. 21. 7d (DK 44 B 6)
4.51 Diogenes Laertius viii. 16
4.52 Diogenes Laertius viii. 10
4.53 Iamblichus *Vita Pythag.* 130
4.54 Aristotle *Nichomachean eth.* v. 8. 1132 b 21 (DK 58 B 4)
4.55 [Aristotle] *Magna moralia* i. 33. 1194 a 29
4.56 Aristotle *Nichomachean eth.* v. 3. 1131 a 25
4.57 Iamblichus *On Nichomachus' Introduction to Arithmetic*, ed. Pistelli, p. 100, 19 (DK 18, 15)
4.58 Archytas *ap.* Porphyry *in Ptol. Harm.* p. 92 (DK 47 B 2)
4.59 Aristotle *Nichomachean eth.* ii. 6. 1106 a 30
4.60 Aristotle *Nichomachean eth.* v. 3. 1131 b 9

CHAPTER FIVE · HERACLITUS

5.1 Diogenes Laertius ix. 1 (DK 22 B 40)
5.2 Diogenes Laertius ix. 1 (DK 22 B 41)
5.3 Archilochus, frag. 103 (Diehl)
5.4 Clement *Strom.* v. 116 (DK 22 B 32)
5.5 Clement *Protrepticus* 22 (DK 22 B 14)
5.6 Clement *Protrepticus* 34 (DK 22 B 15)
5.7 Aristocritus *Theosophia* 68 (DK 22 B 5)
5.8 Hippolytus *Ref.* ix. 10. 6 (DK 22 B 64)
5.9 Diogenes Laertius ix. 8–9 (DK 22 A 1)
5.10 Diogenes Laertius ix. 8 (DK 22 A 1)
5.11 Tzetzes *schol. ad exeg.* II 126 Herm. (DK 22 B 126)
5.12 Clement *Strom.* v. 105 (DK 22 B 30)
5.13 Theophrastus *De vertigine* 9 (DK 22 B 125)
5.14 Plato *Cratylus* 402 A (DK 22 A 6)
5.15 Arius Didymus *ap.* Eus. *P.E.* xv. 20 (DK 22 B 12)
5.16 Clement *Strom.* v. 105 (DK 22 B 31)
5.17 Plutarch *De E* 8, p. 388 E (DK 22 B 90)
5.18 Plutarch *De exil.* 11, p. 604 A (DK 22 B 94)
5.19 Porphyry *in Iliadem* 4, 4 (DK 22 B 102)
5.20 Theophrastus *De sens.* 1–2
5.21 Aristotle *Eth. Eud.* viii. 1. 1235 a 25; Plutarch *De Is. et Os.* 48, p. 370 D; Numenius frag. 16 (Thedinga) *ap.* Chalcidius *in Tim.* c. 297; Simplicius *Categ.* 412, 26 Kalbfleisch (DK 22 A 22). **5.21** represents a composite of these, following Burnet, *Early Greek Philosophy* (London, 1930), 136.

There seems to be no doubt that all refer to something Heraclitus actually said.

5.22 Origen *Contra Celsum* vi. 42 (DK 22 B 80)
5.23 Maximus Tyrius xii. 4, p. 489 (DK 22 B 80)
5.24 Hippolytus *Ref.* ix. 9. 4 (DK 22 B 53)
5.25 Hippolytus *Ref.* ix. 10 (DK 22 B 61)
5.26 Hippolytus *Ref.* ix. 10 (DK 22 B 59)
5.27 Porphyry *in Iliadem* 7, 200 (DK 22 B 103)
5.28 Hippolytus *Ref.* ix. 10 (DK 22 B 67)
5.29 Hippolytus *Ref.* ix. 10 (DK 22 B 60)
5.30 Clement *Strom.* ii. 8 (DK 22 B 17)
5.31 Sextus Empiricus *Adv. math.* vii. 132 (DK 22 B 1)
5.32 Marcus Aurelius Anton. iv. 46 (DK 22 B 73)
5.33 Hippolytus *Ref.* ix. 9 (DK 22 B 50)
5.34 Plutarch *De superst.* 3, p. 166 C (DK 22 B 89)
5.35 Marcus Aurelius Anton. iv. 46 (DK 22 B 73)
5.36 Sextus Empiricus *Adv. math.* vii. 133 (DK 22 B 2)
5.37 Clement *Strom.* ii. 17 (DK 22 B 18)
5.38 Clement *Strom.* iv. 4 (DK 22 B 22)
5.39 Themistius *Or.* 5, p. 69 (DK 22 B 123)
5.40 Plutarch *De Pyth. or.* 21, p. 404 D (DK 22 B 93)
5.41 Plutarch *De Pyth. or.* 6, p. 397 A (DK 22 B 92)
5.42 Hippolytus *Ref.* ix. 9 (DK 22 B 55)
5.43 Sextus Empiricus *Adv. math.* vii. 126 (DK 22 B 107)
5.44 Hippolytus *Ref.* ix. 9 (DK 22 B 51)
5.45 Aristotle *Nichomachean eth.* ix. 2. 1155 b 4 (DK 22 B 8)
5.46 Hippolytus *Ref.* ix. 9 (DK 22 B 54)
5.47 [Aristotle] *De mundo* 5. 396 b 7 (DK 22 B 10)
5.48 Plotinus *Enneads* iv. 8. 1 (DK 22 B 84a)
5.49 Stobaeus *Florilegium* i. 176 (DK 22 B 110)
5.50 Stobaeus *Florilegium* ii. 177 (DK 22 B 111)
5.51 Hippolytus *Ref.* ix. 9 (DK 22 B 58)
5.52 [Aristotle] *De mundo* 6, 401 a 8 (DK 22 B 11)
5.53 Origen *Contra Celsum* vi. 12 (DK 22 B 78)
5.54 Origen *Contra Celsum* vi. 12 (DK 22 B 79)
5.55 Plato *Hippias major* 289 B (DK 22 B 83)
5.56 Sextus Empiricus *Adv. math* vii. 129 (DK 22 A 16)
5.57 Stobaeus *Florilegium* i. 179 (DK 22 B 113)
5.58 Stobaeus *Florilegium* v. 6 (DK 22 B 116)
5.59 Aeschylus *Persians* 818–827
5.60 Diogenes Laertius viii. 9
5.61 Diogenes Laertius ix. 2 (DK 22 B 43)
5.62 Plutarch *Adv. Coloten* 20, p. 1118 C (DK 22 B 101)
5.63 Stobaeus *Florilegium* i. 180a (DK 22 B 115)
5.64 Diogenes Laertius ix. 7 (DK 22 B 45)
5.65 Arius Didymus *ap.* Eus. *P. E.* xv. 20 (DK 22 B 12)
5.66 Clement *Strom.* v. 105 (DK 22 B 36)
5.67 Stobaeus *Florilegium* v. 8 (DK 22 B 118)
5.68 Stobaeus *Florilegium* v. 7 (DK 22 B 117)
5.69 Numenius frag. 35 Thedinga (DK 22 B 77), omitting ἢ θάνατον with Shuster.
5.70 Albertus Magnus *De veget.* iv. 401, p. 545 Meyer (DK 22 B 4)
5.71 Plutarch *Vitae. Coriol.* 22 (DK 22 B 85)
5.72 Stobaeus *Florilegium* i. 178 (DK 22 B 112)

5.73 Hippolytus *Ref.* ix. 9 (DK 22 B 53)
5.74 Hippolytus *Ref.* ix. 9 (DK 22 B 52)
5.75 Stobaeus *Florilegium* iv. 40. 23 (DK 22 B 119)
5.76 Clement *Strom.* iv. 146 (DK 22 B 27)
5.77 Plutarch *Symp.* iv. 4. 3, p. 669 A
5.78 Aetius iv. 7. 2 (DK 22 A 17)
5.79 Clement *Strom.* iv. 49 (DK 22 B 25)
5.80 Schol. Epictet. Bodl. p. lxxi Schenkl (DK 22 B 136). But DK doubt the authenticity of this fragment.
5.81 Clement *Strom.* v. 9 (DK 22 B 28)
5.82 Clement *Paedag.* ii. 99 (DK 22 B 16)
5.83 Stobaeus *Florilegium* i. 179 (DK 22 B 114)
5.84 Diogenes Laertius ix. 1 (DK 22 B 44)
5.85 Proclus *in Alc.* i, p. 525, 21 (DK 22 B 104)
5.86 Clement *Strom.* v. 116 (DK 22 B 34)
5.87 Plutarch *An seni resp.* 7, p. 787 C (DK 22 B 97)
5.88 Strabo xiv. 25, p. 642 (DK 22 B 121)
5.89 Clement *Strom.* v. 116 (DK 22 B 33)
5.90 Galen *De dign. puls.* viii. 773 K (DK 22 B 49)
5.91 Clement *Strom.* v. 60 (DK 22 B 29)
5.92 Homer *Iliad* ix. 411–416
5.93 Clement *Strom.* iv. 16 (DK 22 B 24)
5.94 Homer *Iliad* ii. 480–483

CHAPTER SIX · PARMENIDES

6.1 Plato *Parmenides* 127 B (DK 28 A 5)
6.2 Diogenes Laertius ix. 21 (DK 28 A 1)
6.3 Sextus Empiricus *Adv. math.* vii. 3 and Simplicius *De caelo* 557, 25 (DK 28 B 1)
6.4 Hesiod *Theogony* 22–32
6.5 Proclus *in Tim.* i. 345, 18 Diehl (DK 28 B 2)
6.6 Clement *Strom.* vi. 23 (DK 28 B 3)
6.7 Simplicius *Phys.* 146, 7 (DK 28 B 8, lines 34–36)
6.8 Simplicius *Phys.* 117, 4 (DK 28 B 6)
6.9 Plato *Sophist* 237 A and Sextus Empiricus *Adv. math.* vii. 114 (DK 28 B 7)
6.10 Simplicius *Phys.* 145, 1 (DK 28 B 8, lines 1–21)
6.11 Simplicius *Phys.* 145, 23 (DK 28 B 8, lines 22–25)
6.12 Clement *Strom.* v. 15. 5 (DK 28 B 4)
6.13 Simplicius *Phys.* 145, 27 (DK 28 B 8, lines 26–33), retaining the manuscript reading μὴ ἐὸν in line 33.
6.14 Simplicius *Phys.* 146, 15 (DK 28 B 8, lines 42–49)
6.15 Simplicius *Phys.* 146, 10 (DK 28 B 8, lines 36–41)
6.16 Aristotle *Physics* i. 2. 185 a 12
6.17 Proclus *in Parm.* i, p. 708, 16 (DK 28 B 5)
6.18 Simplicius *Phys.* 30, 17 and 39, 8 (DK 28 B 8, lines 50–61)
6.19 Scholion to DK 28 B 8, lines 56–59. Simplicius *Phys.* 31, 3
6.20 Aristotle *Metaphys.* i. 5. 986 a 31, translated somewhat freely.
6.21 Aristotle *Metaphys.* i. 5. 986 a 23 (DK 24 A 3)
6.22 Clement *Strom.* v. 138 (DK 28 B 10)
6.23 Simplicius *De caelo* 559, 20 (DK 28 B 11)

6.24 Simplicius *Phys.* 180, 9 (DK 28 B 9)
6.25 Aetius ii. 7. 1 (DK 28 A 37)
6.26 Aetius ii. 15. 4 (DK 28 A 40A)
6.27 Simplicius *Phys.* 39, 14 and 31, 13 (DK 28 B 12)
6.28 Aetius ii. 20. 8a (DK 28 A 43)
6.29 Scholion to DK 28 B 8, lines 56–59. Simplicius *Phys.* 31, 3, reading ἑκατέρωσ᾽ with Fränkel.
6.30 Plato *Symposium* 178 B (DK 28 B 13)
6.31 Diogenes Laertius ix. 22
6.32 Caelius Aurelianus *De morb. chron.* iv. 9, p. 116 Sichard (DK 28 B 18)
6.33 Theophrastus *De sensu* 3. I have preferred Theophrastus' version of this fragment to Aristotle's in *Metaphys.* iv. 5. 1009 b 21 (DK 22 B 16).
6.34 Theophrastus *De sensu* 3–4 (DK 28 A 46)
6.35 Aetius v. 30. 4 (DK 28 A 46a)
6.36 Tertullian *De anima* 45 (DK 28 A 46b)
6.37 Plato *Theaetetus* 179 E

CHAPTER SEVEN · ZENO AND MELISSUS

7.1 Plato *Parmenides* 127 D
7.2 Simplicius *Phys.* 131, 9
7.3 Simplicius *Phys.* 109, 34 (DK 30 B 9)
7.4 Simplicius *Phys.* 139, 5 (DK 29 B 2)
7.5 Simplicius *Phys.* 140, 34 (DK 29 B 1)
7.6 Simplicius *Phys.* 140, 27 (DK 29 B 3)
7.7 Aristotle *Phys.* vi. 9. 239 b 14 (DK 29 A 25)
7.8 Simplicius Phys. 1289, 5
7.9 Aristotle *Phys.* vi. 9, 239 b 14 (DK 29 A 26)
7.10 Simplicius *Phys.* 1013, 31
7.11 Aristotle *Phys.* vi. 9. 239 b 5 (DK 29 A 27), translating Ross's text.
7.12 Epiphanius *Adv. haer.* iii. 11
7.13 Aristotle *Phys.* vi. 9. 239 b 33 (DK 29 A 28)
7.14 Aristotle *Phys.* iv. 3. 210 b 22 (DK 29 A 24)
7.15 Aristotle *Phys.* iv. 1. 209 a 23 (DK 29 A 24)
7.16 Simplicius *Phys.* 1108, 18 (DK 29 A 29)
7.17 Diogenes Laertius ix. 25 (DK 29 A 1)
7.18 Plato *Meno* 80 A
7.19 [Aristotle] *De Melisso Xenophane Gorgia* 1. 974 a 1 (DK 30 A 5), retaining ἀπατᾶν at 974 b 6.
7.20 Simplicius *Phys.* 162, 24 (DK 30 B 1)
7.21 Simplicius *Phys.* 29, 22 and 109, 20 (DK 30 B 2)
7.22 Simplicius *Phys.* 110, 2 (DK 30 B 4)
7.23 Simplicius *Phys.* 109, 29 (DK 30 B 3): ἀλλ᾽ ὥσπερ ἔστιν ἀεί, οὕτω καὶ τὸ μέγεθος ἄπειρον ἀεὶ χρὴ εἶναι.
7.24 Simplicius *Phys.* 110, 5 (DK 30 B 5)
7.25 Simplicius *De caelo* 557, 14 (DK 30 B 6)
7.26 Simplicius *Phys.* 111, 18 (DK 30 B 7). I have broken this fragment into three parts. The first appears as **7.26**, the second as **7.30**, and the third as **7.27**.
7.27 See note on **7.26**
7.28 Simplicius *Phys.* 109, 32 (DK 30 B 10)
7.29 Simplicius *Phys.* 109, 34 (DK 30 B 9)

7.30 See note on **7.26**
7.31 Aetius i. 7. 27 (DK 30 A 13)
7.32 Simplicius *De caelo* 558, 19 (DK 30 B 8)
7.33 Aristotle *Phys.* i. 2. 185 a 11. Cf. Aristotle *Metaphys.* i. 5. 986 b 26 (DK 30 A 7).
7.34 Plato *Theaetetus* 183 E

CHAPTER EIGHT · EMPEDOCLES

8.1 Hippolytus *Ref.* vii. 29 and Plutarch *De exilio* 17, p. 607 C (DK 31 B 115)
8.2 Clement *Strom.* iv. 12 (DK 31 B 119)
8.3 Porphyry *De abstinentia* ii. 31 (DK 31 B 139)
8.4 Hesiod *Theogony* 793–804
8.5 Clement *Storm.* iii. 14 (DK 31 B 118)
8.6 Hierocles *Ad carmina aurea* 24 and Proclus *in Cratylum*, p. 97 Pasquali (DK 31 B 121)
8.7 Plutarch *De tranq. an.* 15, p. 474 B (DK 31 B 122)
8.8 Cornutus *Epidrom.* 17 (DK 31 B 123)
8.9 Plutarch *De esu. carn.* ii. 3, p. 998 C (DK 31 B 126). For the image of the cave see Porphyry *De antro. nymph.* 8, p. 61, 19 Nauck (DK 31 B 120).
8.10 Plutarch *Quaest. conv.* v. 8. 2, p. 683 E (DK 31 B 148)
8.11 Diogenes Laertius viii. 77 (DK 31 B 117)
8.12 Sextus Empiricus *Adv. math.* ix. 129 (DK 31 B 137)
8.13 Sextus Empiricus *Adv. math.* ix. 129 (DK 31 B 136)
8.14 Clement *Strom.* iii. 14 (DK 31 B 124)
8.15 Clement *Protrep.* ii. 27 (DK 31 B 145)
8.16 Porphyry *De abstinentia* ii. 21 (DK 31 B 128)
8.17 Schol. Nicander *Theriaca* 452, p. 36, 22 (DK 31 B 130)
8.18 Gellius iv. 11. 9 (DK 31 B 141)
8.19 Plutarch *Quaest. conv.* iii. 1. 2, p. 646 D (DK 31 B 140)
8.20 Aelian *Nat. anim.* xii. 7 (DK 31 B 127)
8.21 Clement *Strom.* iv. 150 (DK 31 B 146)
8.22 Clement *Strom.* v. 122 (DK 31 B 147)
8.23 Diogenes Laertius viii. 62 and Clement *Strom.* vi. 30 (DK 31 B 112)
8.24 Sextus Empiricus *Adv. math.* vii. 122–124 (DK 31 B 2)
8.25 Sextus Empiricus *Adv. math.* vii. 124 (DK 31 B 3)
8.26 Aristotle *De anima* iii. 4. 427 a 21 (DK 31 B 106)
8.27 Aetius i. 3. 20 (DK 31 B 6)
8.28 Plutarch *Adv. Coloten* 11, p. 1113 A (DK 31 B 9), rejecting Diels's emendation of line 5.
8.29 Plutarch *Adv. Coloten* 12, p. 1113 C (DK 31 B 11)
8.30 [Aristotle] *M.X.G.* 2. 975 b 1 (DK 31 B 12)
8.31 Plutarch *Adv. Coloten* 10, p. 1111 F (DK 31 B 8)
8.32 Simplicius *Phys.* 33, 21 (DK 31 B 26, lines 3–12)
8.33 Simplicius *Phys.* 158, 1 (DK 31 B 17, lines 1–8)
8.34 Simplicius *Phys.* 158, 1 (DK 31 B 17, lines 14–26)
8.35 Plutarch *De amic. multit.* 5, p. 95 A (DK 31 B 33)
8.36 Simplicius *Phys.* 158, 1 (DK 31 B 17, lines 27–35)
8.37 Hippolytus *Ref.* vii. 29 (DK 31 B 16)
8.38 Simplicius *Phys.* 1124, 9 (DK 31 B 20)
8.39 Simplicius *De caelo* 529, 1 and *Phys.* 32, 13 (DK 31 B 35)
8.40 Simplicius *De caelo* 587, 18 (DK 31 B 58)

8.41 Aristotle *De caelo* iii. 2. 300 b 30 and Simplicius *De caelo* 587, 1 (DK 31 B 57)

8.42 Simplicius *De caelo* 587, 20 (DK 31 B 59)

8.43 Plutarch *Adv. Coloten* 28, p. 1123 B (DK 31 B 60)

8.44 Aelian *Nat anim.* xvi. 29 (DK 31 B 61), reading στείροις with Diels.

8.45 Plutarch *Max. c. princip. philos. esse diss.* 2, p. 777 C (DK 31 B 27a)

8.46 Plutarch *De fac. lun.* 12, p. 926 E and Simplicius *Phys.* 1183, 30 (DK 31 B 27)

8.47 Hippolytus *Ref.* vii. 29 (DK 31 B 29)

8.48 Aristotle *Metaphys.* iii. 4. 1000 b 12 (DK 31 B 30)

8.49 Simplicius *Phys.* 1184, 2 (DK 31 B 31)

8.50 Aristotle *Metaphys.* i. 4. 985 a 25 (DK 31 A 37)

8.51 Aristotle *De gen. et corr.* ii. 6. 333 a 35 (DK 31 B 37)

8.52 Clement *Strom.* v. 48 (DK 31 B 38)

8.53 Aetius ii. 6. 3 (DK 31 A 49)

8.54 [Plutarch] *Strom. ap* Eus. *P.E.* i. 8. 10 (DK 31 A 30)

8.55 Aetius ii. 11. 2 (DK 31 A 51)

8.56 Aristotle *De caelo* ii. 1. 284 a 25 (after Stocks)

8.57 Aristotle *De caelo* ii. 13. 295 a 19 (DK 31 A 67). But Aristotle mistakes this for an explanation of the *earth*'s staying up.

8.58 Simplicius *Phys.* 381, 29 (DK 31 B 62)

8.59 Proclus *in Tim.* ii. 8. 26 Diehl (DK 31 B 52)

8.60 Diodorus Siculus i. 7, translated by C. H. Oldfather

8.61 Simplicius *De caelo* 530, 5 (DK 31 B 73)

8.62 Simplicius *Phys.* 300, 19 (DK 31 B 96)

8.63 Simplicius *Phys.* 32, 3 (DK 31 B 98)

8.64 Plutarch *Quaest. nat.* 21, p. 917 C (DK 31 B 64)

8.65 Aristotle *De gen. et corr.* 333 b 11

8.66 Aristotle *Phys.* ii. 8. 198 b 17

8.67 Lucretius *De rerum nat.* v. 837–877

8.68 Aristotle *De respir.* 7. 473 a 15 (DK 31 B 100)

8.69 [Aristotle] *M.X.G.* 2. 976 b 23 (DK 31 B 14). I have quoted the line only in part.

8.70 Plutarch *Quaest. nat.* 19, p. 916 D (DK 31 B 89)

8.71 Plutarch *Quaest. nat.* 19, p. 916 D (DK 31 B 89)

8.72 Plutarch *De curios.* 11, p. 520 E, *Quaest. nat.* 23, p. 917 E and [Alexander] *Probl.* iii. 102 (DK 31 B 101)

8.73 Porphyry *De Styge ap.* Stobaeus *Ecl. phys.* i. 49. 53 (DK 31 B 105)

8.74 Theophrastus *De sensu* 7 (DK 31 A 86)

8.75 Aristotle *De anima* i. 2. 404 b 8 (DK 31 B 109)

8.76 Theophrastus *De sensu* 10 (DK 31 B 107). Theophrastus *De sensu* 9 shows that **8.76** immediately followed **8.75** in the original.

8.77 Hippolytus *Ref.* vii. 29 (DK 31 B 29)

8.78 Theophrastus *De sensu* 11 (DK 31 A 86)

8.79 Simplicius *Phys.* 159, 13 (DK 31 B 21)

8.80 Simplicius *Phys.* 159, 27 (DK 31 B 23)

8.81 Diogenes Laertius viii. 59 (DK 31 B 111)

CHAPTER NINE · ANAXAGORAS

9.1 Simplicius *Phys.* 163, 18 (DK 59 B 17)

9.2 Aristotle *De caelo* iv. 3. 302 a 28 (DK 59 A 43)

9.3 Aristotle *Metaphys.* i. 3. 984 a 14 (DK 59 A 43)

9.4 Lucretius *De rerum natura* i. 834–842

9.5 Schol. in Gregor. Naz. xxxvi. 911 Migne (DK 59 B 10)

9.6 Aetius i. 3. 5 (DK 59 A 46)

9.7 Simplicius *Phys.* 164, 22 (DK 59 B 11)

9.8 Aristotle *Phys.* i. 4. 187 a 25

9.9 Simplicius *Phys.* 164, 16 (DK 59 B 3). I have translated Diels's text, but Zeller's τομῇ for the manuscript τὸ μὴ is tempting: "for it is impossible that what is should cease to be through being cut."

9.10 Simplicius *Phys.* 164, 25 (DK 59 B 6)

9.11 Simplicius *Phys.* 175, 11 (DK 59 B 8)

9.12 Aristotle *Phys.* i. 4. 187 b 2

9.13 Lucretius *De rerum natura* i. 875–892

9.14 Simplicius *Phys.* 34, 21 (DK 59 B 4, second half). DK print **9.14** continuously with **9.24** as a single fragment, but H. Fränkel (*Wege und Formen frühgriechischen Denkens*, München, 1955, p. 287) has rightly questioned the wisdom of this.

9.15 Simplicius *Phys.* 155, 26 (DK 59 B 1)

9.16 Simplicius *De caelo* 608, 23 (DK 59 B 7)

9.17 Simplicius *Phys.* 164, 22 (DK 59 B 11)

9.18 Simplicius *Phys.* 164, 22 and 156, 13 (DK 59 B 12)

9.19 Plato *Phaedo* 97 B (DK 59 A 47)

9.20 Aristotle *Metaphys.* i. 4. 985 a 18 (DK 59 A 47)

9.21 Simplicius *Phys.* 300, 27 (DK 59 B 13)

9.22 Simplicius *Phys.* 179, 3 (DK 59 B 15). Diels reads ἡ γῆ after ἔνθα νῦν, but unnecessarily.

9.23 Simplicius *Phys.* 179, 6 (DK 59 B 16)

9.24 Simplicius *Phys.* 34, 28 (DK 59 B 4, first half). See note on **9.14**.

9.25 Aristotle *De partt. animal.* iv. 10. 687 a 7 (DK 59 A 102)

9.26 Plutarch *Vitae. Lysander* 12 (DK 59 A 12)

9.27 Hippolytus *Ref.* i. 8. 7 (DK 59 A 42)

9.28 Aetius ii. 13. 3 (DK 59 A 71)

9.29 Simplicius *Phys.* 35, 13 (DK 59 B 9)

9.30 Hippolytus *Ref.* i. 8. 10 (DK 59 A 42)

9.31 Aetius ii. 20. 6 (DK 59 A 72)

9.32 Aetius ii. 21. 3 (DK 59 A 72)

9.33 Hippolytus *Ref.* i. 8. 10 (DK 59 A 42)

9.34 Hippolytus *Ref.* i. 8. 8 (DK 59 A 42)

9.35 Plutarch *De fac. in orb. lun.* 16, p. 929 B (DK 59 B 18)

9.36 Hippolytus *Ref.* 1. 8. 9 (DK 59 A 42)

9.37 Aristotle *Meteorol.* i. 8. 345 a 25 (DK 59 A 80)

9.38 Diogenes Laertius ii. 12 (DK 59 A 1)

9.39 Plutarch *Vitae. Pericles* 5

9.40 Plato *Phaedrus* 270 A (DK 59 A 15)

9.41 Hippolytus *Ref.* i. 8. 3 (DK 59 A 42)

9.42 Aristotle *De caelo* ii. 13. 294 b 19 (DK 13 A 20), reading ἀθρόῳ with Allan. Cf. [Aristotle] *Probl.* xvi. 8. 914 b 10.

9.43 Diogenes Laertius ii. 9 (DK 59 A 1)

9.44 Plutarch *De fort.* 3, p. 98 F (DK 59 B 21b)

9.45 Sophocles *Antigone* 332–360

9.46 Aetius v. 25. 2 (DK 59 A 103)

9.47 Aristotle *Eudemian eth.* i. 5, 1216 a 11

9.48 Aristotle *Eudemian eth.* i. 4. 1215 b 7

9.49 Cicero *Tusc. disp.* v. 3. 8–9

9.50 Plato *Theaetetus* 174 A (DK 11 A 9)

9.51 Aristotle *Politica* i. 11. 1259 a 9 (DK 11 A 10)
9.52 Sextus Empiricus *Adv. math.* vii. 90 (DK 59 B 21)
9.53 Sextus Empiricus *Adv. math.* vii. 140 (DK 59 B 21a)

CHAPTER TEN · ATOMISM: THE MACROCOSM

10.1   Aristotle *De gen. et corr.* i. 8. 325 a 2 (DK 67 A 7)
10.2   Aristotle *Metaphys.* i. 4. 985 b 4 (DK 67 A 6)
10.3   Aristotle *On Democritus ap.* Simpl. *De caelo* 295, 1 (DK 68 A 37)
10.4   Plutarch *Adv. Coloten* 4, p. 1108 F (DK 68 B 156)
10.5   Simplicius *De caelo* 242, 18 (DK 67 A 14)
10.6   Aetius i. 16. 2 (DK 68 A 48)
10.7   Plutarch *Adv. Coloten* 8, p. 110 F (DK 68 A 57)
10.8   Aristotle *On Democritus ap.* Simpl. *De caelo* 295, 9 (DK 68 A 37), continuing 10.3.
10.9   Theophrastus *De sensu* 60–64 (DK 68 A 135)
10.10 Aristotle *Metaphys.* i. 4. 985 b 12 (DK 67 A 6)
10.11 Theophrastus *De caus. plant.* vi. 1. 6 (DK 68 A 129)
10.12 Theophrastus *De sensu* 67 (DK 68 A 135)
10.13 Aristotle *De gen. et corr.* i. 2. 315 b 6 (DK 67 A 9)
10.14 Aetius i. 15. 8 (DK 68 A 125)
10.15 Galen *De elem. sec. Hippocr.* i. 2 (DK 68 A 49)
10.16 Sextus Empiricus *Adv. math.* vii. 135 (DK 68 B 9)
10.17 Galen *De elem. sec. Hippocr.* i. 2 (DK 68 A 49). Galen is commenting on 10.16, which he has just quoted in part.
10.18 Galileo *Il Saggiatore* in *Opere Complete di Galileo Galilei* (Firenze, 1842), IV, 333, quoted in E. A. Burtt, *Metaphysical Foundations of Modern Science,* Anchor Books edition (New York, 1954), 85.
10.19 Sextus Empiricus *Adv. math.* vii. 137 (DK 68 B 6)
10.20 Sextus Empiricus *Adv. math.* vii. 137 (DK 68 B 6)
10.21 Sextus Empiricus *Adv. math.* vii. 137 (DK 68 B 6)
10.22 Sextus Empiricus *Adv. math.* vii. 139 (DK 68 B 11). I have preferred Bury's ἄλλο τι ⟨ληπτέον⟩ λεπτότερον to Diels's ἀλλ’ ἐπὶ λεπτότερον ⟨δέῃ ζητεῖν, τότε ἐπιγίνεται ἡ γνησίη ἅτε ὄργανον ἔχουσα τοῦ νῶσαι λεπτότερον⟩ on grounds of simplicity. Either reconstruction gives the required sense. Cf. [Hippocrates] *De arte* 11: "What escapes the eye is mastered by the mind's eye."
10.23 Aristotle *Metaphys.* ii. 2. 997 b 35 (DK 80 B 7)
10.24 Galen *De medic. empir.* 1259, 8 Schöne (DK 68 B 125). Kirk and Raven, *The Presocratic Philosophers* (Cambridge, England, 1957), 424, n. 1, very properly question the genuineness of this fragment. It is indeed "odd that Sextus did not quote it."
10.25 Aristotle *Metaphys.* iv. 5. 1009 b 7 (DK 68 A 112)
10.26 Theophrastus *De sensu* 69–70 (DK 68 A 135)
10.27 Sextus Empiricus *Pyrrh. h.* ii. 63 (DK 68 A 134)
10.28 Diogenes Laertius ix. 31 (DK 67 A 1). This unusually detailed account is apparently derived from Theophrastus.
10.29 Aristotle *De caelo* iv. 2. 300 b 8 (DK 67 A 16)
10.30 Aristotle *Metaphys.* xii. 6. 1071 b 31 (DK 67 A 18). In this particular passage Aristotle is speaking of Leucippus and Plato (cf. *Timaeus* 30 A).
10.31 Simplicius *Phys.* 1318, 33 (DK 68 A 58). The word περιπαλάσσεσθαι is printed as DK 68 B 168; the manuscripts have περιπαλαίσεσθαι. Cf. Galen

De elem. sec. Hippocr. i. 2 (DK 68 A 49): "The void is a kind of place in which all these bodies . . . move up and down through all time."

10.32 Plutarch *Quaest. conv.* viii. 3. 3, p. 722 A (DK 59 A 74)

10.33 Aristotle *De anima* i. 2. 404 a 1 (DK 68 A 28)

10.34 Simplicius *Phys.* 327, 24 (DK 68 B 167)

10.35 Diogenes Laertius ix. 35 (DK 68 A 1)

10.36 Aristotle *Phys.* ii. 4. 196 a 24 (DK 68 A 69). Simplicius, in commenting on this passage (331, 16), says that Democritus is meant.

10.37 Simplicius *Phys.* 1153, 22 (DK 68 A 71). Cf. Aristotle *Phys.* viii. 1. 251 b 16 (DK 68 A 71).

10.38 Lucretius *De rerum natura* v. 419–431

10.39 Sextus Empiricus *Adv. math.* vii. 116 (DK 68 B 164). Cf. Aetius iv. 19. 13 (DK 68 A 128).

10.40 Aetius i. 4. 2 (DK 67 A 24)

10.41 Cicero *De fin.* i. 6. 17 (DK 68 A 56)

10.42 Simplicius *De caelo* 712, 27 (DK 68 A 61). Burnet's view that weight is not a property of atoms outside the vortex (*Early Greek Philosophy*, 342 f.) has been widely accepted. But the evidence of Aristotle and Theophrastus is equivocal; Burnet's thesis derives most of its force from Aetius' assertion that "Democritus assigned two properties to atoms: size and shape; Epicurus added to these a third: weight" (i. 3. 18 [DK 68 A 47]) — an assertion similar to many others derived from Epicurean sources intent upon establishing the originality of the master.

10.43 Theophrastus *De vertigine* i, p. 136 Wimmer

10.44 Lucretius *De rerum natura* v. 623–636

10.45 [Hippocrates] *Morb.* IV, xlv (VII. 600 Littré), reading ὑπὸ δίνης for ὑπὸ ὀδύνης with Heidel, "Hippocratea I," *Harvard Studies in Classical Philology* (1914), 173.

10.46 Diogenes Laertius ix. 45 (DK 68 A 1). Cf. Sextus Empiricus *Adv. math.* ix. 113 (DK 68 A 83).

10.47 Aetius i. 26. 2 (DK 68 A 66)

10.48 Aetius i. 25. 4 (DK 67 B 2). Cf. Aristotle *Phys.* ii. 4. 196 a 1 (DK 68 A 68), where, according to Simplicius (*Phys.* 330, 14), Democritus is meant.

10.49 Aristotle *Phys.* ii. 4. 195 b 36 (DK 68 A 68)

10.50 Simplicius *Phys.* 330, 14 (DK 68 A 68)

10.51 Aetius ii. 7. 2 (DK 67 A 23)

10.52 Hippolytus *Ref.* i. 13. 2 (DK 68 A 40). I have rearranged the order of the sentences slightly.

10.53 Aetius i. 5. 4 (DK 70 A 6)

10.54 Diogenes Laertius ix. 33 (DK 67 A 1)

10.55 Hippolytus *Ref.* i. 13. 4 (DK 68 A 40)

CHAPTER ELEVEN · ATOMISM: THE MICROCOSM

11.1 [Hippocrates] *De carn.* 2–3 (VIII, 584 Littré)

11.2 Aristotle *De caelo* iv. 6. 313 a 16

11.3 Lucretius *De rerum natura* vi. 476–480

11.4 Aetius v. 19. 6 (DK 68 A 139), reading εἰδέων ἀνάρθρων with Diels.

11.5 Censorinus *De die natali* 4, 9 (DK 68 A 139)

11.6 Lactantius *Inst. div.* vii. 7. 9 (DK 68 A 139)

11.7 Aristotle *De respir.* 4. 471 b 30 (DK 68 A 106)

11.8 Diodorus Siculus i. 8 (DK 68 B 5), translated by C. H. Oldfather

11.9   Aelian *Hist. anim.* xii. 16 (DK 68 A 151)

11.10   Plutarch *De sollert. anim.* 20, p. 974 A (DK 68 B 154)

11.11   Stobaeus *Ecl. eth.* ii. 9. 5 (DK 68 B 176)

11.12   Stobaeus *Ecl. eth.* ii. 8. 16 (DK 68 B 119)

11.13   Clement *Strom.* iv. 151 and Stobaeus *Ecl. eth.* ii. 31. 65 (DK 68 B 33). Cf. [Hippocrates] *Nomos* 2: "Learning becomes second nature."

11.14   Philodemus *De music.* iv. 31, p. 108, 29 Kemke (DK 8 B 144). Cf. Plato on the rise of history *(Critias* 110 A) and Aristotle on the rise of philosophy *(Metaphys.* i. 2. 982 b 11).

11.15   Stobaeus *Ecl. eth.* ii. 31. 47 (DK 68 B 189)

11.16   Stobaeus *Flor.* i. 210 (DK 68 B 191). This fragment is continued in 11.34.

11.17   [Hippocrates] *Morb. sacr.* xvii

11.18   Theophrastus *De sensu* 58 (DK 68 A 135). Cf. Aristotle *De anima* i. 2. 404 a 27 (DK 68 A 101).

11.19   Stobaeus *Flor.* iv. 40. 21 (DK 68 B 288): νόσος οἴκου καὶ βίου γίνεται ὅκωσπερ καὶ σκήνεος.

11.20   Clement *Paedag.* i. 6 (DK 68 B 31)

11.21   Stobaeus *Ecl. eth.* ii. 7. 3 i (DK 68 B 170)

11.22   Stobaeus *Flor.* iii. 1. 27 Hense (DK 68 B 187)

11.23   Aristotle *De anima* i. 3. 406 b 15 (DK 68 A 104)

11.24   Aristotle *De caelo* iii. 8. 306 b 35

11.25   Plutarch frag. *De libid. et aegr.* 2 (DK 68 B 159)

11.26   Stobaeus *Flor.* iii. 10. 65 (DK 68 B 223)

11.27   Stobaeus *Flor.* iii. 4. 72 (DK 68 B 198)

11.28   Stobaeus *Flor.* iii. 10. 43 (DK 68 B 219)

11.29   Stobaeus *Flor.* iii. 17. 38 (DK 68 B 233)

11.30   Stobaeus *Flor.* iii. 5. 27 (DK 68 B 211)

11.31   Stobaeus *Ecl. eth.* ii. 33. 46 (DK 68 B 188). Cf. Clement *Strom.* ii. 130 (DK 68 B 4).

11.32   Demokrates 24 (DK 68 B 74)

11.33   Demokrates 34 (DK 68 B 69)

11.34   Stobaeus *Flor.* iii. 1. 210 (DK 68 B 191), continuing 11.16. See 11.84.

11.35   Porphyry *De abst.* iv. 21 (DK 68 B 160)

11.36   Stobaeus *Flor.* iii. 18. 30 (DK 68 B 234)

11.37   Stobaeus *Flor.* iii. 20. 56 (DK 68 B 236)

11.38   Demokrates 35 (DK 68 B 70)

11.39   Demokrates 49 (DK 68 B 83)

11.40   Stobaeus *Flor.* iii. 7. 74 (DK 68 B 126)

11.41   Demokrates 24 (DK 68 B 59)

11.42   Stobaeus *Ecl. eth.* ii. 31. 72 (DK 68 B 183). I have omitted the first sentence.

11.43   Stobaeus *Flor.* iii. 29. 66 (DK 68 B 242)

11.44   Stobaeus *Flor.* iv. 26. 26 (DK 68 B 280)

11.45   Stobaeus *Flor.* iii. 4. 24 (DK 68 B 208)

11.46   Stobaeus *Flor.* 16. 18 (DK 68 B 228). τύπος is employed in its technical sense here; cf. Theophrastus *De sensu* 52 (DK 68 A 135).

11.47   Stobaeus *Ecl. eth.* ii. 31. 66 (DK 68 B 182). The remainder of the text is corrupt.

11.48   Stobaeus *Flor.* iii. 29. 88 (DK 68 B 243). The text is corrupt.

11.49   Stobaeus *Flor.* iii. 29. 63 (DK 68 B 240)

11.50   Stobaeus *Flor.* iii. 29. 64 (DK 68 B 241)

11.51   Stobaeus *Ecl. eth.* ii. 31. 56 (DK 68 B 178)

11.52   Stobaeus *Ecl. eth.* ii. 15. 57 (DK 68 B 179)

11.53   Demokrates 57 (DK 68 B 91)

11.54 Demokrates 58 (DK 68 B 92)
11.55 Demokrates 59 (DK 68 B 93)
11.56 Demokrates 60 (DK 68 B 94)
11.57 Stobaeus *Flor.* iv. 24. 33 (DK 68 B 278)
11.58 Stobaeus *Flor.* iv. 24. 31 (DK 68 B 276)
11.59 Stobaeus *Flor.* iv. 24. 32 (DK 68 B 277)
11.60 Stobaeus *Flor.* iii. 7. 25 (DK 68 B 214)
11.61 Demokrates 78 (DK 68 B 111)
11.62 Stobaeus *Flor.* iii. 18. 35 (DK 68 B 235)
11.63 Demokrates 3 (DK 68 B 37)
11.64 Plutarch *De prof. in virt.* 10, p. 81 A (DK 68 B 146)
11.65 Dionysius, Bishop of Alexandria, in Eus. *P.E.* xiv. 27. 4 (DK 68 B 118)
11.66 Stobaeus *Flor.* iii. 40. 7 (DK 68 B 247)
11.67 Diogenes Laertius ix. 38 (DK 14, 6)
11.68 Demokrates 23 (DK 68 B 57)
11.69 Demokrates 71 (DK 68 B 105)
11.70 Demokrates 6 (DK 68 B 40)
11.71 Stobaeus *Flor.* iv. 52. 40 (DK 68 B 297)
11.72 Stobaeus *Flor.* iii. 4. 73 (DK 68 B 199)
11.73 Stobaeus *Flor.* iv. 44. 67 (DK 68 B 290)
11.74 Stobaeus *Flor.* iv. 1. 43 (DK 68 B 252)
11.75 Stobaeus *Flor.* iv. 40. 20 (DK 68 B 287)
11.76 Stobaeus *Flor.* iv. 1. 34 (DK 68 B 249)
11.77 Stobaeus *Flor.* iv. 1. 40 (DK 68 B 250)
11.78 Stobaeus *Flor.* iv. 1. 46 (DK 68 B 255)
11.79 Stobaeus *Flor.* iv. 1. 42 (DK 68 B 251)
11.80 Stobaeus *Flor.* iv. 2. 15 (DK 68 B 257)
11.81 Stobaeus *Flor.* iv. 2. 17 (DK 68 B 259)
11.82 Stobaeus *Flor.* iv. 5. 44 (DK 68 B 262)
11.83 Stobaeus *Flor.* iii. 38. 47 (DK 68 B 245)
11.84 Stobaeus Flor. iii. 1. 210 (DK 68 B 191), continuing **11.34.**
11.85 Stobaeus *Flor.* iii. 7. 31 (DK 68 B 215)
11.86 Stobaeus *Ecl. eth.* ii. 9. 3 (DK 68 B 174)
11.87 Demokrates 72 (DK 68 B 72)
11.88 Stobaeus *Ecl. eth.* ii. 31. 59 (DK 68 B 181)
11.89 Demokrates 27 (DK 68 B 62)
11.90 Stobaeus *Flor.* iv. 5. 46 (DK 68 B 264)
11.91 Demokrates 11 (DK 68 B 45)
11.92 Demokrates 9 (DK 68 B 43)
11.93 Demokrates 26 (DK 68 B 61)
11.94 Demokrates 13 (DK 68 B 47)
11.95 Stobaeus *Flor.* iv. i. 33 (DK 68 B 248)

CHAPTER TWELVE · PROTAGORAS, ANTIPHON, AND CALLICLES

12.1 Plato *Protagoras* 314 E
12.2 Plato *Protagoras* 318 A
12.3 Plato *Protagoras* 327 C
12.4 Plato *Protagoras* 325 C
12.5 Plato *Protagoras* 328 B
12.6 Sextus Empiricus *Adv. math.* vii. 60 (DK 80 B 1)

12.7 Plato *Cratylus* 385 E. Cf. Plato *Theaetetus* 152 A.
12.8 Plato *Theaetetus* 152 B
12.9 Plato *Theaetetus* 170 A. The context shows, I think, that this was Protagoras' own view, not merely one which Plato attributes to him for the sake of his argument.
12.10 Plato *Theaetetus* 161 B
12.11 Plato *Theaetetus* 166 C
12.12 Plato *Protagoras* 322 B
12.13 Oxyrhynchus Pap. xi n. 1364, ed. Hunt, Frag. A (DK 87 B 44)
12.14 Continuation of above
12.15 Continuation of above, omitting Col. 4, lines 9-32
12.16 Continuation of above. The text of the closing sentences is largely conjectural.
12.17 Plato *Gorgias* 482 C

CHAPTER THIRTEEN · REACTION

13.1 Diogenes Laertius ii. 40
13.2 Plato *Apology* 26 B
13.3 Plato *Apology* 18 A
13.4 Aristophanes *Clouds* 366–411
13.5 Plutarch *Vitae. Pericles* 5 (DK 59 A 16)
13.6 [Hippocrates] *Morb. sacr.* 1
13.7 Herodotus *Histories* iii. 33
13.8 Aristophanes *Clouds* 816–829
13.9 Plato *Apology* 23 C
13.10 Aristophanes *Clouds* 960–1023
13.11 Aristophanes *Clouds* 1062–1082
13.12 Gorgias *Encomium on Helen* 2, 5–8, 14, 12, 15–16, 18–21 (DK 82 B 11)
13.13 Diogenes Laertius ix. 51 (DK 80 B 4)
13.14 Sextus Empiricus *Adv. math.* ix. 18 (DK 84 B 5)
13.15 Sextus Empiricus *Adv. math.* ix. 54 (DK 88 B 2)
13.16 Aristophanes *Clouds* 1409–1432
13.17 Plato *Protagoras* 316 C
13.18 Plato *Meno* 91 B
13.19 Plato *Republic* 492 A
13.20 Thucydides *History of the Peloponnesian War* v. 89–111, translated by R. Crawley
13.21 Thucydides *History of the Peloponnesian War* iii. 40, translated by R. Crawley
13.22 Thucydides *History of the Peloponnesian War* iii. 44–48, translated by R. Crawley

EPILOGUE

1 Plato *Republic* 358 E
2 Plato *Republic* 359 B
3 Plato *Laws* 886 C
4 Plato *Laws* 889 A

APPENDIX A · THALES OF MILETUS

1 Herodotus *Histories* i. 74 (DK 11 A 5)
2 Aristotle *De caelo* ii. 13. 294 a 28 (DK 11 A 14)
3 Aristotle *Metaphys.* i. 3. 983 b 6 (DK 11 A 12)
4 Seneca *Quaest. nat.* iii. 14 (DK 11 A 15)
5 Aristotle *De anima* i. 2. 405 a 19 (DK 11 A 22)
6 Aristotle *De anima* i. 5. 411 a 7 (DK 11 A 22)

APPENDIX B · GORGIAS, ON NATURE

1 Sextus Empiricus *Adv. math.* vii. 65–86 (DK 82 B 3)

INDEX

Aeschylus
on the impregnation of Earth, 8
warns against excess, 99

Air
supports the earth, 30–31, 46, 189–190
the primary stuff of the world-order, 41–43, 49
and soul, 47–50
and intelligence, 47–50, 98
one of the four elements, 157

Alcmaeon
on health as equality of powers in the body, 35
on the opposites, 118

Analogy
mechanical *vs.* biological, 27, 83–84
of microcosm and macrocosm, 35, 48–50, 168–169, 215
use of mechanical analogies by the medical writers, 26–27, 210, 211; by Anaximenes, 42–43; by Empedocles, 163–164, 168–169; by Anaxagoras, 190; by Democritus, 207
use of biological analogies by Hesiod, 27; by Anaximander, 48; by the Pythagoreans, 75; by the atomists, 212–213
use of satirized by Aristophanes, 260

Anaxagoras
relation to Empedocles, 175
life of, 175, 188–189
relation to Parmenides, 175, 193–194
theory of *homoiomerai*, 176–177
on the infinitely small, 177–180
on mind, 181–185
on the heavenly bodies, 185–188
trial of, 188–189
association with Pericles, 188–189
on man, 190–191
on the philosophic life, 191–192
on sense-perception and thought, 193–194
explains freak of nature naturalistically, 261

Anaximander
date of, 23
on the infinite, 23–24
on formation of the world-order, 25–26
on the vortex, 26–27
on the heavenly bodies, 27–29
on the earth's support, 29–30
draws the first map, 31–33
on the origin of life, 33–34
on the injustice of the opposites, 34–36
on justice in the world-order, 34–38
on thunder and lightning, 39
on the death of the world-order, 39–40
on earthquakes, 315 (note on Reference 3.12)

Anaximenes
on the infinite, 41–43
on compression and dilation of air, 42–43
on the heavenly bodies, 44–46
on air and intelligence, 46–49

Animals
absence of justice among, 17–18, 254, 271
generated spontaneously, 33, 51, 190
as the teachers of men, 218

Antiphon
on natural *vs.* man-made law, 250–252
appeals to self-interest, 251–252

Aretē
meaning of, 239
transmission of, 243–244

Aristocracy
relation of Pythagoras to, 79
relation of Pindar and Heraclitus to, 105
values of, 105

Aristophanes
lampoons Socrates in *Clouds*, 259–266
on natural philosophers as atheists, 259–263
rails against the new education, 264–266
attacks the sophists, 266–268

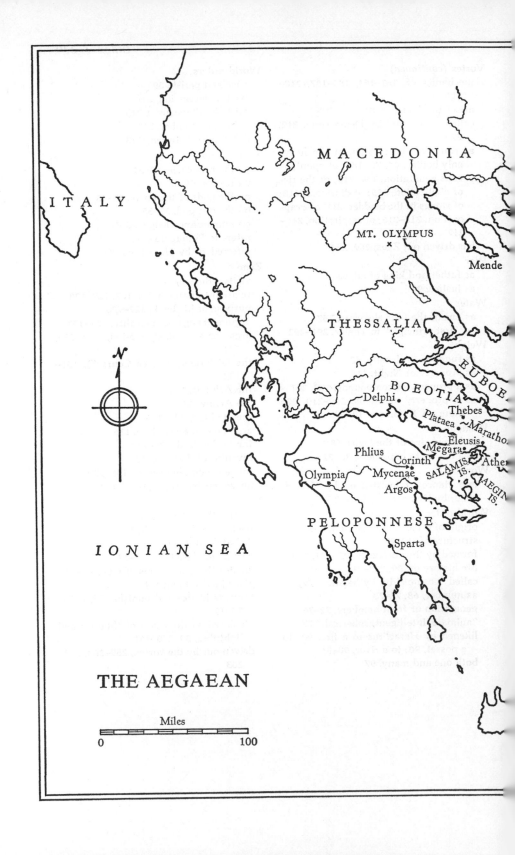

ITALY

MACEDONIA

MT. OLYMPUS
×

Mende

THESSALIA

EUBOEA

BOEOTIA
Delphi
Thebes
Plataea
Marathon
Eleusis
Megara
Phlius
Corinth
Athens
Olympia
Mycenae
SALAMIS
IS.
AEGINA
IS.
Argos

PELOPONNESE

Sparta

IONIAN SEA

THE AEGAEAN

Miles

0   100

BLACK SEA

THRACE

Bosporus

Abdera

PROPONTIS

SAMOTHRACE
IS.

IMBROS IS.

Lampsacus

Hellespont

MNOS
IS.

Troy

PHRYGIA

TENEDOS
IS.

MYSIA

Mytilene

AEGAEAN SEA

Pergamum

LESBOS IS.

LYDIA

Magnesia

Chios

Clazomenae

CHIOS
IS.

IONI

Colophon

SAMOS IS.

Ephesus

Priene

CARIA

Miletus

DELOS IS.

PAROS IS.

Halicarnassus

CLADES

SPORADES

COS IS.

Cnydus

RHODES

CRETE

SOUTHERN ITALY AND SICILY